Malcolm Root's

RAILWAY PAINTINGS

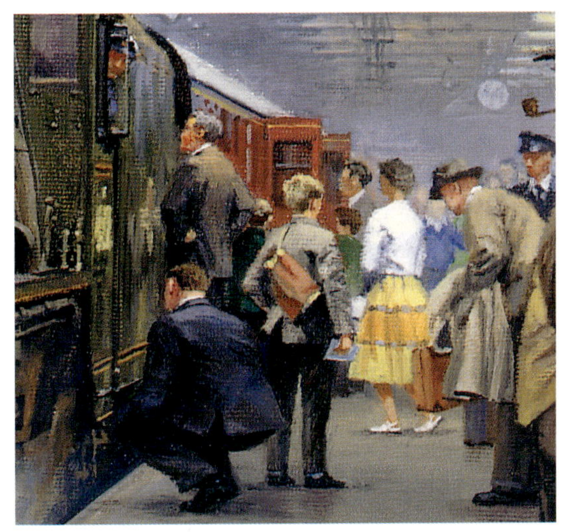

To Anne & Barry
With Best Wishes
Malcolm Root.

TEXT BY

TOM TYLER

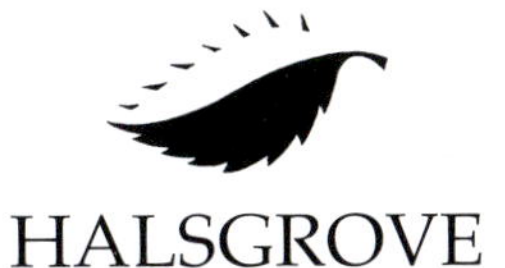

HALSGROVE

First published in 2004 by Halsgrove. Reprinted 2006

British Library Cataloguing-in-Publication Data
A CIP record for this title is available from the British Library

ISBN 1 84114 366 9
ISBN 978 1 84114 366 8

HALSGROVE
Halsgrove House
Lower Moor Way
Tiverton, Devon EX16 6SS
T: 01884 243242
F: 01884 243325
www.halsgrove.com

Printed and bound in Italy by D'Auria Industrie Grafiche Spa

ARTIST'S ACKNOWLEDGEMENTS

I have never regretted our decision to paint full time. I say 'our' for without the support of my wife and two children this would not have been possible. They sacrificed many things in the early years and I would like to take this opportunity of thanking them.

When I set out on the precarious path and all the uncertainties that come with being a professional artist, some 25 years ago, I was totally unaware of the diversity of people that I would meet. This has been an unexpected bonus, for I have struck up many true friendships with people whose knowledge of railways and transport in general is far greater than my own. Railway expertise does not come any greater than that of Richard Hardy, whose memory for detail never ceases to amaze me, and who has so kindly written the foreword for this book. To Richard I offer my sincere thanks. Similarly I would like to thank Bob Clow who has put me right many times on railway operation when I thought a picture was complete! John Hill has always been both a true friend and an unceasing source of information, as have the many photographers, especially Tom Boustead. My thanks also go to Andy Wyatt of CCI whose expertise in photographic reproduction has contributed to the quality of this book. Finally I am grateful to Colchester Museums and JARVIS plc for allowing me to reproduce their paintings, and to the other owners of the paintings that appear in this book.

Foreword

by RHN Hardy

This is a wonderful collection of railway paintings. I say this with complete confidence for, although I am no artist, the railway was my working life for forty-two years. In my twenties, I worked for and suffered under a truly great Locomotive Superintendent who bred in us the need to use 'the seeing eye'. If LP Parker was alive today he would have appreciated Malcolm's great work. He was a practical and severely critical perfectionist and he would have looked for and found, with inward satisfaction, the small but essential points of detail that play such an important part in the creation of the atmosphere of railway life. 'LP' would have blown a couple of smoke rings from his pipe and said: 'Quite good, Root, but tell me why is the fireman of the A1 making smoke at High Dyke?' Of course, Root knew why and said so, and got a very searching look for his pains which was followed by: 'Root, ride with that man and put him right for the future.' But an artist can, to some extent, do as he pleases, and what is a bit of a trail of smoke amongst friends.

There are few of Malcolm's paintings that do not tell the tale. They can speak to one. Look at the frontispiece and one hears the soft-beat Drummond M7 pattering gently away in the snow from Corfe Castle. One is there, on the job, and yet I have not been to Corfe for seventy-four years. Look too at 'Foggy Arrival'. Here comes old D16 2564, once a Super Claud that I knew only too well as 8833. She rolls easily and silently towards the murky Norwich platform, siderods ringing gently, the big Westo pump beating quietly and perhaps a few strong beats at the chimney top to take the train in. Marvellous but, if that is not enough to make the picture live, look over on the right where a railwayman with a paraffin handlamp is walking along the catwalk. Nothing in itself but the artist has not forgotten the tiny pin-prick of light that signifies that the lamp is doing its work. Here is a true work of art.

Down to Folkestone Harbour where the old Stirling R1s with their free-steaming Wainwright boilers reigned supreme, burning brickettes and low-grade Kent coal. Malcolm has them leaving the harbour and taking that memorable dash at the 1-in-30. Many a time, when I was in charge at Stewarts Lane, I have watched those little heroes fighting their way up the last length of that impossible gradient to the junction sidings while we waited on 70004 to take their 'Arrow' empties down to Dover. Look at them and then listen to Peter Handford's CD and you will be doubly rewarded.

Malcolm takes us into backwaters away from today's world of steam. We go to colliery sidings or to Braintree Loco, home to two engines, or to Wrabness where the little 'Westo Goods' is crossing over with the driver crouching against his 'spectacle' to see where he is going, inevitable with a low boiler and cab with a high footboard. And then again, here is Brell Ewart's *Royal Duchess*, 6233, in all her glory, hauling the Queen's beautiful train along the coast of North Wales. I could go on but that would never do. This book will give you all great joy and, I, for one, will banish the pressures of retirement to relax, to learn, to use my 'seeing eye' time and again and to marvel at the artist's practical knowledge as well as at his sublime ability. One day, perhaps, he will create a Copley Hill GN Atlantic pounding up from Holbeck past the shed with the 'Pullman' or a Robinson '4-cylinder', blackened by hard war-time service, roaring up the long grade from Sheffield to Woodhead with a heavy train: that will be the day!

RHN Hardy

RHN Hardy

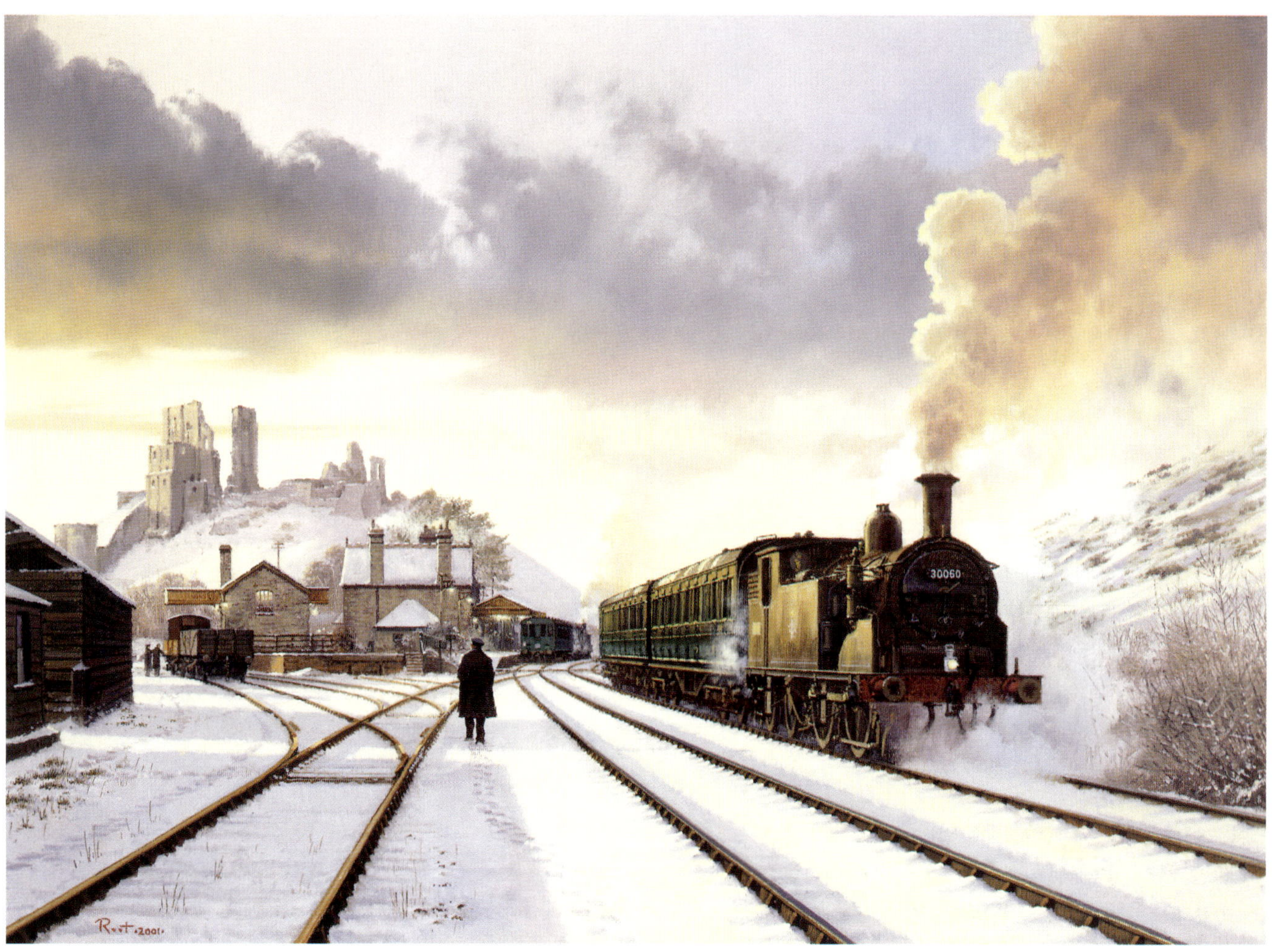

Winter at Corfe Castle

Painted 2000

A wonderful evocative scene on the branch line that runs from Worgret Junction, past Corfe Castle to Swanage and the sea. At first the line was intended to carry stone quarried from the Isle of Purbeck, but by the time it was built in 1885 the Victorian holiday by the sea was firmly established, and I know my father travelled by train to Swanage in the 1890s. Corfe Castle was originally Norman, but rebuilt and expanded in the late fourteenth century. Because it held out so successfully in the Civil War against Parliament, it was demolished in revenge in 1646, leaving the impressive ruin seen today. The two-coach train leaving Corfe is pulled by a M7 0-4-4 locomotive, first introduced on the LSWR in 1897 and designed by Dugald Drummond.

Introduction

Britain was a world pioneer in the development of the railway, and as with most pioneering enterprises there was a considerable degree of haphazard planning involved, if not actual chaos. Duplication, failed financial projects, fatally faulty structures, and the battle of the gauges all featured in the history of the first 70 years of the railways. By the end of the First World War, during which the railways had risen to the demands of a national emergency in a magnificent manner, it was clear that some drastic action was long overdue. During the war over 120 railway companies had been put under the control of the Railway Executive Committee. When the war finished, the railways were suffering from huge exertion, lack of manpower and investment, and a government which did not pay its debts to the embattled railway companies with any semblance of punctuality. The railways passed out of government control on 15 August 1921. Immediately the Railway Act was passed, requiring all the companies to be amalgamated into four regional companies by June 1923.

Most of the paintings in this wonderful collection cover the period from June 1923, through the Nationalisation in 1948, to the end of steam on British Railways in the 1960s. They remind us of the way in which railways affected almost every community in the British Isles. Small branch lines wound round the hills and up the valleys, bringing transport and communications to villages and hamlets previously served by the horse and cart. When each modest passenger train arrived at a country station, at least six people would be involved. On the train would be a driver, fireman and guard. On the station a stationmaster, a porter/ticket collector, and a signalman who would often be level crossing keeper as well. In between trains the staff kept their station tidy, washing down paintwork and tending flowerbeds.

Out in the countryside people regulated their days by the punctual passing of the trains. A distant whistle at a crossing would herald the train's approach, long before the white smoke could be seen. Children would run to field fence or garden hedge to watch. Even the smallest tank engine with a single coach had a majesty and fascination, proving man's superiority over the lie of the land and the elements, and speaking of far horizons, bustling cities and holiday haunts.

Malcolm Root's pictures bring back to us all these memories, particularly the important details of this past way of life. The mechanism of the signals, the carriage lamps, the nature of station architecture, passengers' luggage are all faithfully recreated, as well as the utterly accurate details of the locomotives and trains themselves. You can almost smell the mixture of steam, smoke and hot oil, and hear the rhythm of wheels on the jointed track. More than that, every painting is a beautiful picture, reminding us of the skill of the artist, and reflecting his deep love of railways and everything linked to them. I hope you will enjoy the collection as much as I do. I must record my grateful thanks to Roland Niblett, who has proof read the text and made suggestions as a result of his great experience of the railways, and also to my wife and daughter who have given great assistance with this project, the latter taming my computer with consummate skill! As usual the mistakes are all my own work.

Tom Tyler

Artist's Introduction

From the times when cavemen first applied paint to cave walls, art has been used to record momentous occasions as well as everyday life. Along with the written word, much of our history can be determined from pictorial records. In the days long before photography the only way of preserving for posterity the character and appearance of our forebears was by painted portraits.

With the coming of the impressionist movement, self-expression added yet another and welcome dimension, and freed artists from the tight restraints of representational art. What, you might ask, has this to do with railway art? From the time Trevithick's locomotive first moved under its own power, steam has had an unequalled fascination for young and old alike. It is not surprising then that artists have felt the need to try to capture the movement of rods, the steam and the smells that the steam locomotive encapsulates. This has been achieved in both impressionistic and representational styles very successfully. Probably the most famous railway impressionist picture of all is 'Rain, Steam and Speed' by JMW Turner. In recent years two artists more than any others have, in my opinion, been the catalysts for a new generation of railway artists. Terence Cuneo and David Shepherd have both set new standards, having applied their exceptional talents to railway art.

Many years ago, as a child, I tried to emulate the works of Vic Welch whose bold railway pictures adorned my board books! However, it was the impact of a picture by Terence Cuneo, 'Evening Star', that started the creative juices flowing, and from that point on an uphill struggle to produce accurate ellipses for wheels had begun! I left school in 1967 having enjoyed my art lessons. This coincided with the end of steam on British Railways and I found painting and drawing railways a way of replenishing my thirst for steam. Railway artists generally fall into two categories – the artist who is interested in railways, and the railway enthusiast who tries his hand at art. Perhaps I fall somewhere in the middle for my interests in both art and railways have followed a parallel path from a very early age.

I made reference earlier to impressionism and realism. I would describe myself as someone who paints fairly realistically, with a small amount of exaggeration. Could this be considered a concession to impressionism? Certainly railways are a very technical subject, and one in which draughtsmanship plays an important part. During the 1970s my involvement with railway preservation armed me with vital technical and engineering knowledge that I hope is reflected in some way in my paintings.

If this book can be looked at and enjoyed, and in some pictures a story told or a nostalgic memory rekindled, then I will have achieved my goal. It is not intended to be a technical book, but one which reflects something of the railways that I loved.

Malcolm Root

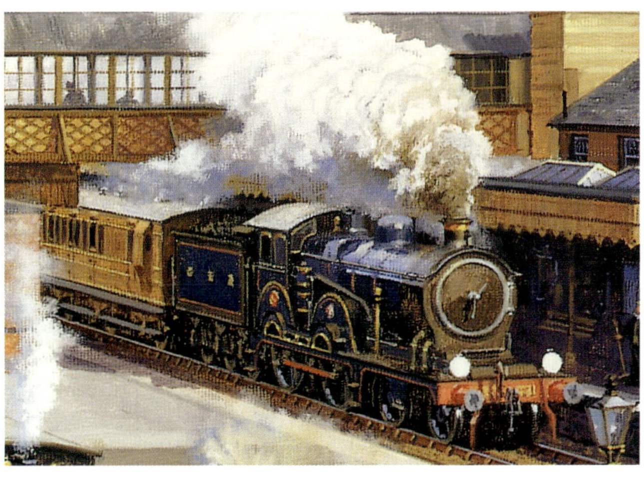

The Paintings

Constable Country

Painted 1993

The River Stour, which forms the boundary between the counties of Essex and Suffolk, flows past Flatford Mill, a favourite setting for the artist John Constable. A few miles further downstream the river reaches its estuary at Manningtree, and here it is crossed by the tracks of the old Great Eastern Railway. Trains heading for Colchester and London pass through Manningtree station and then head up Dedham Bank, past the signal box, which also bears the name of the village, a mile or so to the north-west. This lovely painting reminds us how often the railways cut through some of the most beautiful tracts of our British countryside, giving railway passengers views never enjoyed by those hurtling along hedge-enclosed roads.

The picture shows a classic scene in the late 1950s, with Britannia Pacific class locomotive number 70003, *John Bunyan* in the usual British Railways livery, hauling an express consisting of nine coaches, which will have started from Norwich, calling at Ipswich, Colchester and Chelmsford on its way to Liverpool Street, the London terminus. The Britannia class of express passenger locomotives were designed by RA Riddles and introduced as the first of twelve new British Railways types in 1951. In all 55 of the class were built, all at Crewe. Despite some early criticism the engines performed well during their comparatively short working lives, and were to be found operating on express trains all over the BR network, although it was in the East of England where they made their biggest impact. They had a total weight of about 141 tons, a boiler pressure of 250 psi and a tractive effort of 32 150lbs.

Two of these impressive locomotives were saved from the scrap yard, number 70000 *Britannia* which originally found a home on the Severn Valley Railway and number 70013 *Oliver Cromwell* which is to be found at the Bressingham Hall Steam Museum in Norfolk, where it is on static display. Here you can climb into the cab and be reminded of the majesty and power of the last of the steam locomotives. This arresting painting is a fitting tribute to the last decade of the steam engine and its contribution to the history of railways.

Dedham Bank will be remembered by steam locomotive crews as a place where teamwork was essential. The driver would be trying to get the best from his locomotive while the fireman would be hard at work with the shovel on the climb from Manningtree. I, however, remember it for a very different reason. Many years ago while driving my Morris Marina a loud crack had told me that a rear spring had broken. Fortunately this occurred near the spot in the painting. I watched the trains (by this time class 47s) until aid arrived.

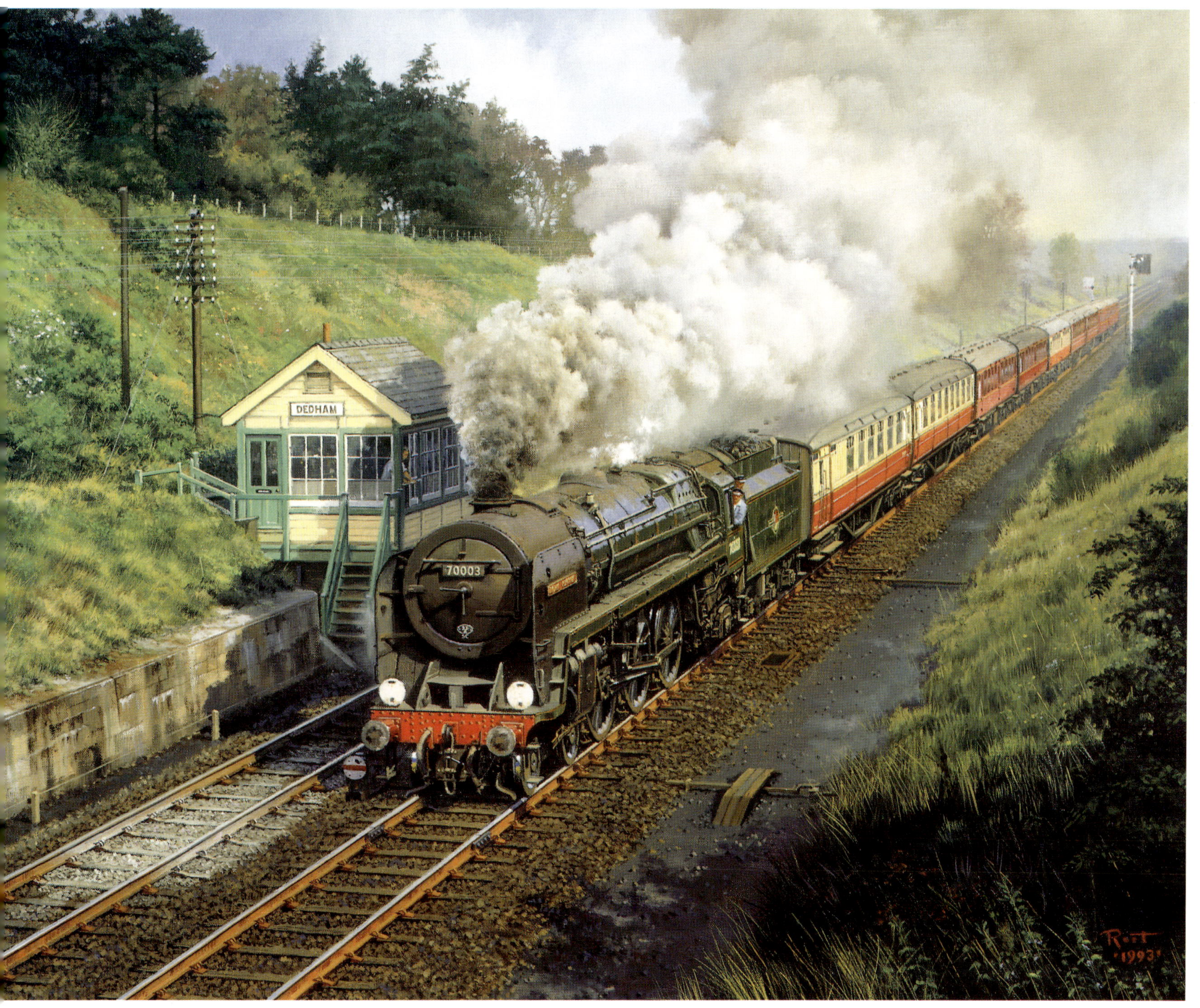
DEDHAM
70003
Root
1993

Wrabness in the Snow

Painted 1996

I visited Wrabness on one of the hottest days of summer 2003, and a bit of snow would have been most welcome! The end of the platform and the bridge in the distance remain the same, but otherwise much has changed since the time of the scene Malcolm has painted. The track seen leaving the main line just beyond the waiting locomotive, and heading to the right, was the siding that led down to the War Department loading bays.

The line that branched off the London to Ipswich main line at Manningtree and terminated at the North Sea coast at Harwich has always been most important as Harwich is the east coast equivalent of Dover. I recently travelled from Harwich to the Hook of Holland at a steady 45mph on the Stena Sealink and this emphasised what a good route the Liverpool Street–Harwich–Hook route continues to be for those going to the continent. At Parkeston Quay (see page 112) one only has to walk a couple of hundred yards from the train to get on board ship. Liverpool Street Station might not seem as glamorous as Victoria, but the boat train service was equally efficient.

The Wrabness signal box may be covered in snow, but the glow of the light inside, and the smoke emerging from the tall stove pipe indicate that the signalman, like his many colleagues up and down the country, knew how to make himself comfortable. Signalmen, with the safety of the railway in their hands, had to be very methodical and constantly alert. However as they spent long hours in their signal boxes there was a strong incentive to import some creature comforts such as a comfortable chair and tea-making equipment. The locomotive waiting patiently for the right of way is a J15 class 0-6-0 probably built around the turn of the twentieth century, and still giving good service.

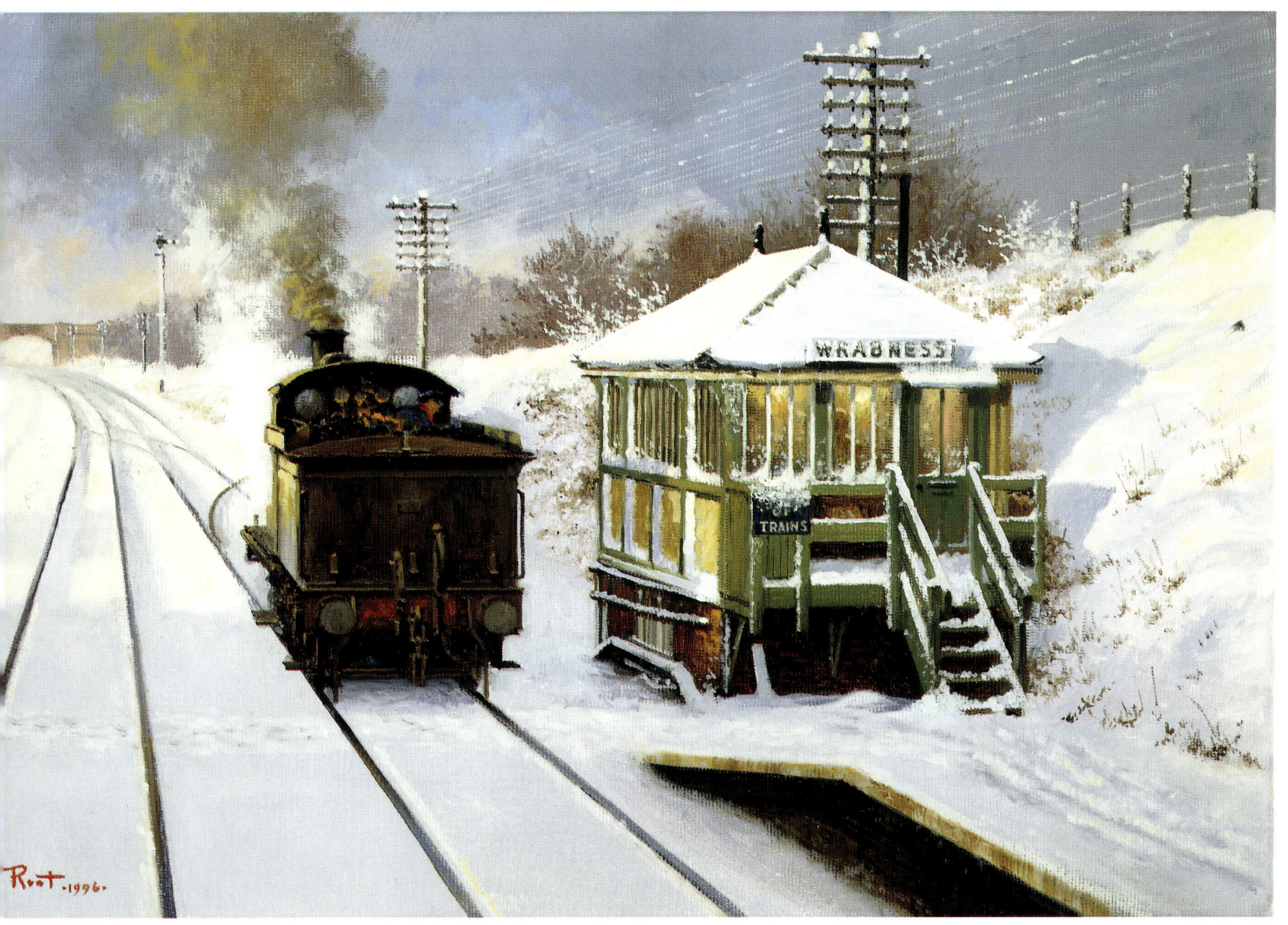
WRABNESS
TRAINS
Root. 1996.

Wisbech and Upwell Tramway

Painted 2001

Tramways were to be found all over the country linked to a variety of industries, and providing links to either main line railways or port facilities. The Wisbech and Upwell Tramway was constructed to supply transport for passengers and freight. In an area of great horticultural significance this tramway provided transport for fruit and vegetables to the main line station at Wisbech. Here the carefully packed wagons would be shunted on to the main line, and taken to destinations all over the country. To ensure the produce arrived in the best possible condition, speed and careful handling were essential. The tramway was first opened in July 1883, and was equipped with Y6 (GER G15) 0-4-0 steam-powered tram engines designed by TW Worsdell. By 1903 more powerful engines were needed, and the J70 (GER class C53) 0-6-0 steam tram engines were added to the repertoire. Both these types of engine worked the tramway throughout its life until the introduction of diesels in 1952. The scene is set towards the end of the tramway's history in about 1950 with the J70 engine in British Railways livery. The line finally closed in May 1966.

The Revd W Awdry who wrote the *Thomas the Tank Engine* stories was vicar of one of the parishes close to the Wisbech and Upwell Tramway, and must have delighted in the trains that meandered along this whimsical little railway. In fact his character Toby the Tram Engine is based on the steam tram engines used for so many years to haul the trains.

The lorry that has brought the precious fruit from the orchard is an ERF of 1938 vintage, a flat truck powered by a Gardner Diesel engine as so many lorries were. Fork lift trucks were not in widespread use so the loading is done by hand, and with much care. In those days the apples might be Adam's Pearmain, Blenheim Orange, Lady Henniker, Cox's Orange Pippin, or Kings Acre Pippin, along with the most popular variety, Bramley. Like the tramway these are treasures of an age now gone. Nowadays everything seems to be Golden Delicious, standardised and without any distinctive character!

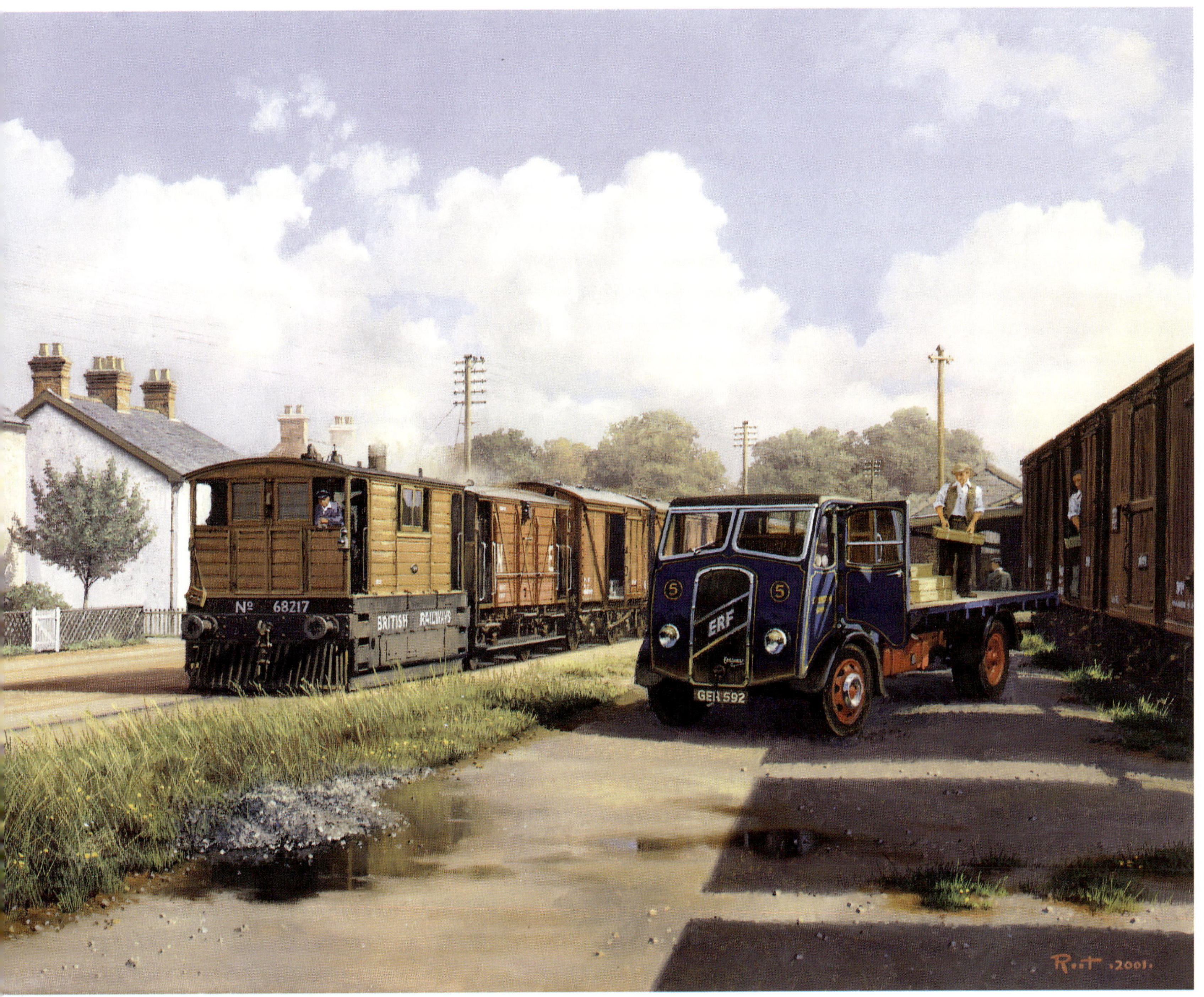
Nº 68217
BRITISH RAILWAYS
ERF
GER 592
Root 2001

Foggy Arrival

Painted 1996

However much we may look back to the 'good old days', and I do frequently, we have to admit that Clean Air Acts and anti air pollution policies have made smog a thing of the past. Where there was smoke in abundance, as for example at large railway stations, foggy conditions often prevailed, particularly at night. Norwich, one of the more remote cathedral cities geographically, was connected to the rapidly expanding railway network by 1850, with lines via Ipswich to London, and across country to the west to meet the main northbound route at Peterborough. Further lines laid in the next fifty years linked Norwich to Cromer and other towns in north Norfolk, making the station at Norwich Thorpe ever more important.

Station platforms were often notably chilly and draughty places, and East Anglia with its keen east winds can be especially raw in the winter. With the onset of a foggy dusk, the heart of many a traveller has been lightened at the sight of the approaching train. Few used to congregate in front of the small fire in the otherwise pretty cheerless waiting room, and so the train promised warmth, a comfortable seat, and with a bit of luck privacy as well. In the days when trains had compartments, the Englishman – and woman – would go to great lengths to try to secure a compartment and hold it against all-comers. Luggage could be scattered on all the seats, and the blinds immediately pulled down. There was then only the door out to the corridor to be guarded – if the train had a corridor. Ian Hay in *The Safety Match* gives a lovely account of two children inventing a recent, horrible and wildly infectious illness to rid their compartment of an unwanted fellow traveller. Having secured the castle against invaders, travellers could sink back into those old padded seats – it was horsehair wasn't it? – and try to generate the maximum fug until their destination was reached.

The Great Eastern Railway's Claud Hamilton class of 4-4-0 locomotives were designed by James Holden and first introduced in 1900. They were intended for express passenger work, and in all over 100 were built. The class took its name from the original engine number 1900 which bore the name *Claud Hamilton* after the chairman of the GER. Considered one of the most handsome designs, later rebuilds in the 1930s and 40s did not improve their good looks, and the last one was scrapped in 1960, with sadly none surviving in preservation.

At first sight this scene appears relatively straightforward to paint, as there is little or no detail in much of the picture. Restraint has to be shown in not including too much detail, for to do so would lessen the impact of the painting. It is however vital to include some features – in this case a station lamp and signals – at varying distances to give the necessary depth, and to show the thickness of the fog. In the distance strategically-placed lights highlight the locomotive front and add a welcome reflection to the rails.

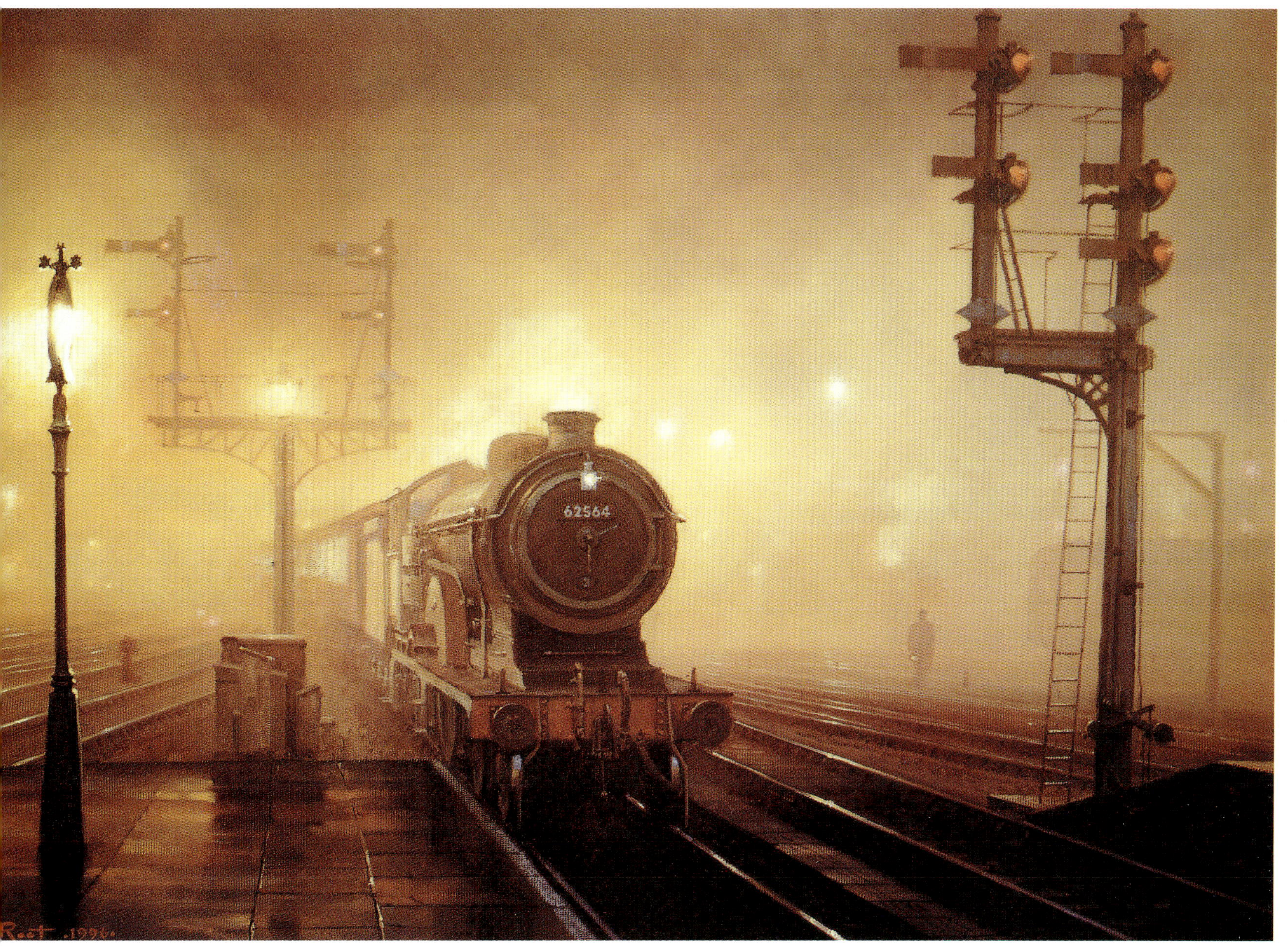
62564
Root .1996.

Barnstaple Bridge

Painted 1998

The London & South Western Railway, later to become part of the Southern Railway, had an interesting history in the West Country. Always under the shadow of the Great Western Railway in this area, it still managed to build a main line from London via Salisbury to Exeter by 1860. It then proceeded to connect to a number of east Devon and west Dorset seaside towns. Beyond Exeter, Plymouth was the next goal, and after trying a route via Yelverton, the LSWR took a northern route round the edge of Dartmoor and came down the Tamar Valley to Plymouth from the north. This resulted in a small town like Tavistock having two stations served by two railways, and trains from London arriving at both Exeter and Plymouth from opposite directions, which could be a bit confusing for travellers! Beyond Plymouth the LSWR sneaked down into north Cornwall, and eventually came to a full stop by the sea at Padstow. This rather meandering line served a lot of popular holiday areas including Barnstaple which had its junction near Yeoford.

The Southern Railway had some difficulty keeping up with its larger rivals, but nevertheless established its named trains such as the Atlantic Coast Express which ran all the way down to Padstow, while the Devon Belle was the western equivalent of the Brighton and Bournemouth Belles, and terminated at Ilfracombe.

In this painting West Country class 4-6-2 number 34041 *Wilton* heads the London-bound Devon Belle slowly over Barnstaple Bridge, with the river Taw below. The train comprises six Pullman coaches with a special observation coach at the rear from which excellent views could be obtained. The Pullman coaches had a distinctive luxury with table lamps, veneered panelling and a feeling of grand opulence.

The streamlined Pacific locomotives were designed by Oliver Bulleid when he was Chief Mechanical Engineer of the Southern Railway. The first of these remarkable 'air smoothed' locomotives, a Merchant Navy class, appeared surprisingly in 1941. It had a number of novel features, and 20 were built by 1945. In that year a smaller version of the Merchant Navy class loco was produced, being two feet shorter, and more importantly 14-tons lighter, and was thus able to serve all the branch lines of the railway. These locos were called Battle of Britain and West Country classes. Most of the locomotives had their streamlined casings removed when rebuilt in later years, but they proved their worth by working well right up to the end of the steam era, and at least eight of the Bulleid Pacifics have been preserved and continue to work.

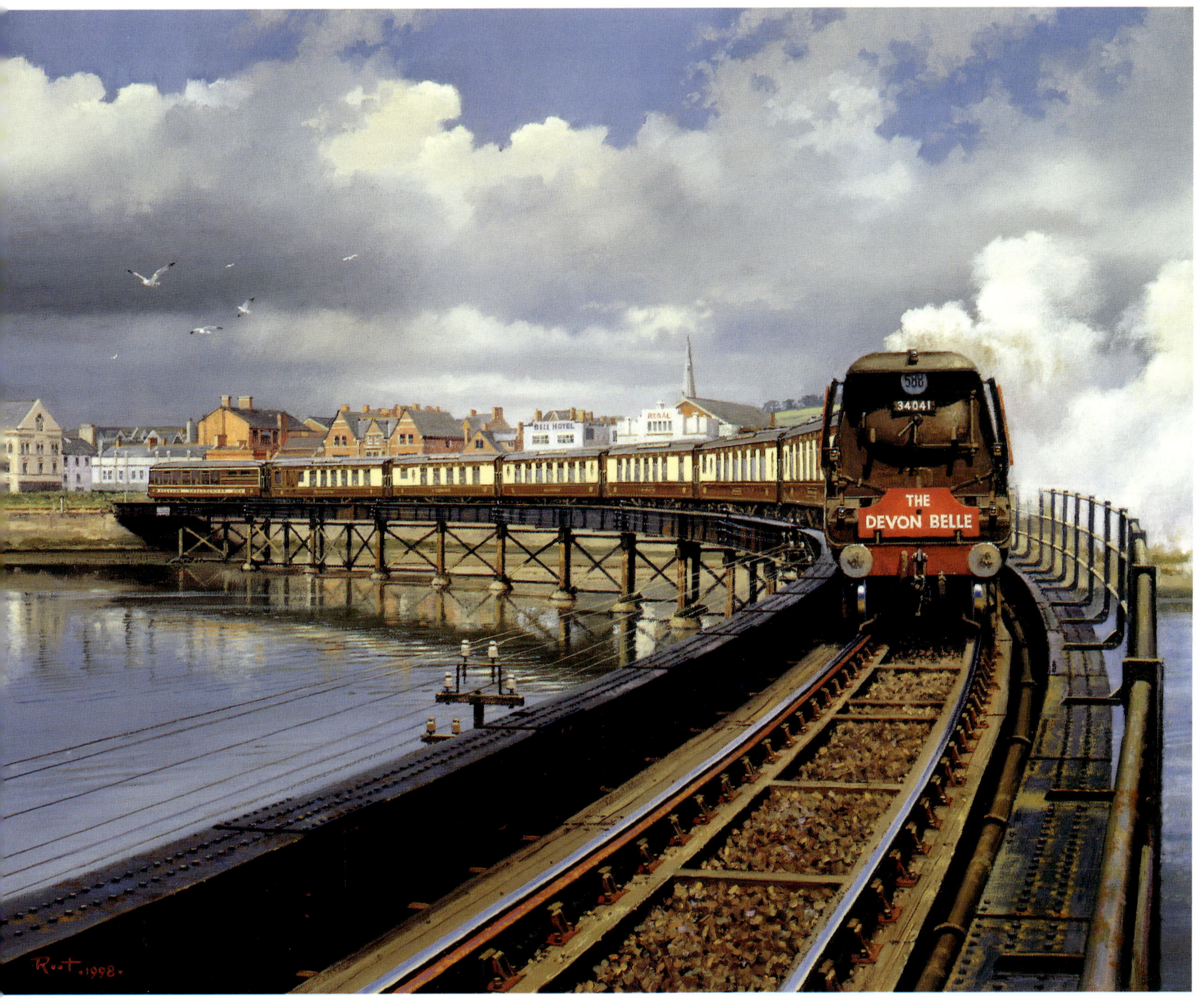
THE
DEVON BELLE
34041
588
BELL HOTEL
REGAL
Root. 1998.

Grit and Determination

Painted 1994

Although the route from London Liverpool Street to Norwich appeared predominantly flat, there is quite a gradient up to Bethnal Green, soon after leaving the terminus. As engines have the additional task of getting their express trains up to speed as quickly as possible this means a lot of hard work at the start of the journey, and Malcolm Root has captured the scene magnificently as the locomotive 2859 B17 class 4-6-0 *East Anglian* accelerates with its six-coach train of the same name, at the start of its journey via Ipswich to Norwich.

The B17 class locomotives were conceived by perhaps the greatest CME of the age of steam, Sir Nigel Gresley, along with the North British Locomotive Company, and were first introduced in 1928. They weighed in at nearly 116 tons, and had a tractive effort of 25 380lbs. Seventy-three of the class were built, but they were to a certain extent supplanted by the arrival of the B1 class in 1942. In the 1930s when streamlining of locomotives was all the rage, two of the B17 class, 2859 *East Anglian* and 2870, *City of London*, were given a streamlined casing similar to that of the much more famous A4 Gresley Pacifics. However they still ran in green livery, unlike the blue of the larger Pacifics, and were in some ways a foretaste of things to come in British Railways days. Their casings were removed in 1951. Both engines were based at the Norwich shed, from which the East Anglian Express originated.

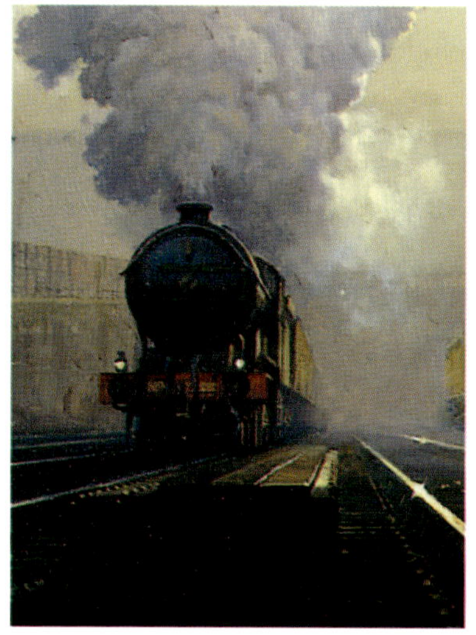

Malcolm Root has dedicated this superb picture 'to the people of the East End of London, who were to suffer so much in the years to follow,' and who also showed such grit and determination. Bethnal Green, which is the setting for this picture, lies to the north-east of London's East End, but not so far from the docks which were a prime target for German bombers. On the left of the picture can be seen a local train in the care of a B12 class locomotive, originally designed by Holden and introduced in 1911. They were specifically intended for the London to Harwich boat trains.

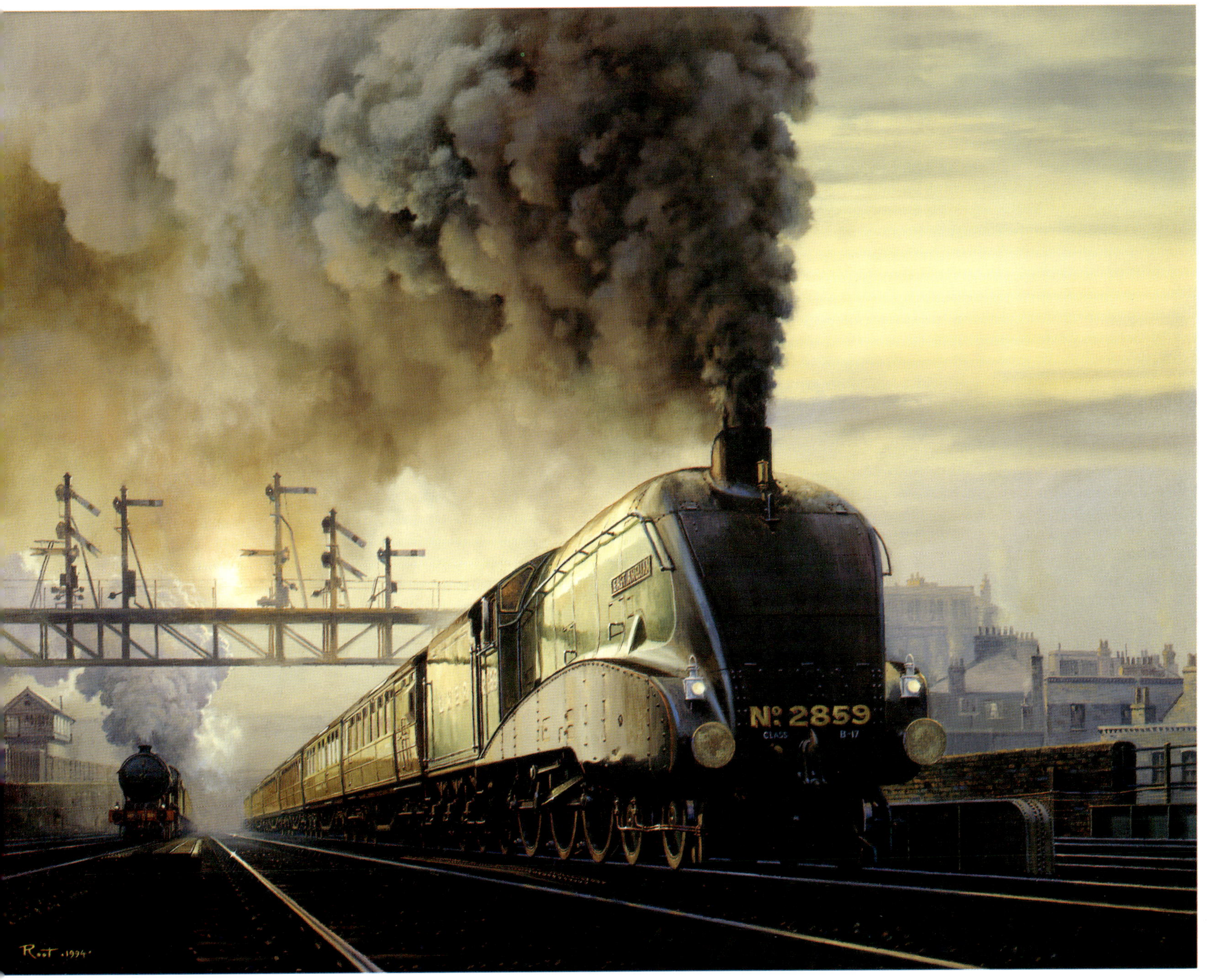
Nº 2859
CLASS B-17
Root .1994.

Greta River Bridge

Painted 2000

Nothing could be in greater contrast to the last picture than this beautiful rural scene in the Lake District. On the flat plains of East Anglia the railways could run straight from one town to the next, whereas up in the Lake District they had to twist round the hills and negotiate the lakes, often following winding river valleys and crossing and re-crossing rushing rivers as they tried to find a foothold for the rails. This lovely picture shows the Penrith to Cockermouth railway running through the Greta River gorge just to the east of Keswick. Here, between Keswick and Threlkeld stations, there were two short tunnels and many bridges, of which several were of the bowstring girder under-line design shown so vividly in the painting. The railway builders had a great advantage over their fellows on roads and canals as they could lay the track complete as they progressed, and thus use trains to bring up heavy materials for construction such as metal bridge girders. All over the country, from the mighty Forth Bridge to the smallest branch line, bridges like this one, a fascinating variety of design and construction, were to be found all along the railways. Incidentally, this bridge and its companions were designed by the railway engineer Thomas Bouch, who designed the ill-fated Tay Railway Bridge, and also drew up plans, never used, for the Forth Bridge.

The start of this well-known branch line was a railway connecting Cockermouth and the port of Workington on the western coast of the Lake District. In November 1864 the line between Cockermouth and Penrith was completed, going via Keswick, and the junction with the main West Coast line from London to Scotland was effected. Passenger traffic was first carried in January 1865, and the line was to carry both freight and passengers in reasonable quantities until it was eventually closed just over 100 years later in 1972. For those going on holiday it offered a foretaste of the marvellous scenery in the Lake District as it wound its way through river gorges and past Bassenthwaite Lake.

The locomotive shown is an 0-6-0 LNWR 18-inch goods class. These engines were nicknamed 'Cauliflowers' because of the company's coat of arms emblazoned on the driving wheel splashers. These robust engines were the staple motive power on this railway for very many years. Originally introduced in 1880 to a design by FW Webb they weighed about 53 tons, and over three hundred of the class were built. It is perhaps rather typical that while the man watches the train go by, the lady is reading her map!

'Where do you get the ideas for your paintings?' is an often-asked question. Some pictures are based on photographs. This has to be the case as much of our railway heritage has long disappeared. Some are complete fiction leaving the onlooker to ponder, and to use his superior knowledge to pinpoint the location! Occasionally a setting presents itself so perfectly that a picture is bound to follow. This example happened when on holiday in the Lake District, near Keswick. Alas the bridge now carries only a footpath, but with the addition of an LNWR 0-6-0 a picture can be made.

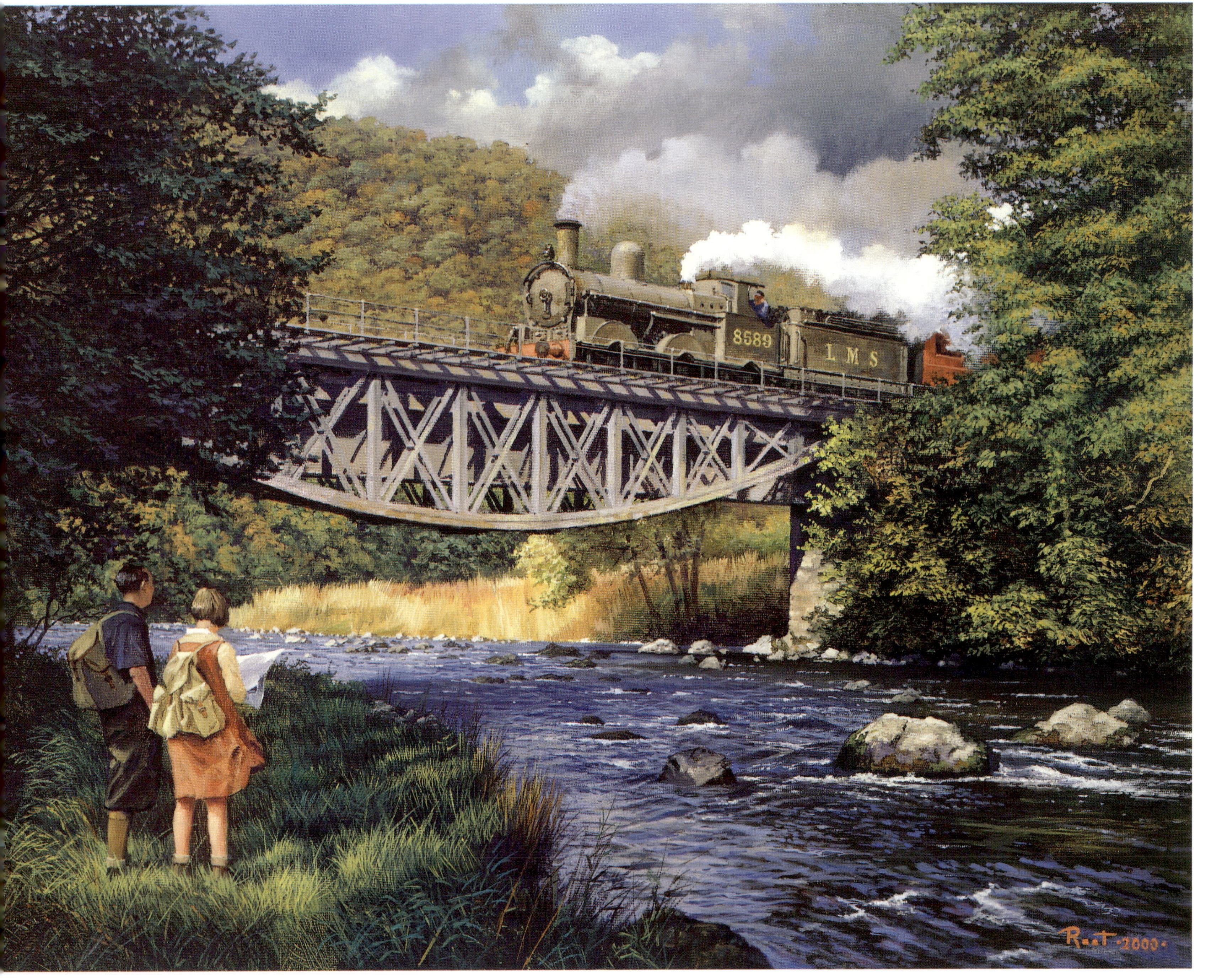
8589
LMS
Root 2000

Snow Princess

Painted 2000

Although the scene in this striking picture is only twenty-five miles from that depicted on the previous page, there could not be a greater contrast. Here the mighty LMS Pacific *Princess Margaret Rose* thunders north towards Shap in Cumbria with a London to Scotland express. It is the late 1930s when the race to the north was in full swing, and competition between the LMS and its eastern rival the LNER was at its peak. One of the problems running long-distance non-stop trains was providing water for the locomotives. By the later 1930s efficiency of locomotive engineering meant that sufficient coal for the journey could be carried. The water problem had been solved by laying water troughs along the track so that locomotives could pick up water while still travelling at speed. To provide such troughs a stretch of absolutely level track at least a mile in length was required, which was not so easy in the north of England. At Dillicar near Tebay in present-day Cumbria, such a level stretch existed where the railway ran up the valley of the River Lune alongside Jeffrey's Mount.

It was the fireman's duty to spot the marker post, giving warning of the trough, and to lower the water scoop which was located just behind the centre wheels of the tender. The system was so efficient that many hundreds of gallons could be taken on board in a mere minute or less. Indeed it was too efficient sometimes, as the spray could drown anyone foolhardy enough to stick his head out of the leading coach window. The water troughs had to be kept free of solid ice, unless they were warmed by steam pipes.

The LMS Princess Royal class 4-6-2 Pacific locomotives were designed by Sir William Stanier and the first was introduced in 1933. They were powerful express passenger engines weighing nearly 160 tons. Number 6203 *Princess Margaret Rose* was built in 1935, and there were thirteen in the class altogether, of which one, *Princess Anne* was originally a steam turbine experimental engine, later to be rebuilt as a conventional engine. Sadly it was destroyed in the terrible Harrow and Wealdstone railway accident of 1952. No 6203 was preserved and put on static display at Butlins Holiday Camp, Pwllheli, North Wales, and was later restored to mainline operation in 1990.

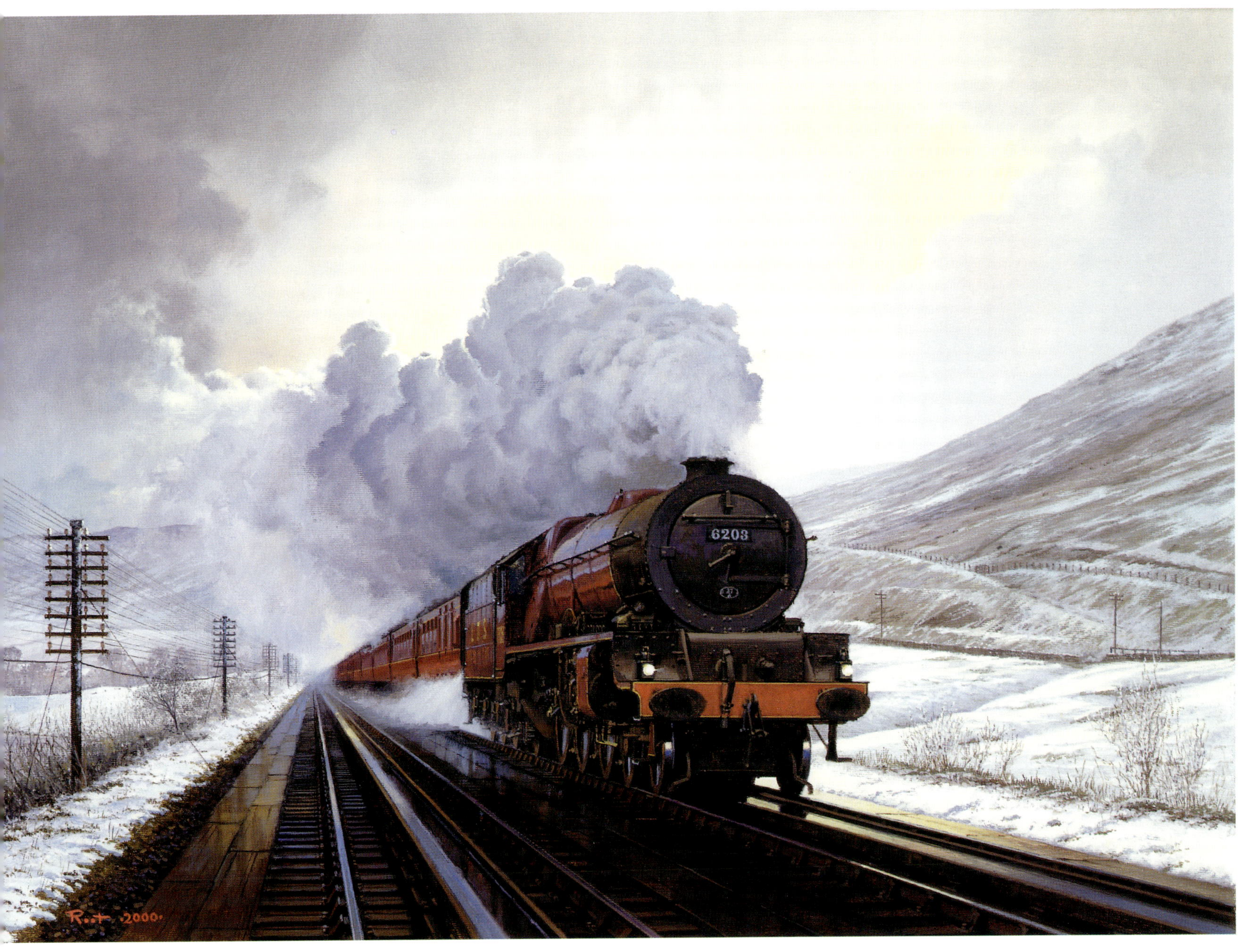
6203
Root 2000

Priory Halt

Painted 1994

Again a great contrast, as a local train on the Manningtree to Harwich branch of the Eastern Region of British Railways drops in to Priory Halt, just west of Wrabness (page 4) and close to the river Stour. Throughout the country there were sidings and halts which served local factories, and where local trains stopped to transport the workforce on a daily basis. Between Priory Halt and the river was to be found a very discreet factory belonging to the Royal Ordnance, and manufacturing munitions. In all 350 people worked at the factory and they had their own social club and other facilities. It does not appear on the map of 1914, but was built shortly afterwards. It possibly had its own jetty by the river suitable for barges, as well as several railway sidings which were served by two fireless 0-4-0 steam locomotives charged from a boiler house within the complex. Local people remember the trains stopping regularly although this was never shown on timetables. The first station platform was built of wood, later replaced with concrete. Two old carriage bodies were pressed into service as station buildings. Today nothing remains of the halt at all, and the broken-up concrete has been used to surface a nearby track. The Royal Ordnance factory buildings still exist, but somewhat modified, and used for storage purposes.

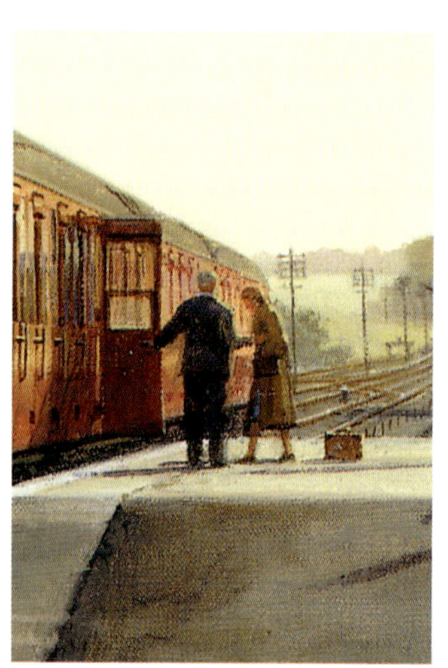

The three-coach train waiting at the halt is in the care of an N2 class 0-6-2 tank engine number 69502, designed by Sir Nigel Gresley. A development of the earlier Great Northern Railway N1 design by Ivatt, the first locomotives were introduced in 1920. In all 107 were built. Some of the engines had a distinctive condensing pipe connecting the side of the smoke box with the front of the water tank, for use on tunnelled lines in the London area. The locomotives, weighing 70 tons and with a tractive effort of 19 945lbs, were ideal on the old LNER. I have a particular affection for this engine, as Hornby produced a Dublo model of it attired in the livery of all the four main railway companies, as well as BR, and it hauled the goods train round my layout for many years – and still does!

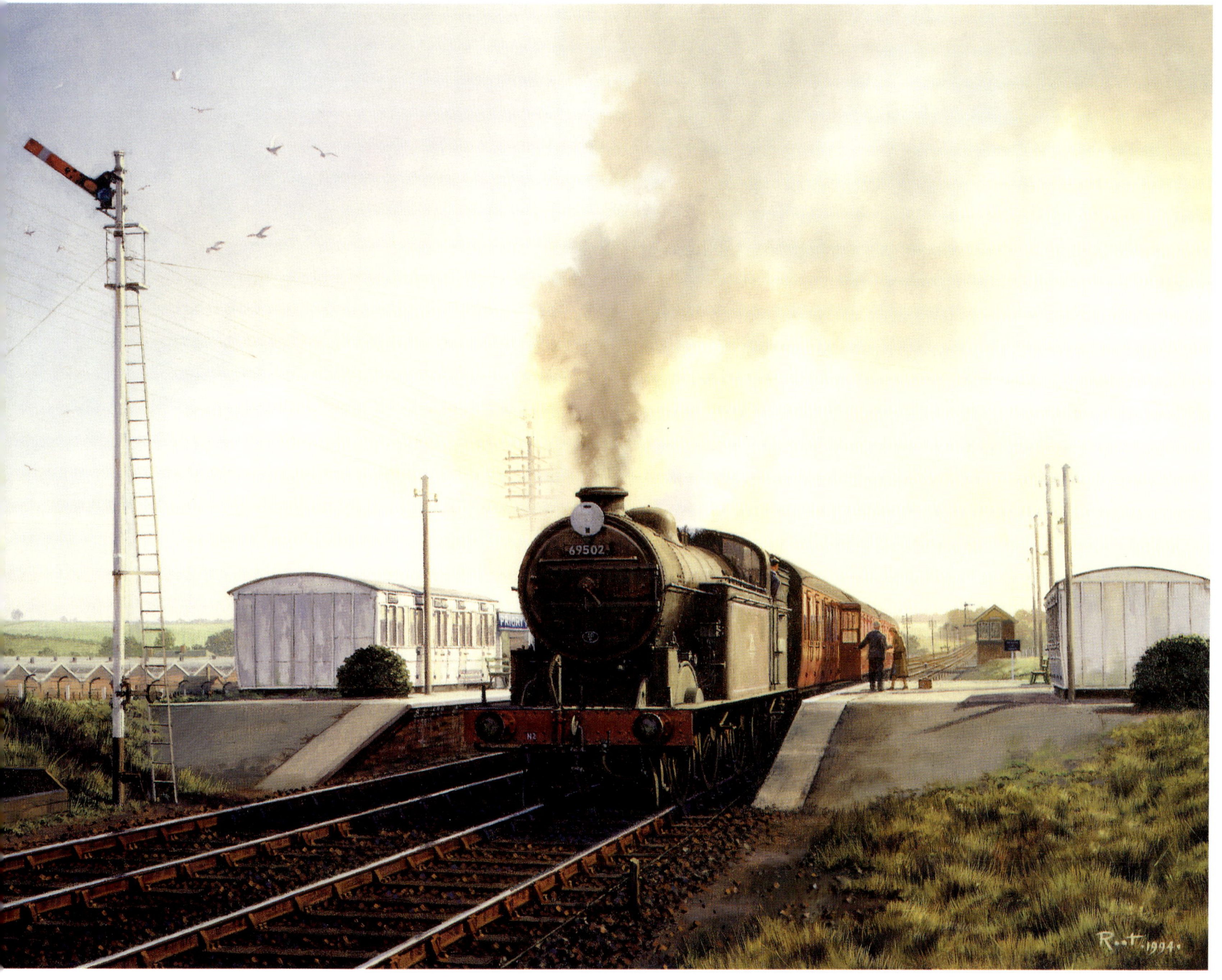
69502

Gleneagles

Painted 1996

The world famous golf club at Gleneagles in Scotland was designed by James Braid and opened first in 1919. Adjacent to the equally famous Gleneagles Hotel it is situated just south-west of Auchterarder, beside the main A9 trunk road, and also by good fortune, the main railway between Stirling and Perth. We have seen that it was quite usual for factories and other industrial sites to have their own railway halts, but there cannot be many golf clubs that can boast their own stations, and especially a station as spectacular as Gleneagles with its two storey buildings and unusual footbridge. It is to be noticed that at the time this painting depicts, the 1960s, the extra tracks in to the station platform on the left-hand side have already been removed. Given such excellent communications it is easy for large numbers of visitors to reach the golf club when major tournaments are being played there.

When the four major railway companies were created in 1923 there was some overlap between the territories of the LMS and the LNER, and this was particularly so in Scotland where the LNER pushed as far north as Mallaig on the west coast, while the LMS headed for the north-east, going via Inverness to Wick. Gleneagles was thus sited on the old LMS main line, but with the coming of British Railways integration took place, and so it is not surprising to find a train hauled by an ex-LNER locomotive heading south out of the station. South of Stirling there would be a choice of routes, via either Glasgow or Edinburgh, and depending on that, a different terminus in London.

This is a very fine portrait of Sir Nigel Gresley's A4 Pacific 60024 *Kingfisher*. When originally built the A4s had valances which covered the top half of the driving wheels and the valve gear. These had to be removed when maintenance was required, and this was time consuming, especially for hard-pressed shed staff during the war. For this reason the valances were removed during the war and never replaced. Anyway, after the war the A4s ran with equal efficiency without their valances, and continued in service until replaced with diesels in the 1960s. Six of the class are preserved including *Mallard* and *Sir Nigel Gresley* and of these six one is in Canada and one in the USA. They were introduced in 1935, and *Mallard*'s record of 126mph for a steam engine, in July 1938, remains unbroken.

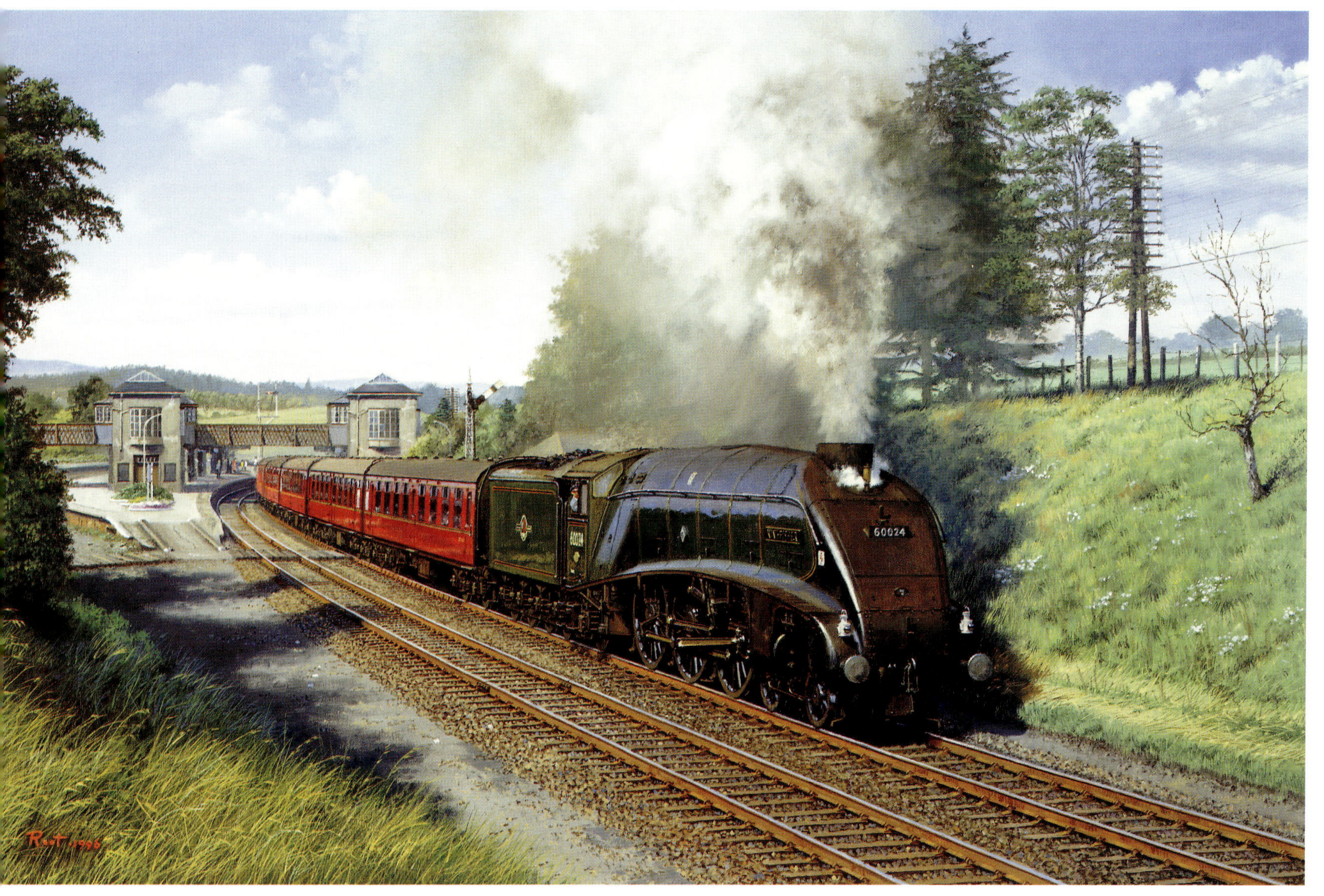
60024

Nearing Departure

Painted 2001

Of the ten or so London terminus stations, four, namely Paddington, Euston, Kings Cross and Victoria had an early prominence allowing them to develop into the flagship stations of the four great railway companies from 1923 onwards. As early as 1832 the directors of the London & Birmingham Railway were looking at a number of possible sites, but were hampered by the decision of the government that for safety reasons railway trains must be kept away from the City of London and Westminster. This explains why the main stations in London are all sited in a ring around the capital. Having looked at a site at Chalk Farm, the directors of the L&BR decided it was economically sensible to build an extension down to Euston Grove, even though this meant overcoming the problem of a steep gradient, Camden Bank. The solution was to take the locomotives off the trains at Chalk Farm, and then run them down the bank to the new Euston Station in the charge of a brakeman. On leaving the station the trains were hauled up the bank on cables wound in by a stationary engine at Chalk Farm. This also solved the problem of bringing locomotives within the sacred ring! The new station at Euston cost £39 850 to build, but the directors also commissioned the architect Philip Hardwick to create a Doric masterpiece, the Euston Arch, which with its lodges cost an amazing £35 000.

There must have been an almost spooky feeling about being towed silently out of the old Euston station on the end of a cable! What a contrast to the power and simmering majesty of the mighty LMS Princess Coronation Pacific ready to tackle Camden Bank with a full head of steam. This class of locomotive, designed by Sir William Stanier, was first introduced in a streamlined version in 1937, but somehow did not look nearly as convincing as Gresley's A4s. Some of the class were built without streamlining, and looked much better in my opinion, so when it was found that maintenance was very difficult the casing was removed from all the locomotives. The *Duchess of Sutherland* shown in British Railways livery in the painting was built in 1938, but the scene is late 1950s, when she hauled the Royal Scot train from Euston to Glasgow in about 6.5 hours. This titled train, inaugurated in 1927, had to be hauled over the summits at Shap and Beattock, and all of the *Duchess*'s 40 000lbs of tractive effort were needed. The *Duchess of Sutherland* was preserved and spent some time at Bressingham Hall where I was lucky enough to ride on her footplate before 'Health and Safety' put an end to such a memorable experience.

The sight of a 'named' train passing at speed was always something special. The headboard was often adorned with crests or flags and the carriage boards announcing start and destination points somehow seemed to set these trains apart from the rest. They don't come any more famous than the Royal Scot seen here complete with tartan headboard awaiting departure from Euston. I recall having some difficulty in sourcing the information necessary to paint the headboard which appears so large in the painting. Fortunately help was at hand with the expert and willing help of the National Railway Museum, who soon put me right.

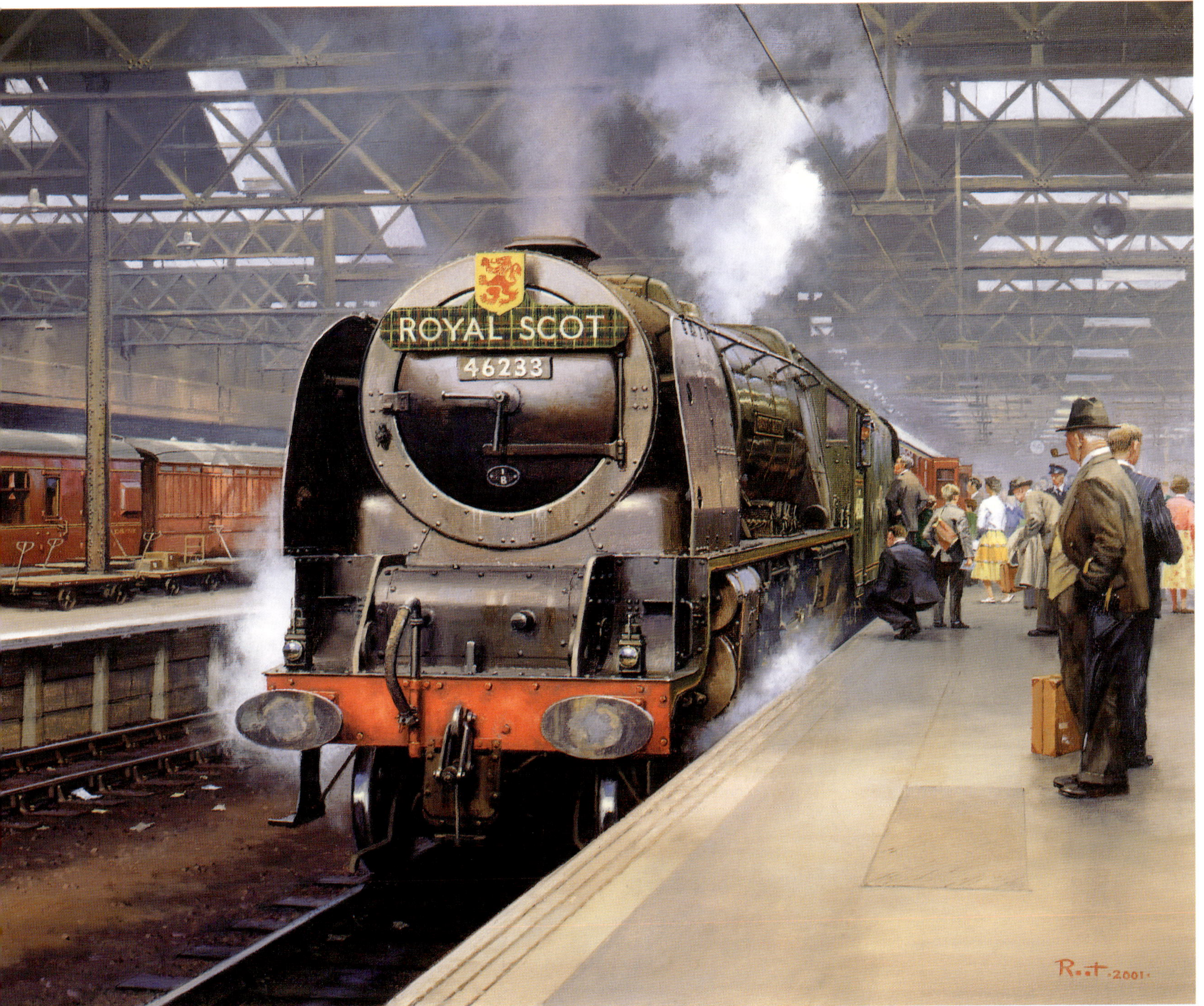
ROYAL SCOT
46233
Root 2001

Topping Up the Tank

Painted 1996

Ventnor, on the south coast of the Isle of Wight, was served by two railway stations in its heyday, but the main station which was the southern terminus for the Isle of Wight Railway was the more important, and of special character. Trains coming from Ryde on the north coast, where they connected with steamers from the mainland, passed through Brading and Sandown, and then began a climb through Shanklin. They then plunged through the long tunnel under St Boniface Down, and finally emerged out of breath right into Ventnor station, nearly 300 feet above sea level. The sea was less than half a mile away to the south! It is said that chalk excavated when the tunnel was built was used in the construction of the goods shed at the southern end of the station. In the late 1800s a non-stop Ryde to Ventnor train christened 'The Invalid Express' did the 12 miles in 21 minutes, which must have been very exciting for the invalids travelling to the famous sanatorium at Ventnor for the good of their health. One suspects a few may have expired in the final tunnel without ever reaching the promised land!

Before the amalgamation of the railways in 1923 the Isle of Wight was served by three principal railways, all built between 1860 and 1900. In 1923 the Southern Railway took over, and inherited a wide variety of locomotives and rolling stock, most of it worn out. Because the traffic on the Island railways was light and seasonal, the policy of the SR was to 'pension off' suitable locomotives and rolling stock from elsewhere, and thus for a period from the mid 1930s to the mid 1960s ex-LSWR 02 class 0-4-4 tank engines became the Island's standard locomotive on all routes. These locomotives, designed by W Adams, were first introduced in 1889, with a second batch made in 1923, and those used on the Island weighed in at about 48 tons, nearly two tons more than the others, due to being fitted with a larger bunker. They were also named after the places served by the railway, and in the painting number 29 *Alverstone* is seen getting a much needed drink from the water column at the south end of Ventnor station. The tunnel is out of sight to the left, and St Boniface Down in the background. In this scene from the 1950s it is good to see the much missed red K2 telephone box in a prominent position. I wonder where it is now?

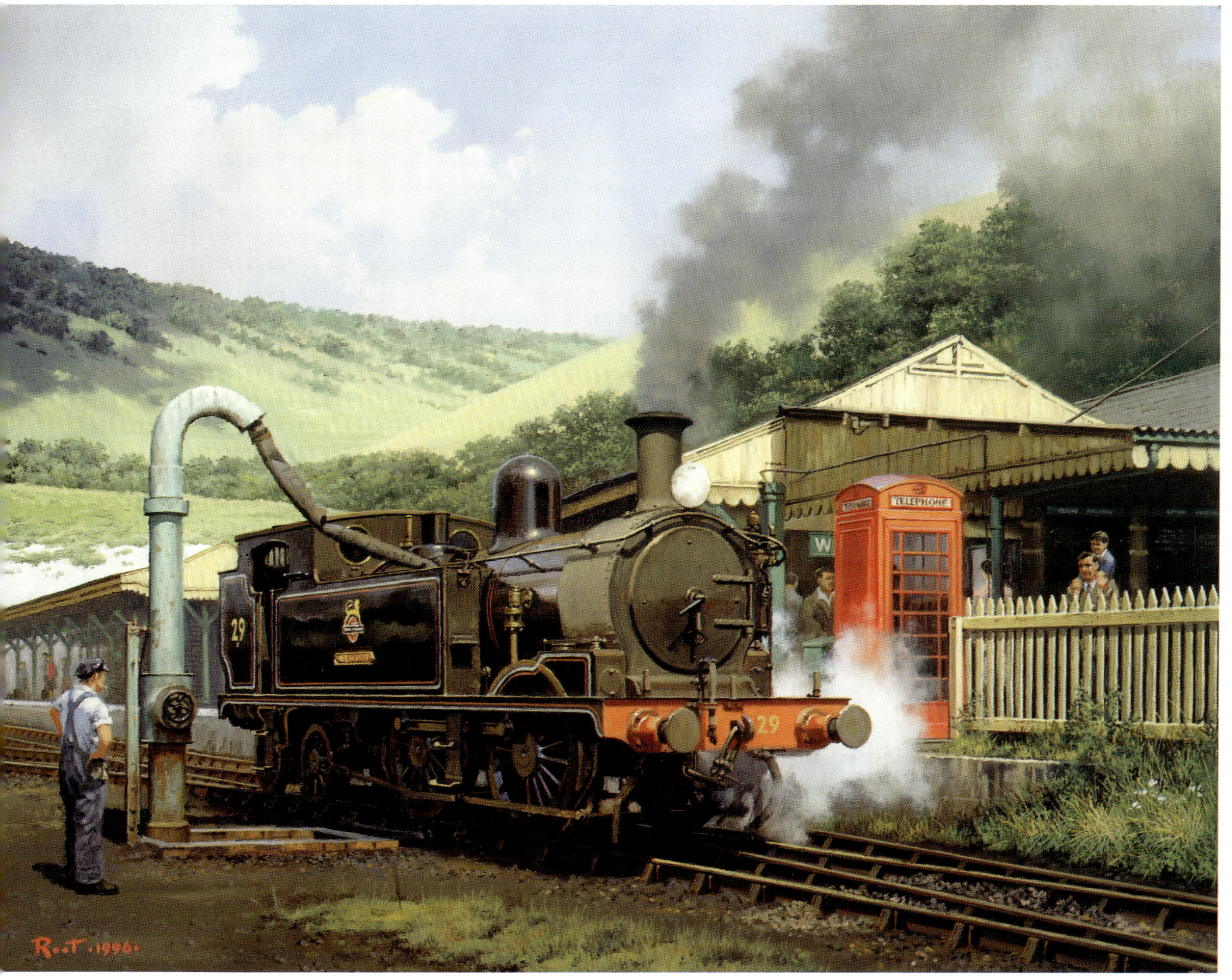
TELEPHONE
29
29
Root. 1996.

Monday Morning

Painted 1998

Monday morning, and just to add to the feeling of gloom it is also raining, so coats and brollies are the order of the day. I do not know any artist who conveys wetness as well as Malcolm does, with the hazy background, lights reflecting on wet platform surfaces, and sodden sleepers. Because London was not only the capital city of England, but the capital of an empire that stretched all over the world, it had huge importance down the centuries, and every self-respecting railway company wanted its line to terminate in the city. Hence the ring of London stations, and the web of railways coming into London from every direction except actually up the Thames! This in turn meant that many of London's millions of workers could escape from the congested built-up areas and live an hour's journey away along one of the many railway lines. Here a train prepares to leave Bishop's Stortford on its 45-minute journey via Bethnal Green to London Liverpool Street. My grandfather would have boarded its predecessor at Hoddesden and travelled to work at his office in the City of London in the 1880s! Commuting to work is not such a new occupation, as the desire to live outside the sprawling capital and to bring up one's children in a country environment must go back nearly 150 years.

The commuter train is hauled by Britannia class loco 70007 *Coeur-de-Lion*. Although the Britannia class locomotives were designated mixed traffic they were largely used on express passenger services. With the exception of the *Duke of Gloucester* it was the largest of the BR standard locomotives. In all 55 of the class were built at the old locomotive works at Crewe (details of the class are given on page 2). The painting conveys well the majesty of these last of the great steam locomotives to thunder along British railways.

'Coeur de lion' or Lionheart was the nickname of King Richard I, who also had a Great Western Railway King class loco named after him. Compared too favourably to his brother John, and especially in films about Robin Hood, Richard actually spent only nine months of his ten-year reign in England. The rest of the time he was either fighting in the Holy Land or in prison in Austria! It seems very unfair that he should have had two magnificent locomotives named after him, when much better kings only achieved one!

As if Monday morning is not depressing enough, it is also raining. It is not yet fully light and this coupled with the dull weather presents a gloomy scene. To emphasise the cold and damp some warmth needs to be added to the picture, and I did this by highlighting the signal box interior. With the wet look picture it is an advantage to include verticals to make reflections, and here they are provided by the signal box and its step supports. I wanted to separate the engine from the signal box, and the fact that steam lingers on cold days gave me an authentic way to do this.

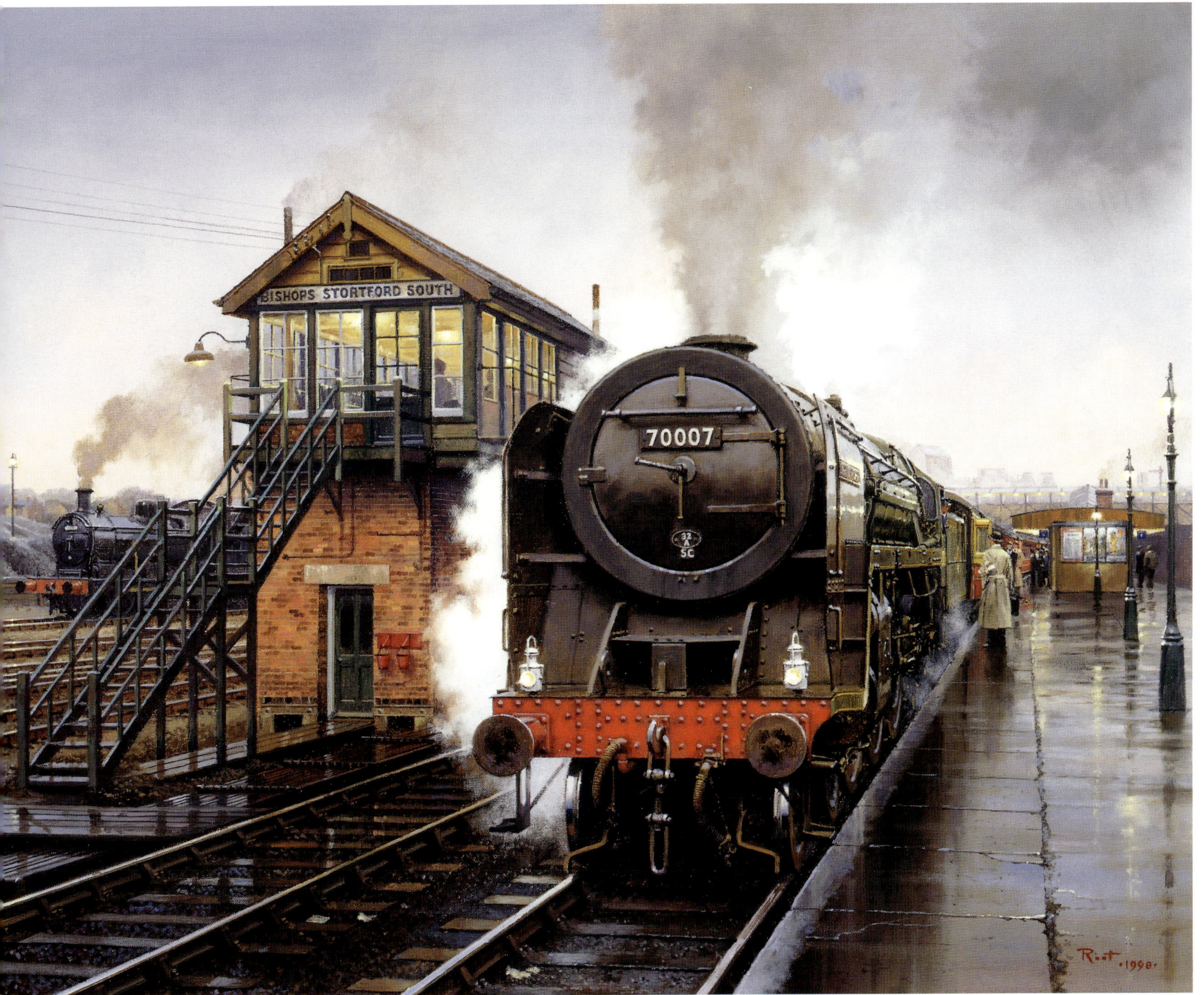
BISHOPS STORTFORD SOUTH
70007
Root 1998

All Out Effort

Painted 2001

Isambard Kingdom Brunel was an engineer of amazing genius, but he also had some notable and very costly failures such as the *Great Eastern*, the broad gauge, and the atmospheric system. As the Great Western Railway developed, Brunel was required in 1844 to construct the section between Exeter and Plymouth in South Devon. The first part, via the Exe estuary, the seashore at Dawlish, and the Teign estuary was relatively easy. Beyond Newton Abbot any fairly direct route involved crossing the southern foothills and river valleys of Dartmoor with steep gradients.

Brunel was attracted by the atmospheric system of railway patented by Clegg and Samuda, where a train is pulled along by suction using continuous pipes, a shoe-type piston on the train, and stationary pumping engines. Brunel decided this would solve his problems, and the system was installed between Exeter and Totnes. The system was up and running by November 1847, somewhat delayed, and for a time worked well with 64mph being attained on one occasion. But there were too many parts to go wrong and deteriorate, especially the vital leather seals, and by June 1848 even Brunel had to admit failure. It was a great blow to his reputation and personal finances, and it left the company with a large loss of perhaps £400 000, and a single line with some very heavy gradients, which were to tax locomotives to the limit for many years to come. Chief among these were the Dainton banks, with Dainton tunnel at their peak.

In this spectacular painting we see BR King class 6023 *King Edward II* dragging the down Cornish Riviera Express up Dainton bank past Stoneycombe quarry in the early 1950s, and needing all of its 40 300lbs of tractive effort to do so. Until the coming of the Kings, larger trains had to be double-headed to cope with the 1-in-36 gradient. Being born and brought up a couple of miles from Dainton, I spent many childhood hours marvelling at the mighty engines, and I can remember heavy goods trains not only being double-headed, but with a banker on the back. This may have been partly to prevent trucks running away if a coupling broke, as it did on at least one occasion. I was most impressed by the mess it made!

The King class locomotives introduced in 1927 to a design by CB Collett, were a natural development from the Castles and their predecessors, and weighed about 135 tons. They were the pride of the GWR, and when *King George V* went to visit the USA the engineers over there were amazed at its performance. In all thirty of the class were built, of which sadly only three are now preserved, *King Edward II* being one of the lucky ones. The Cornish Riviera Express was inaugurated on 1 July 1904, and became one of the country's most famous titled trains, covering the distance from Paddington to Plymouth in 4 hours, and on to Penzance. The performance of the Kings has only recently been superseded by the HSTs of our own day.

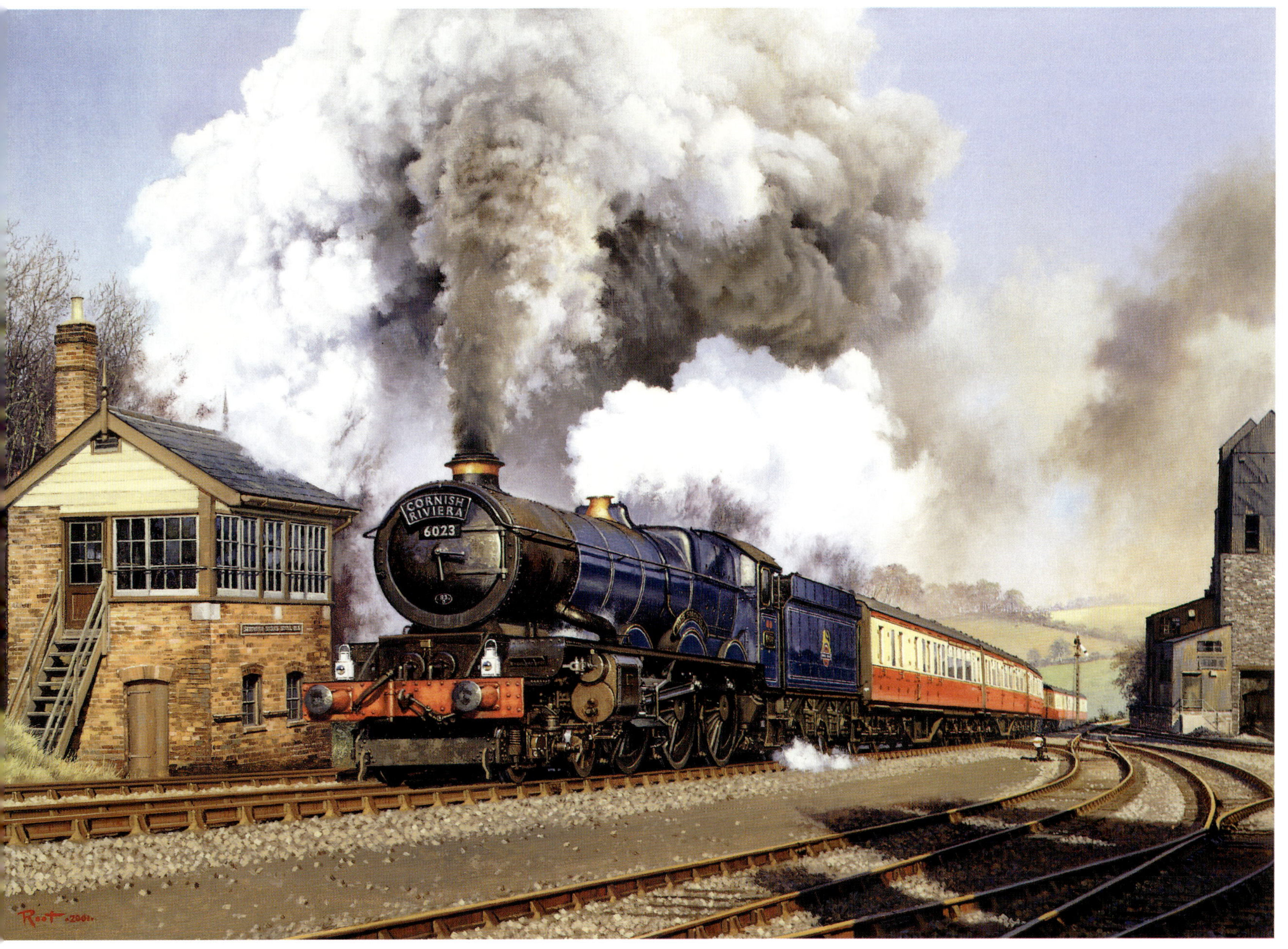
CORNISH RIVIERA
6023
Root 2001

Cleaning the Ash Pit

Painted 1996

One of the fundamental principles of running a railway was that locomotives and their crews operated out of a running shed which was strategically positioned for the route they had to serve. Unless they were engaged on a long-distance run, loco and crew would return to the shed, and after their shift would normally be able to go home to their families. The locomotive would be cleaned and serviced by a team of fitters and cleaners who knew each engine in their care. As the whole health and power of an engine depended on the strength of the fire in the firebox, care had to be taken to dump clinker and ash after each run, in order to keep a 'clean fire'. Then a good fire could be built up when required. It was usually the job of the shed labourer to clear ash, though when pressed he would be aided by the engine cleaner. The cleaner, usually just starting his railway career would be happy to do this if it meant more pay (the labourer's pay being that of an adult). Ashpans were cleaned and ash and clinker deposited where the engine stood, often into the pit between the rails. Just enough steam pressure would be retained to drift on to a nearby siding, or into the engine shed, to rest for the night. The mixture of ash and clinker was used to surface the yard areas as it would stop weeds growing, and had to be dumped somewhere! It really had no other commercial use.

This scene is described as 'somewhere in Great Western territory', but such a scene would be found every day all over the country. The clue is the locomotive which is just preparing to be serviced, a GW 4-6-0 modified Hall class 6990 *Witherslack Hall*, originally designed by CB Collett and introduced in the modified form by Hawksworth in 1944. The class were highly successful general-purpose locomotives, and over 300 were built, which operated all over the Great Western territory. They weighed in at 121 tons, and developed 27 275lbs tractive effort. The Halls worked to the end of the steam era and eighteen were saved from scrapping, of which seven were modified Halls.

No less important to the GWR is the locomotive on the right of the painting, the ubiquitous 2-6-2 Prairie tank engine, which was also designed by CB Collett, and found all over the Western Region. Introduced in the 1930s, well over 200 were built, and they worked very hard with both local passenger and goods trains, as well as giving a helping hand up the Dainton bank! In the distance on the left of the picture can be seen a Castle resting in the gloaming, but I cannot read its name or number! Only one of the seven railwaymen in the picture is actually working, but then it is the end of the day, so that is to be expected.

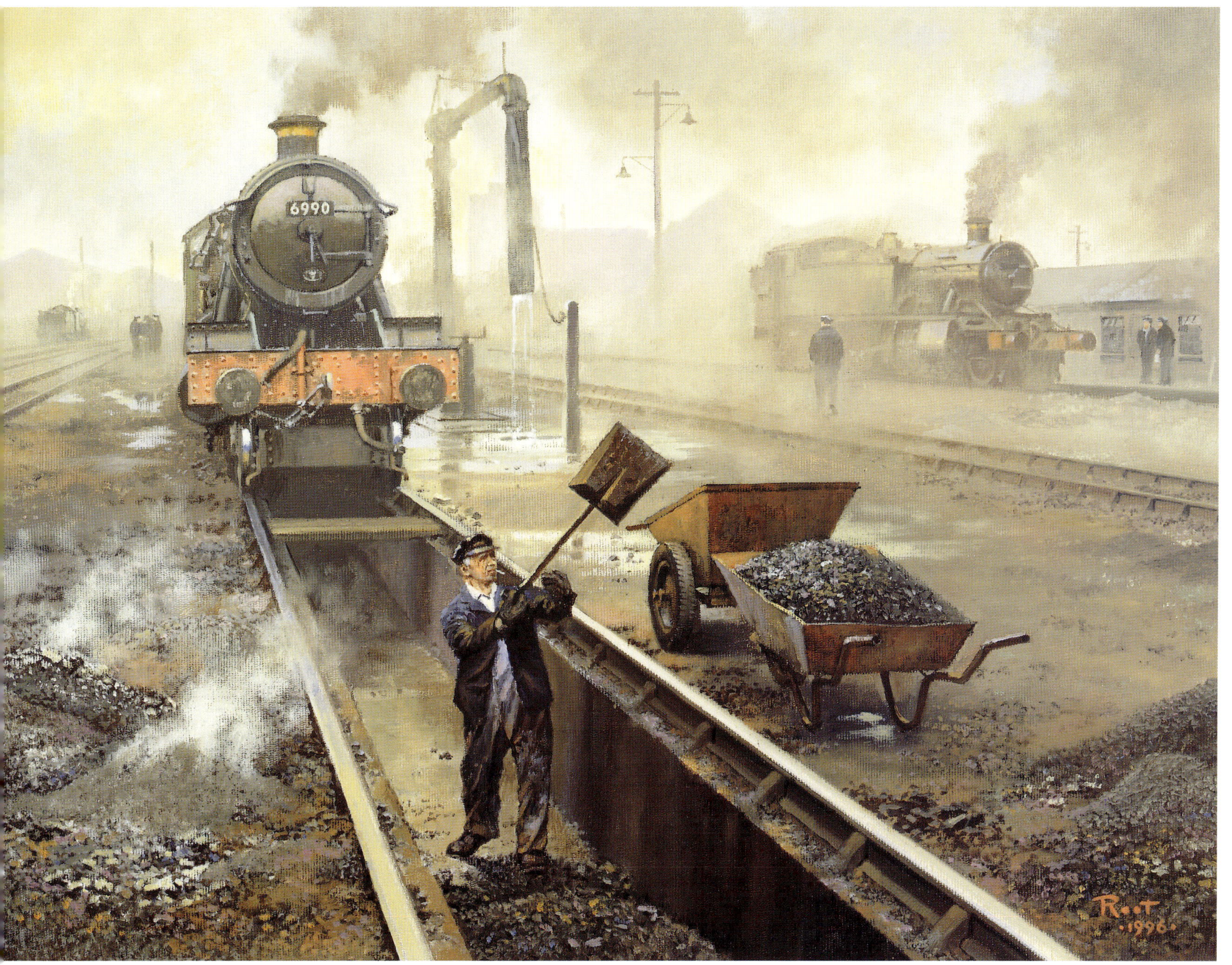
6990
ROOT
·1996·

Ely Evening

Painted 1998

For nearly nine hundred years the great cathedral and surrounding city of Ely have stood like a raised island above the flat surrounding fens. In fact before the fens were drained, the great cathedral floated like a ship surrounded by water. It was a remote place, hideout for Hereward the Wake, and a place where abbot and monks had little to distract them from their prayers. The fens were drained, providing fertile land for agriculture, and a main stagecoach route preceded the coming of the railway. In fact Ely became a very important junction with the main line from London coming in via Cambridge, and then routes going out to Newmarket, Norwich, Kings Lynn and Peterborough. In this evening scene we see a London to Kings Lynn train passing the Ely South signal box on its way into Ely station in the mid 1980s.

The debate about steam versus diesel went back a good many years. The *Modern World Book of Railways* published in 1948 reveals that by using diesel electric locomotives on the run between London and Derby the LMR saved 13 000 tons of coal in a year. The use of diesel shunters balanced 50 tons of oil used against 600 tons of coal. Given the quick start up time, lack of fuel consumption when not in use, abolition of the overworked fireman, lower weights and so on, the battle was really over before it even started, hard as it is for me to admit it!

Here one of the most successful and widespread of all the diesels, a Class 47, is heading the train. The Class 47 were the most numerous class of main line diesel locomotives with over 500 being built, and could be found throughout the British Railways network. Many variations occurred, but the major difference was between those locomotives which retained steam heating equipment and those which had it removed, and can be identified by the lack of a steam pipe on the buffer beam. Constructed at Crewe and containing Brush equipment, the Class 47 locomotives weighed between 111 and 123 tons in running order, and were introduced in 1962. They were rated at 2750 hp, which gave them a tractive effort of 62 000lbs, – compared to the 40 300 of the GWR King class loco. Their fuel tanks held 765 gallons, giving them a considerable range. They were lighter and shorter than the most powerful of the steam locomotives, and also had the great advantage of being able to be driven from either end of the locomotive, so that turntables became a thing of the past. The design of the diesel locomotive also gave the driver an unrivalled view of the road ahead, as well as a degree of comfort never found in a steam locomotive. However much one loves steam locomotives, the above advantages cannot be ignored, and explain the rapid changeover to diesel traction.

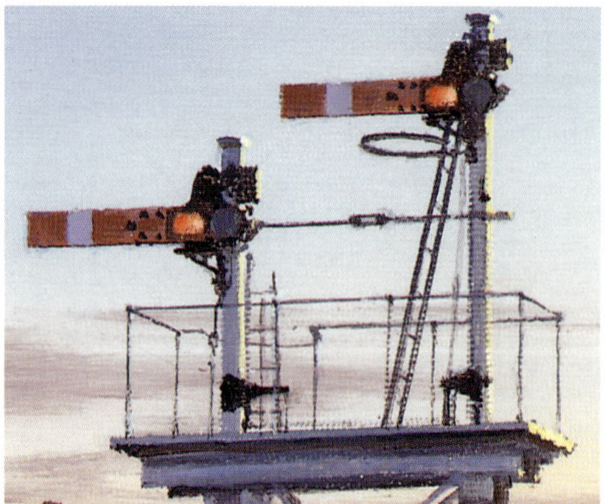

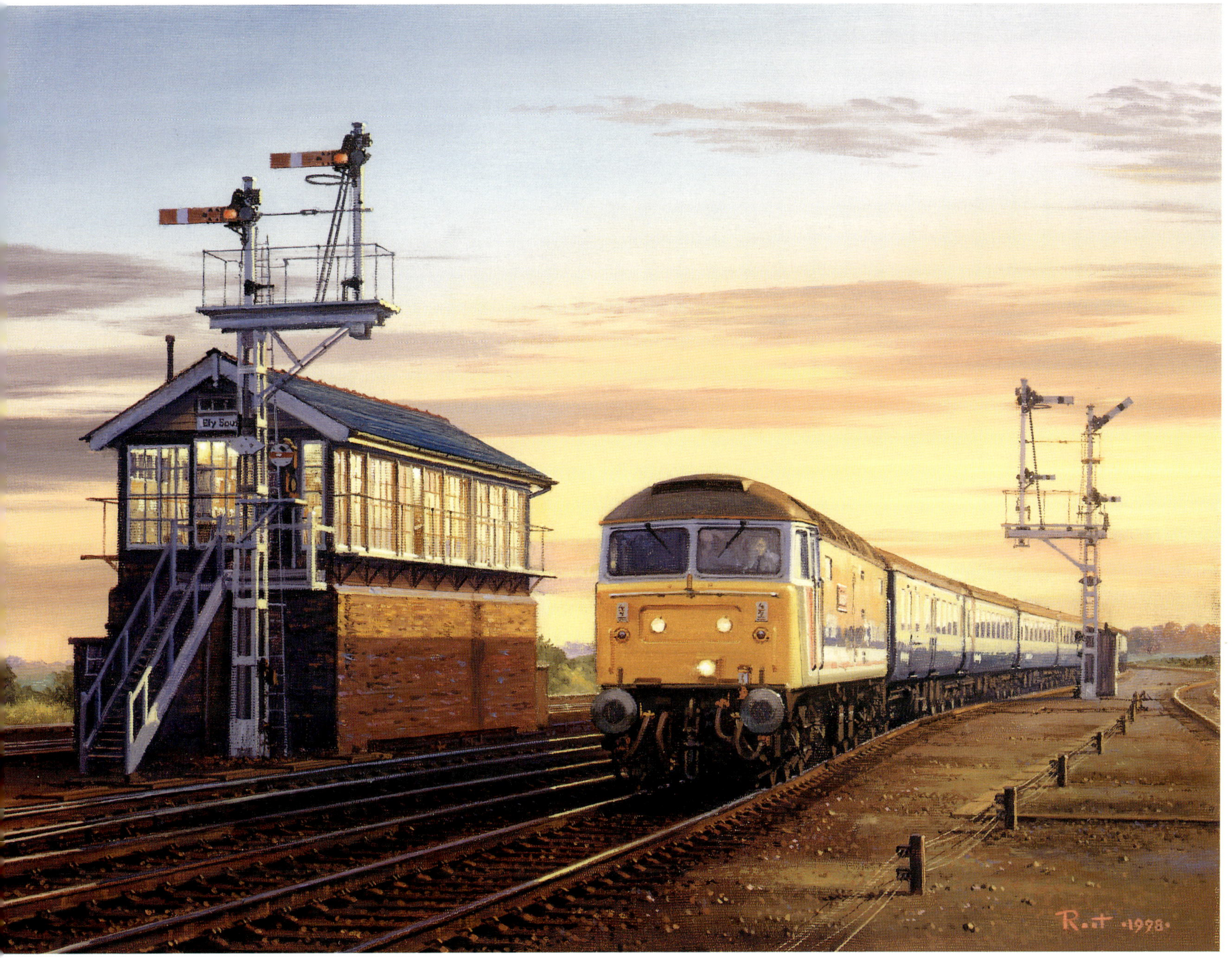
Root ·1998·

Norfolk Charabanc

Painted 2000

There are many places in the British Isles where road and rail, and even canal and river, run side-by-side, the first three using the valley carved by the river as the natural route to avoid hills. Here the road and railway make use of the narrow strip of level land between low hills and the sea, and once again the temptation to make a race of it has proved too great. The charabanc driver has seen the smoke of the train in his small mirror and pressed his foot further down on the accelerator, and the driver of the locomotive has spotted the two vehicles ahead, and realising one is the despicable charabanc which takes passengers away from the railways, has gently opened his steam regulator to give the old lady a bit more speed. At least the rails are smooth, unlike the road surface, so the passengers on the train are likely to enjoy the race more than those being rattled around on the bus! I think the Darracq behind has given up the contest, and the passenger is admiring the thundering locomotive above him as it passes by.

The scene is on the north Norfolk coast, probably heading east towards Sheringham on what is now the beautiful preserved North Norfolk Railway. This line was part of the old Eastern & Midland Railway of 1882 vintage, which was bought up by the Midland & Great Northern Railway in 1893. It had its administrative headquarters at Kings Lynn, and its own locomotive works at Melton Constable, where its beautiful 'autumn leaf' yellow-liveried locomotives were built and maintained. In 1923 the Midland & Great Northern was inherited jointly by the LMS and LNER but retained much of its original character. In 1935 the concern was handed over to the LNER.

The locomotive in this picture winning the race is a Beyer Peacock 4-4-0. The class was first introduced in 1882 at a cost of £2000, but from 1895 Midland C-type boilers were substituted, and Johnson's preferred Salter spring-balance safety valves fitted on the dome, with a single lock-up valve in a distinctive brass casing on top of the firebox. Number 30, seen in the picture, also has a weatherboard on its tender, and is provided with a tablet exchanger on both sides so that it can run tender first when required. Fifteen locomotives in this handsome class were built, and many of them saw long service in northern East Anglia. Number 30 was scrapped in 1933. The date for this scene would be about 1920. It is strange, but only last week I found myself speeding up a bit alongside a train on the way home from Felixstowe!

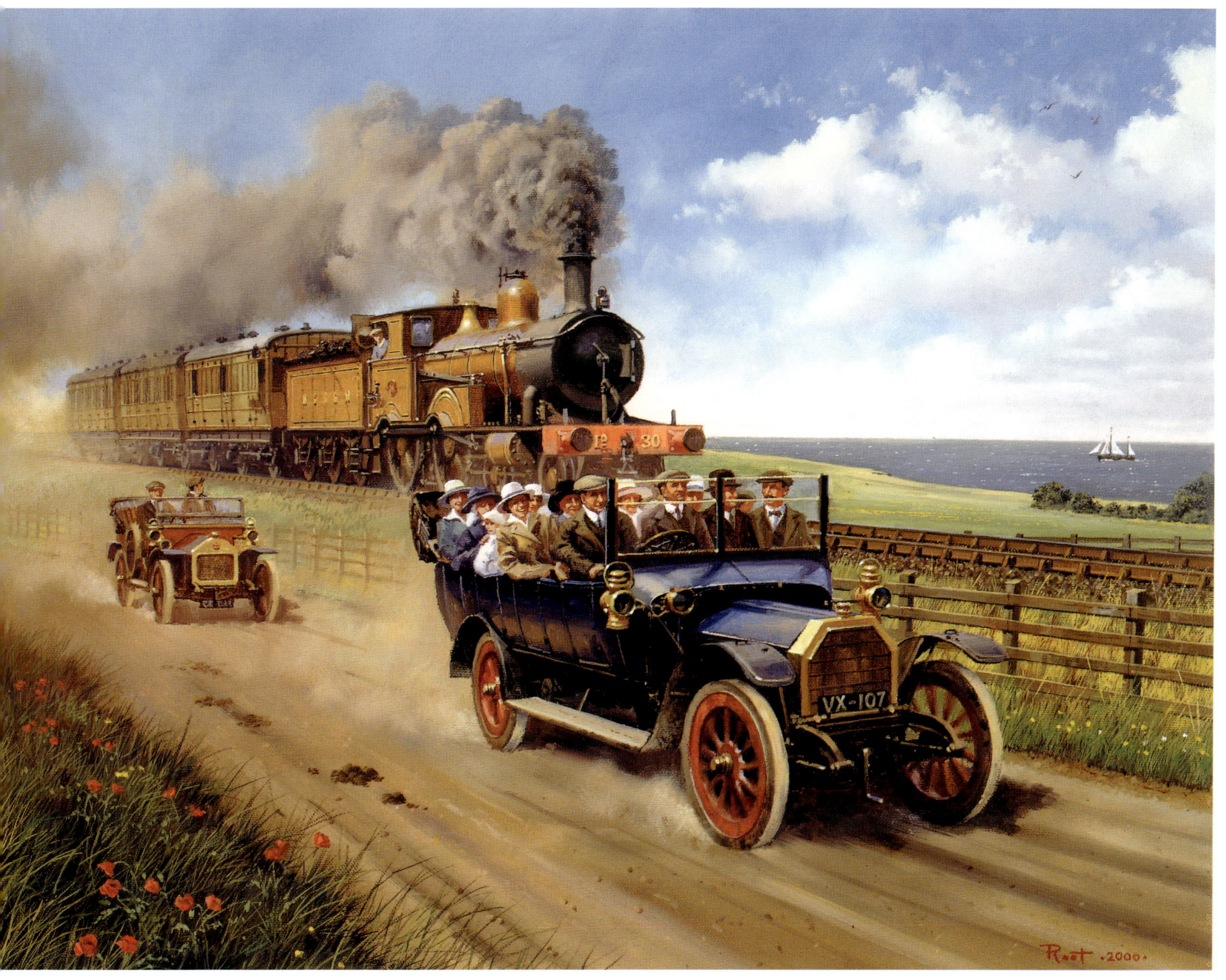
VX-107
Root ·2000·

Great Eastern Splendour

Reproduced by permission of Colchester Museums. Painted 1987

The Great Eastern Railway came into existence in 1862 as an amalgamation of five smaller railway companies, the earliest of which had been founded in 1834. Grandiose designs were whittled down, often due to financial stringency, but the GER was able to establish a network of railways to serve East Anglia, working out of the Liverpool Street station terminus in London. Two factors helped this railway: firstly the relatively flat land which it traversed, secondly the rapid expansion of built-up areas in Essex and Hertfordshire which generated a steady increase in commuting into London, and increasing numbers of profitable suburban trains. By 1910 the GER was firmly established under the chairmanship of Lord Claud Hamilton, and was financially sound. Its route to Harwich and from there to the Continent was very popular, and the main line via Ipswich and Norwich to the north Norfolk coast carried a lot of general as well as holiday traffic. In addition there was a link as far north as York helping to provide industrial traffic. It was a thriving railway that made its contribution to the efforts of the First World War, and was then swallowed up into the London & North Eastern Railway in 1923.

East Anglia is not all flat, and at Colchester, scene of this picture, the railway came along the side of a hill above the ancient town, and the station was on a fairly sharp curve. As a result it was always hampered by speed restrictions. Although work started before the war it was not until 1962 that the rebuilding of the station, along with the elimination of the curve, was completed. The present-day station is not the striking building Malcolm has depicted.

The locomotive shown is a GER D15 Claud Hamilton class 4-4-0 designed by James Holden and introduced in 1900. It has been described as one of the most handsome locomotives ever built. It is interesting that from an early date motor cars were styled to make them look more graceful, but railway locomotives remained essentially functional. The introduction of streamlining in the 1930s to give the appearance of speed was little more than a publicity stunt. It did little to enhance performance. Yet the locomotive did have a great sense of power and grace, and this was recognised and enhanced by livery and lining. The dark blue, red and polished brass of the GER was very distinctive, and the Claud Hamilton class with large driving wheels and an almost transatlantic flavour to the cab was very striking, and had a long life in service. The D15s weighed 91 tons including the tender, and developed a tractive effort of 17 096lbs. The GER experimented with oil burning, but as North Sea oil had not arrived, coal still held the advantage. Only one engine in the class had a name, and that was *Claud Hamilton* itself, named after the chairman of the railway.

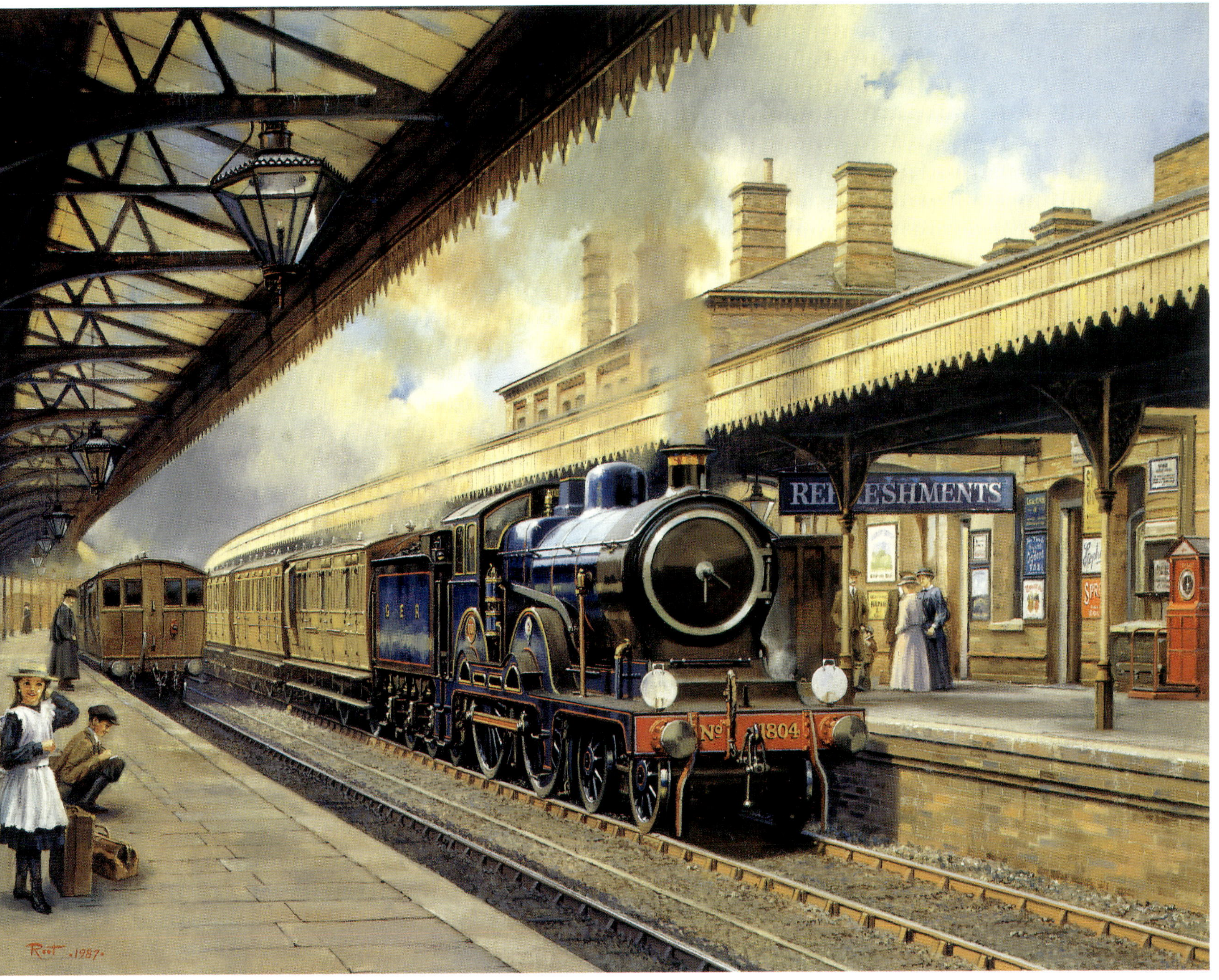
No 1804
G E R
Root .1987.

Night Freight

Painted 1997

It is late evening and foggy at Shrewsbury station, and the platforms are deserted except for two passengers and a well-dressed porter. The railways never sleep, and the scene is dominated by a goods train which has emerged out of the murk, and is passing slowly through the station on the middle track, the driver keeping a sharp lookout for the all important signals. The railways were born because of the need to move goods traffic, especially coal and mineral ore, and the first ones were small processions of wagons pulled by horses. It was the need to move coal from the Durham mines that caused the Stockton and Darlington railway to be built, and the engine *Locomotion* to achieve an astonishing 15 miles per hour! From that moment onwards goods traffic became of vital importance to the growing railways, and especially the transport of coal, which was the power source for the nation.

The handling of goods traffic by the railways was almost a world in itself. Thousands of industrial sites, large and small, had their own sidings connected to the railway network, and many also owned their own goods wagons, specially adapted for the commodity they had to transport. All these wagons had to be picked up and then sorted in huge marshalling yards, where overseers made up long trains with the trucks in the right order, using teams of small shunting engines like a shepherd using his sheep dogs. Finally the complete train would be coupled up to a mixed traffic engine like the GWR Hall class, or if it were an especially heavy train a 2-8-0 or even a 2-10-0 heavy goods locomotive would be employed. The night hours were the best for moving goods, for then passenger traffic was at a minimum, and the slower goods trains would not hold up other traffic. I can remember hearing the distinctive sounds of truck couplings banging into each other during the night, when staying near a railway. Each goods train started with a busy engine, and then, after a long succession of lifeless trucks came the guard's van, with its lights and promise of a small snug stove within.

The locomotive steaming through Shrewsbury is GWR 4-6-0 5904 *Kelham Hall* which was designed by Collett, and built in 1931. It was in service for 32 years, and must have covered a lot of miles in that time (see page 30 for details of the Hall class locomotives).

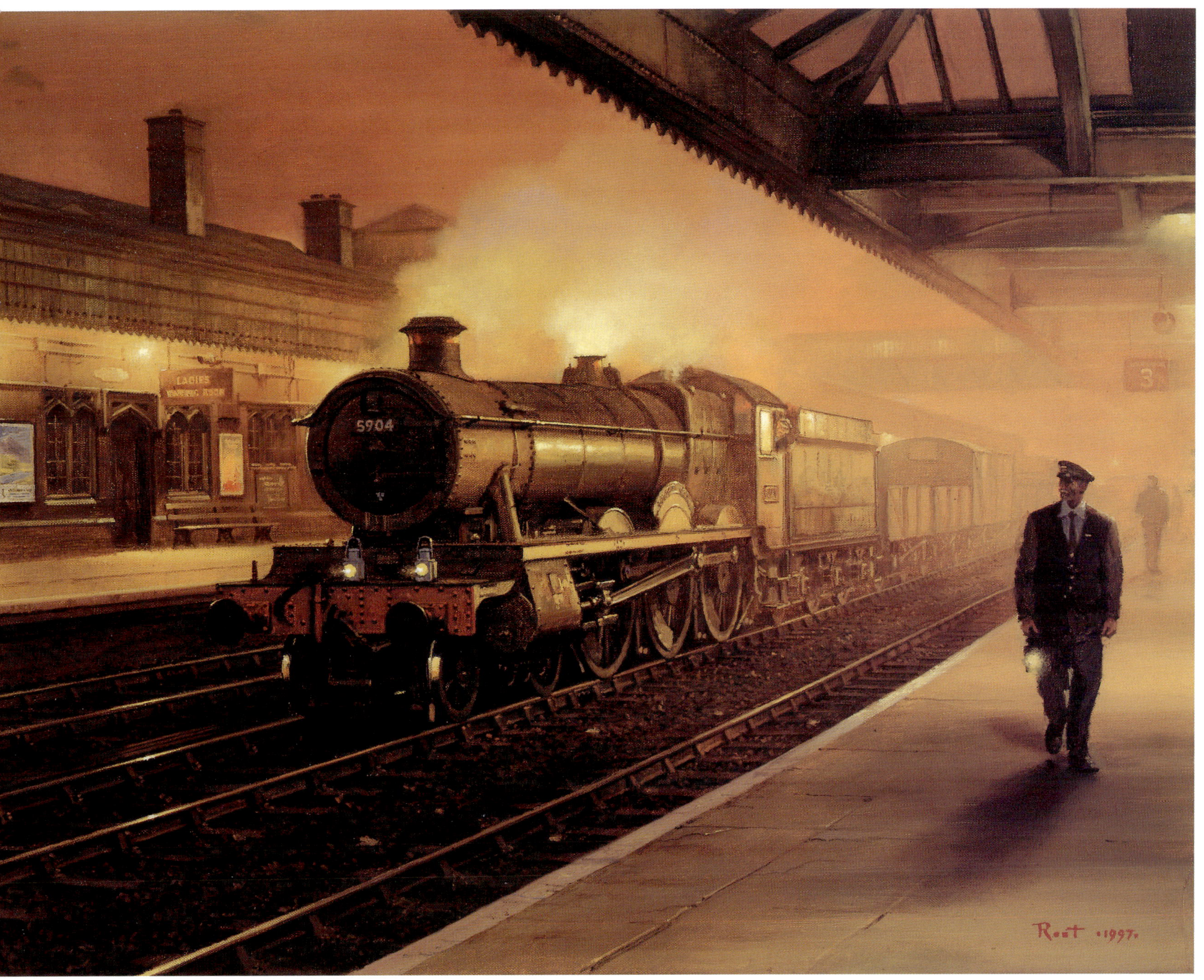
5904
3
Root ·1997·

257 Squadron

Painted 2003

This painting is set in 1964 and carries very sad undertones for lovers of steam locomotives, for it is near the end of steam traction on British Railways, and the background is the locomotive depot at Eastleigh in Hampshire, known for its major locomotive works. The locomotive shown, Bulleid Pacific 34072, *257 Squadron* was built at Brighton Works and completed in April 1948, just in time to become part of British Railways. *257 Squadron* was first based at Dover, and worked the Continental boat trains to London Victoria, a very glamorous service indeed. One of its main duties appears to have been the Night Ferry. The electrification of the Kent lines in 1958 resulted in the stable of steam locomotives being dispersed to other parts of the Southern Region and *257 Squadron* became based at Exmouth Junction. This was the Southern Region's main locomotive depot for the West Country, and the locomotives worked trains from Salisbury to Plymouth, and throughout North Devon and North Cornwall. *257 Squadron* appears in a number of photographs taken in the Ilfracombe area. In 1964 the locomotive was moved to Eastleigh shed, and in the autumn of that year was withdrawn, being sent to Woodham's scrapyard in March 1965.

Further details of the Merchant Navy class and other Bulleid Pacifics are given on page 10. Of the three streamlined locomotive types produced by the LNER, the LMS and the SR it has to be said that the SR Pacifics were the least attractive (although the artist would disagree with me) being irreverently referred to as 'spam cans'. However in the case of the Bulleid Pacifics the so-called streamlining was a way of both saving weight and improving the profile of the whole train. As was the case with the LMS locomotives, many were rebuilt with the streamlining removed, and turned out to be very handsome locomotives.

The Battle of Britain class was introduced in 1946, by which time the war was won, and the strategic importance of this great air battle could be properly assessed. It seemed very appropriate to commemorate the battle by naming a class of locomotive after the principal squadrons of the Royal Air Force which had taken such an epic part in defending Britain in 1940. 257 Squadron first flew Hurricanes and later Typhoons.

To some they were ugly and temperamental, to others they were the epitome of Southern Railway design. I confess to being of the latter opinion. Being a great admirer of OVS Bulleid, and having a father who was associated with 257 Squadron during the war, this was a painting waiting to happen. The choice for the setting was not a difficult one as much memorable time had been spent at Eastleigh in my youth, while on holiday. The rust on the shed behind the engine and the ash and clinker in the foreground give an opportunity to add colour to represent grime.

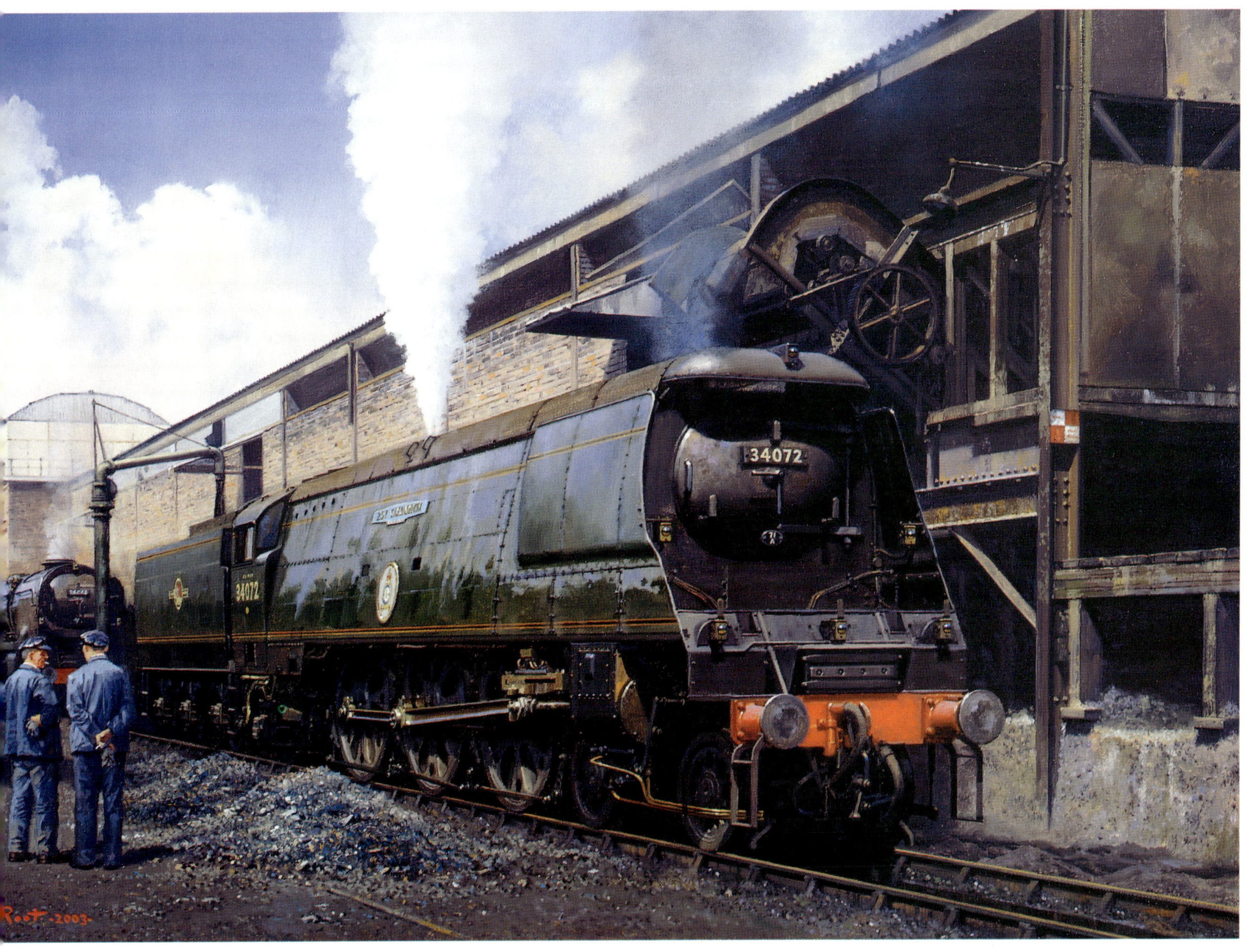
34072
34072
Root 2003

Cambrian Local

Painted 1996

This is the first of three paintings which portray the beautiful Cambrian coast railway, part of which ran from Dovey Junction north along the coast of Wales to Pwllheli. Most of this line was built in the 1860s, and it was a considerable engineering feat, with the crossing of the estuary at Barmouth (see page 60), and skirting round the Dovey estuary to Aberdovey. In addition there were places where the railway had to be cut into the cliff above the sea, and twice, in 1883 and 1933, rock falls caused locomotives to derail and plunge down the cliffs killing the crews. The painting shows one of the many bridges along the line, this one taking the railway across a small river near Tal-y-bont a couple of miles north of Barmouth. As is usually the case, the passing of a train is infinitely more interesting for a few seconds than catching minnows in the river as far as the children are concerned. The railway bridge is a simple girder bridge used to span many a river and stream. In 1923 the Cambrian Coast line was absorbed into the Great Western Railway, and the director of publicity for the GWR recognising the scenic merits of this lovely area published *Rambles around the Cambrian Coast* in 1936, written by Hugh Page and costing 6d! It is a lovely little book, and gives a great deal of information for those people travelling by train and shanks's pony! The scene here would be just off walk number 5, which looks extremely strenuous.

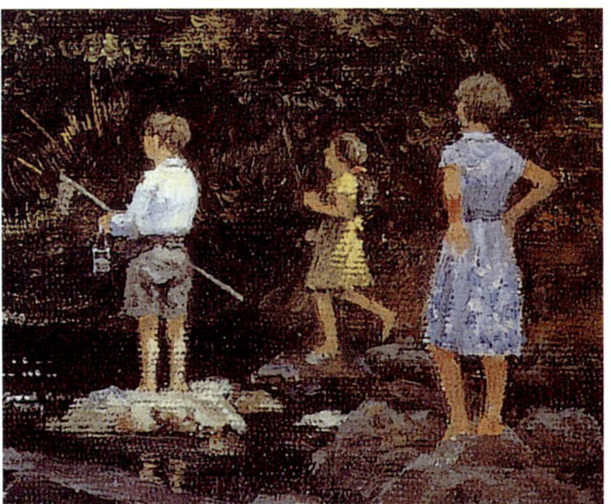

The route from Dovey Junction to Pwllheli was a single line, and was worked using the electric token system with passing loops, although some sections were double track, and were worked using the absolute block system. The train in this picture is in British Railways livery, giving a date in the 1950s, before Dr Beeching effected his drastic cuts to branch lines all over the country. The locomotive is a well-known workhorse of the GWR having been designed by CB Collett, and first introduced in 1930. Known as the 22xx or 2251 class, this 0-6-0 tender locomotive was one of 120 built. The locomotive was an updated version of the famous Dean Goods 0-6-0, which served for so many years on the GWR.

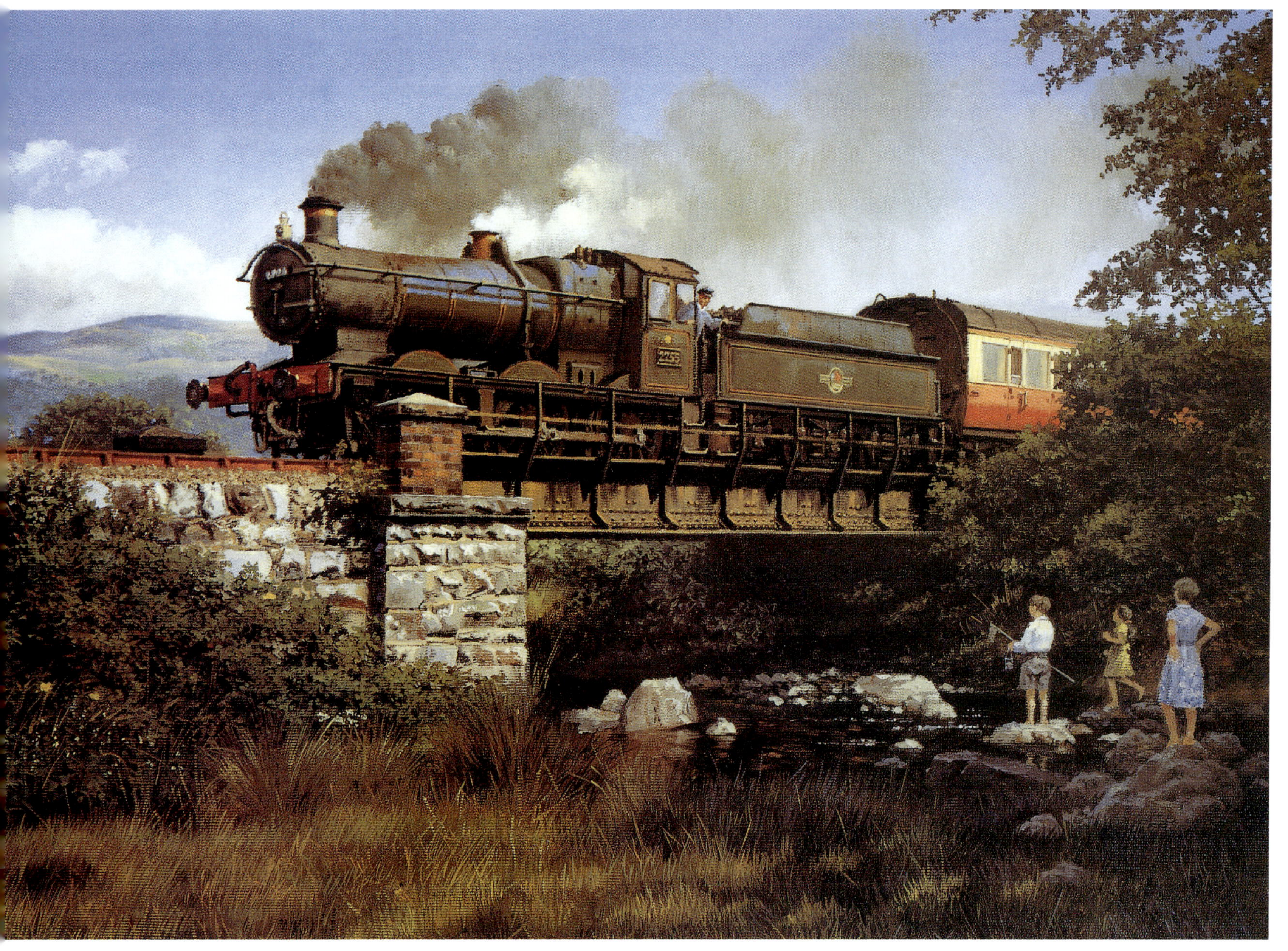

Crossing the Clyde

Painted 1990

From the beginning, the railways were funded privately with the purpose of making a profit for their shareholders. To do so they had to carry passengers and freight, and thus needed to be connected to major centres of population and industry. It is not surprising therefore to find that by 1848 a railway linked London and Glasgow. This route involved three companies, the London & North Western, the Lancaster & Carlisle Railway, and the Caledonian Railway. These lines, in British terms at least, were mountain railways topping summits of 304 metres at Shap, and 309 metres at Beattock. At Beattock and Tebay stations banking engines waited on duty into the 1960s to assist heavy trains up the gradients. North of Carlisle the hills were partly traversed using the river valleys of the Annan and the Clyde and once again we find river, road and railway keeping close company up the valleys, and crossing and re-crossing one another. The scene shown in this picture is near Crawford, where the river Clyde runs between Tewsgill Hill on the east side, and the Lowther Hills to the west.

By 1926 the three-year-old London Midland & Scottish Railway was in urgent need of a new and more powerful express locomotive for the West Coast route. Sir Henry Fowler's original proposals were overruled by the board and the resulting compromise was the three-cylinder 4-6-0 Royal Scot class locomotive based on a simple design. Fifty of the class were produced in 1927, and a further twenty in 1930. Number 46113 *Cameronian* created a world-record run by hauling a train from London to Glasgow non-stop in April 1928, a distance of 401 miles. *Royal Scot* herself was sent to the Chicago World Fair in 1933, and then toured 11 200 miles in North America, including crossing the Rocky Mountains unaided with its train. Like the GWR *King George V*, the *Royal Scot* was presented with a bell to commemorate the achievement. The Royal Scot class proved a very successful locomotive, solving the problem of the steep gradients of the West Coast route for many years. In the picture we see ex-LMS 46112 *Sherwood Forester* heading for Glasgow with a train of eight coaches.

Two of the class have been preserved, *Royal Scot* and *Scots Guardsman*. *Royal Scot* with its original maroon livery and numbered 6100 has been on show at Bressingham Hall near Diss, in Norfolk, where it still impresses with its clean lines and sense of power. At the time of writing it is undergoing restoration.

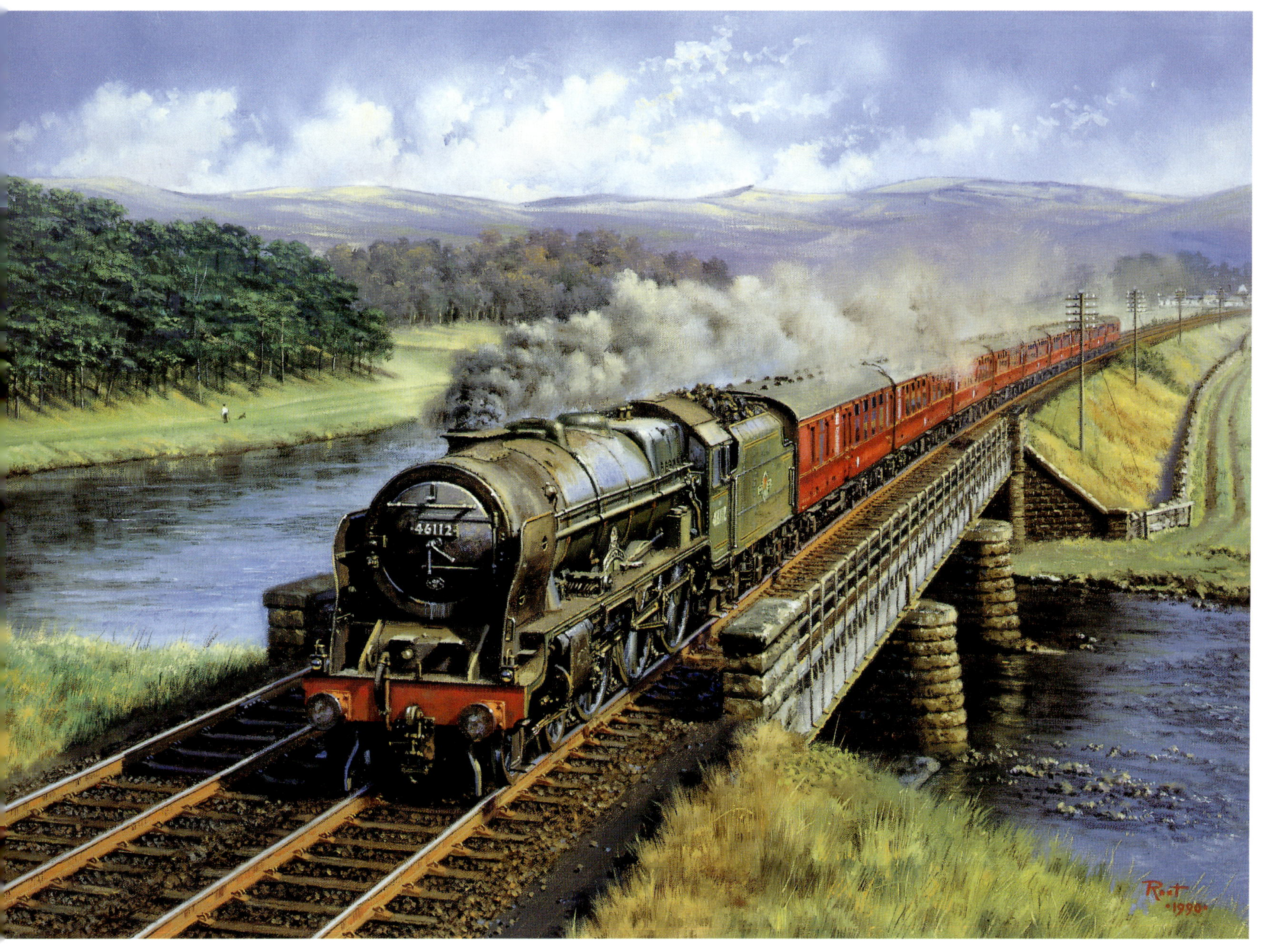
46112
Root
1990

Queen of Scots

Painted 1999

A fall of a few inches of snow not only casts a white quilt over the countryside, transforming everything one sees, but it also muffles sound, preventing echoes and producing a remarkable stillness. Even the steady exhaust beat of an express locomotive travelling at speed sounds different, less staccato. The picture is of a famous stretch of railway line, but not for any particular scenic interest. It was near here, on Stoke Bank, that the Gresley A4 Pacific *Mallard* achieved her world steam speed record in July 1938, thundering along at 126mph.

Here we see the northbound Queen of Scots Pullman express passing under the impressive signal gantry at High Dyke after emerging from Stoke tunnel with the morning sunshine glistening on the fresh snow. The date is the early 1950s, and the blue livery of the locomotive is very attractive, contrasting nicely with the chocolate and cream of the Pullman coaches. The Queen of Scots express superseded the Harrogate Pullman in May 1928, and travelled a 450 mile route from Kings Cross to Glasgow via Edinburgh. The use of Pullman trains largely derived from the arrival of an American General Manager for the Great Eastern Railway in 1914, Sir Henry Thornton. Being used to the comfort of Pullman travel, he ordered Pullman coaches for selected express trains, and the Harrogate Pullman was one of the results of this policy. The Queen of Scots carried on the tradition.

The first A1 Pacifics to run on the East Coast Route were designed by Sir Nigel Gresley. Edward Thompson, who succeeded him as CME produced his own one-off version. His successor, AH Peppercorn, produced his own very successful class of A1 locomotive as shown in the painting. Introduced in 1948, just before nationalisation, the locomotives had a tractive effort of 37 400lbs, giving them excellent pulling power, even in the snow! In all 49 of the class were built, and they served very efficiently until the end of the steam era on British Railways.

Although only used for a short time, the standard British Railways blue seemed to suit the LNER and Bulleid Pacifics well. The children's railway books of the 1950s always showed the principal classes in blue, so I think this painting can be attributed partly to nostalgia. The juxtaposition of the brown and cream Pullmans with the blue locomotive is a harmonious one and contrasts well with the hues of the snow. One interesting feature of snow scenes is that the reflected light shows up detail otherwise hidden, examples being the underside of the boiler and the wheels.

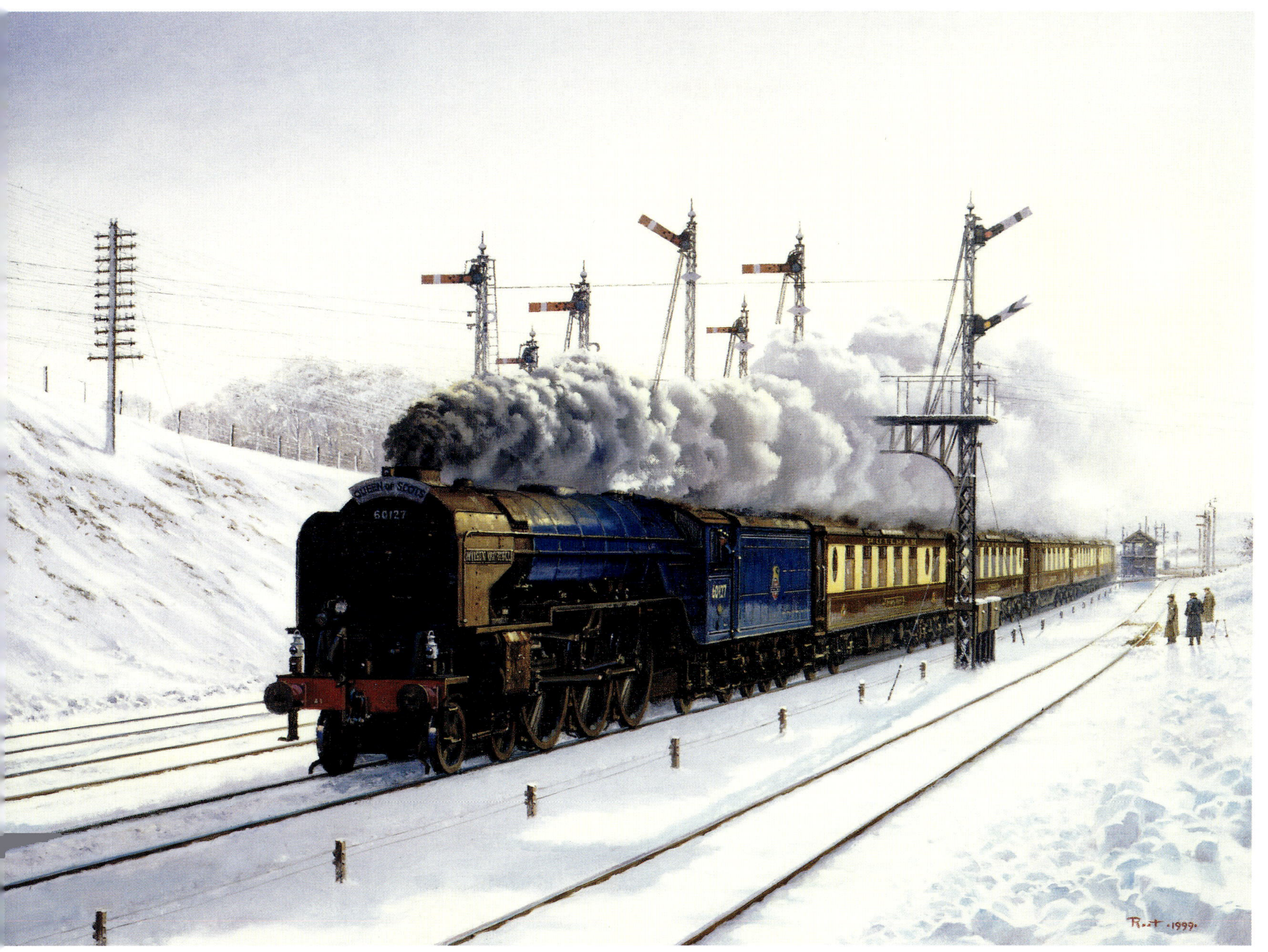
QUEEN of SCOTS
60127
60127
Root ·1999·

Tender First

Painted 1990

Once again a great contrast to the previous scene. Here we have a bright late summer day, and instead of the main line to the north a quiet section of the single track Colne Valley Railway. This line left the Great Eastern main line at Marks Tey, and then having crossed north over the impressive viaduct at Chappel, the Colne Valley proper forked left and followed the River Colne through Halstead and Sible Hedingham to Haverhill. The Colne Valley Railway was completed by 1863, and like the Mid Suffolk Light Railway was never part of the Great Eastern Railway, remaining independent until it was incorporated as part of the LNER in 1923. The line closed for passenger traffic in 1961, and was finally closed to all traffic in 1965. Now part of the line has again been reopened as a preserved steam railway, so that trains can once again meander along part of the beautiful Colne valley.

The original line was very lightly laid, and the weight of trains had to be curtailed, so that the J15 0-6-0 tender locomotive as shown here, designed by TW Worsdell and introduced in 1883, was ideal for the line and its bridges, weighing just 68 tons. The train is a pick-up goods train serving the light industries in the towns along the line. There was one particular problem in running tender first, and that was coal dust from the tender blowing into the cab. Knowing engine crews would damp down the surface of the coal with a hosepipe before starting on their journey. Running in this way was necessary when there was no turntable available. Locomotives would run round their trains using a loop line.

On certain small railways like the GWR Ashburton branch, trains simply ran in reverse with the locomotive behind. Small passenger trains called Auto Trains were used, and the driver controlled the train from the front of the carriage, while the locomotive pushed the train, cab first from behind. The driver had a brake lever and a regulator connected right through the carriage to the lever in the cab. The problem was that a regulator needed very gentle control and the linkage on this system always had slack in it, with noisy and wasteful results. Crafty engine crews would disconnect the control linkage, and the fireman in the cab would then watch the end of the linkage, and move the regulator gently by hand according to the drivers instructions!

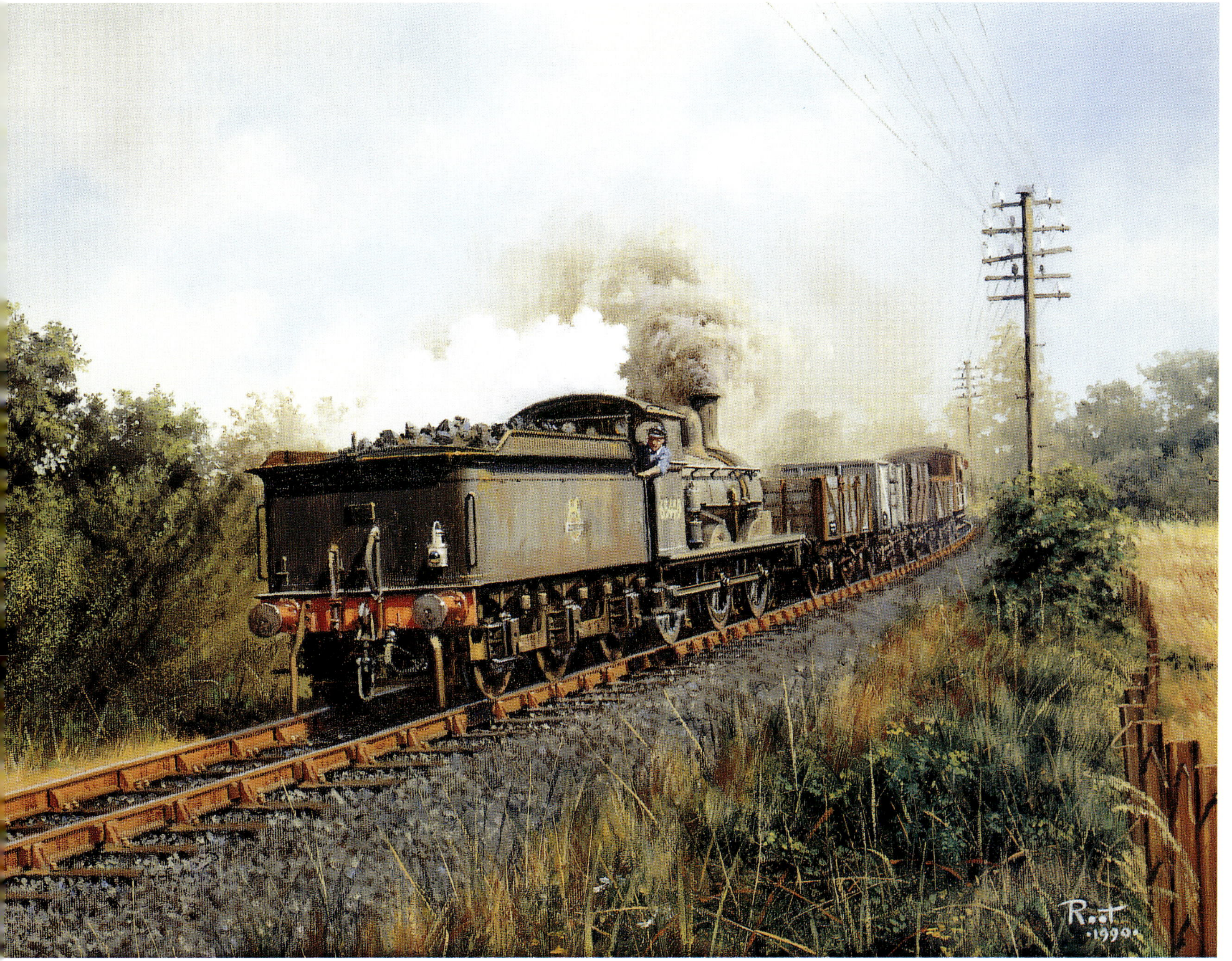
Root
·1990·

Chilly Morning

Painted 1982

The Southern Railway as established in 1923 fanned out from London in a great semicircle from the Thames in the east to the Thames at Reading in the west. It also stretched west of Salisbury, but here became curiously intertwined with the GWR (see page 10). The lines around the southern sector of London served a double function. Firstly, they brought into the capital an army of workers every day, and took them home again each evening, and this service encouraged the suburbs of London to grow ever outwards year by year. Secondly, the railway served the ports and seaside towns of the south coast, and through the ports passengers could travel to the continent and even further afield. Both ports and seaside towns grew and prospered thanks to their rail links to London. The Southern Railway was largely an amalgamation of the London & South Western Railway, the London Brighton & South Coast Railway, and the South Eastern & Chatham Railway, and it was not always a happy union! Traffic managers on the new Southern had to decide which of two competing routes to Portsmouth should be preferred, and came down in favour of the direct route via Guildford, thus downgrading the old Mid-Sussex line through Horsham. Guildford, with lines also running to Dorking in the east and Aldershot in the west, became an increasingly important station, and our scene shows a train pausing there on a very chilly morning in the early 1960s. One passenger at least will be very glad to get on board a warm, steam-heated train!

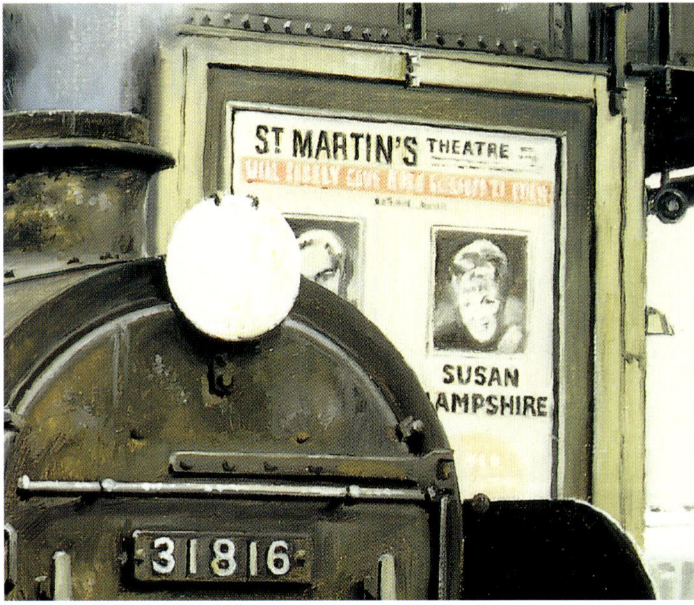

The locomotive, badly in need of a good clean and polish in these last years of the steam era, is a Southern N class 2-6-0 designed by one of the great CMEs of the steam age, REL Maunsell, and first introduced in 1917. No wonder it is showing its age after about 40 years in active service. Designed as a mixed-traffic engine for the South Eastern & Chatham Railway, it weighed about 61 tons, and had a good tractive effort. Some of the class, which numbered 86 in all, were specially built to work the Tonbridge to Hastings line, and were designated N1 and had three cylinders. Maunsell went on to design the famous Lord Nelson and Schools classes of locomotives for the Southern Railway, and the N class can be seen as a step towards these later locomotives. The chimney and smoke deflectors helped to make these engines easily recognisable as Southern.

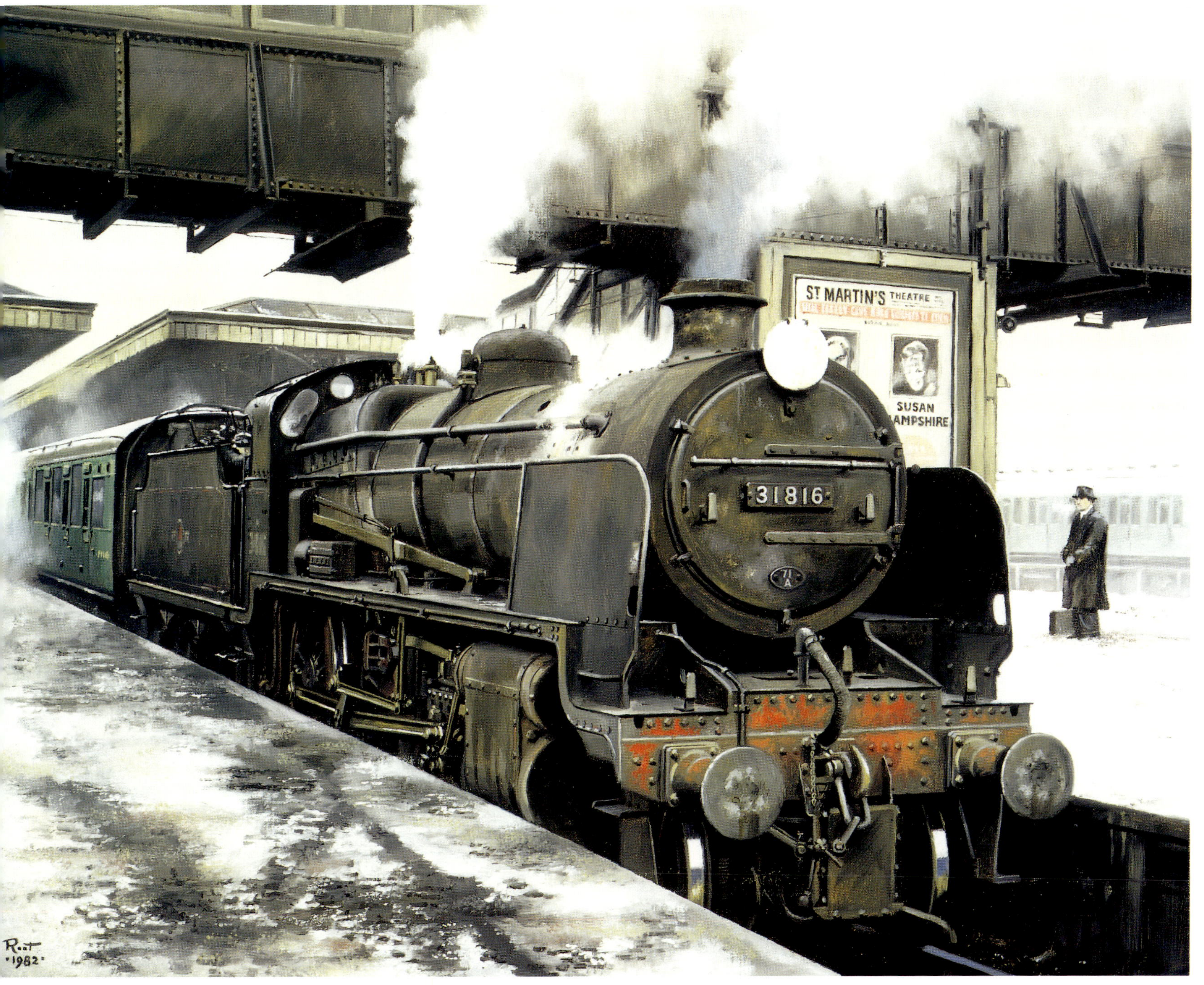
ST MARTIN'S THEATRE
SUSAN
31816
Root 1982

Royal Progress

Painted 2002

The major development of the railways in Britain almost exactly coincided with the reign of Queen Victoria, and therefore it was not surprising that the young queen made her first journey by rail on 13 June 1842, travelling from Slough to London Paddington. Windsor Castle was a favourite residence of Victoria, and the GWR soon extended the line to a small terminus station in Windsor, built with an opulence worthy of the queen. Apart from touring the country, Victoria was able to travel easily to her other favourite retreats at Balmoral and Osborne House. In an era when the condition of the roads often varied from bad to worse, Victoria was also able to enjoy a degree of luxury when she travelled which was unparalleled.

This magnificent painting commemorates a special tour of North Wales made by Queen Elizabeth II as part of her Golden Jubilee Year celebrations, and also marks 160 years of royal trains. It was also the first time for 35 years that a royal train had been steam hauled, and the honour was given to LMS Pacific 4-6-2 6233 *Duchess of Sutherland* (see page 22). This famous locomotive was acquired by the Princess Royal Class Locomotive Trust from Bressingham Hall in 1998, and has had a three-year restoration project costing about half a million pounds. The royal train included the Queen's Saloon and that for the Duke of Edinburgh which were converted to royal use for the Silver Jubilee in 1977. Diesel class 47 47787 *Windsor Castle* brought up the rear, and was used to reverse the royal train for servicing purposes. The tour started near Holyhead and finished at Crewe. It was certainly a memorable occasion, but may sadly be the last time a royal train is ever steam hauled.

At present the whole future of the royal train is 'under serious review'. It will be tragic as the royal train has provided our hard-working royal family with a much-needed haven when working round the country. I remember creeping down through a wood in South Devon just after the war ended to see the royal train which had been shunted up the Ashburton Branch of the GWR for the night, a favourite spot beside the beautiful River Dart. The railway authorities laid a cinder track beside the railway for a mile or so in order that King George VI could enjoy his early morning run.

This painting, commissioned by Brell Ewart, chairman of the Princess Royal Class Locomotive Trust, hangs in the Duke of Edinburgh's saloon on the royal train.

Not only is this picture historic in that it shows the Royal Train being hauled by steam in modern times, it is also a tribute to the steam preservation movement. The locomotive is doing what it was designed to do efficiently and without fuss, moving swiftly and with an even patterned trail of steam from the chimney showing that all is well mechanically. What a sight the Duchess of Sutherland *made conveying Her Majesty along the North Wales coast that day!*

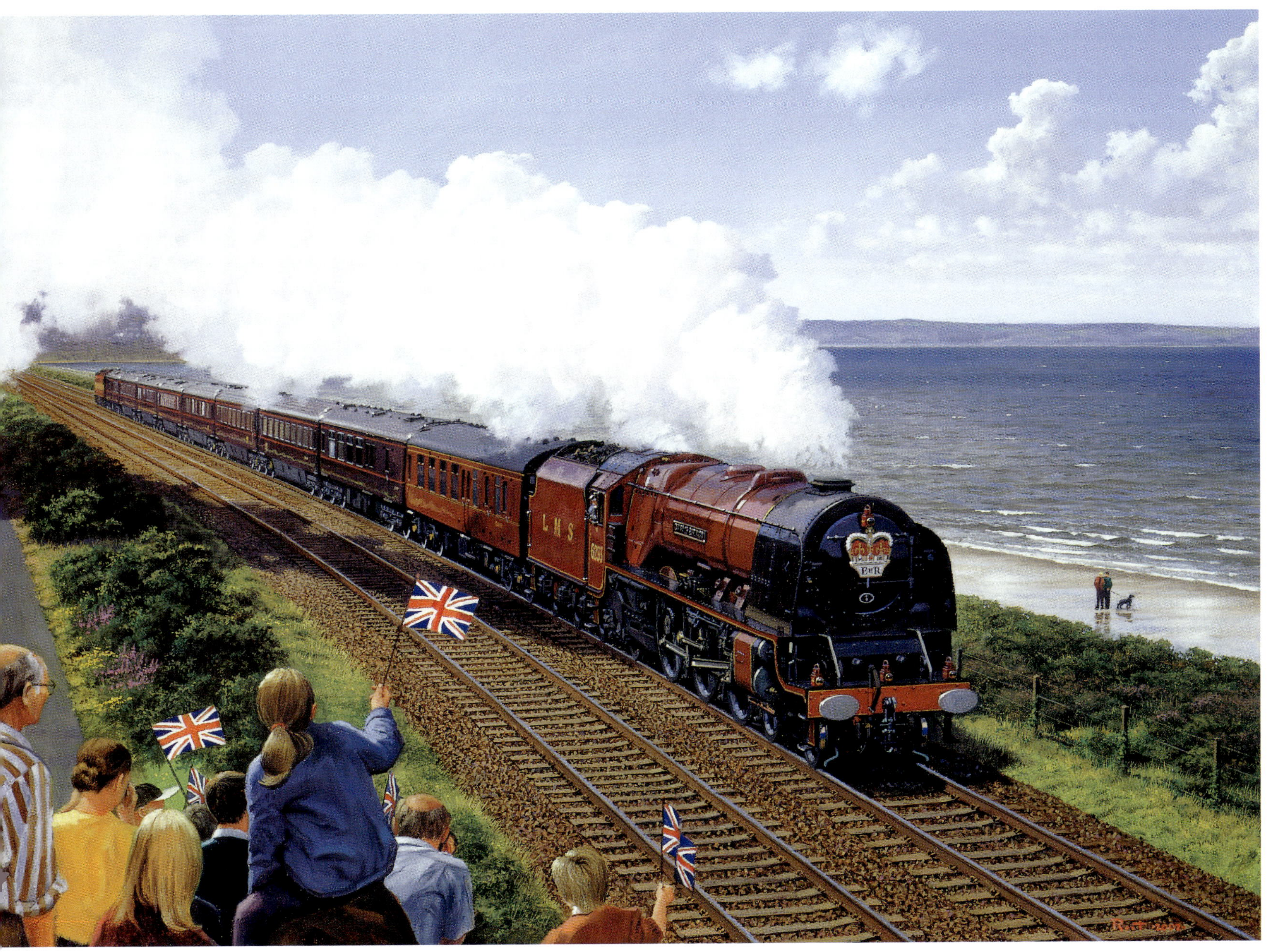
L M S

'May I Look Around?'

Painted 1988

How different from the pomp and circumstance of the last painting. Like a jigsaw puzzle with some pieces large and flamboyant, and some small and almost insignificant, so the railways combined the large and grand with the small and domestic, yet all were necessary to complete the total picture. Here we see a very quiet corner of the locomotive depot at Braintree, situated on the railway linking up with the ex-GE main line at Witham, in Essex, and running through Great Dunmow to connect with the main line at Bishop's Stortford. Now most of the branch line has been closed, and Braintree is the terminus. The scene is the late 1950s, and a young train spotter is politely asking permission to look round. At small stations such as this everyone knew everyone else, and vandalism was almost unheard of, so the member of the engine's crew taking a break from replenishing the tanks has no hesitation in giving permission. I can remember endless hours spent poking about in similar situations, but it was the locos themselves rather than their numbers that held the fascination for me.

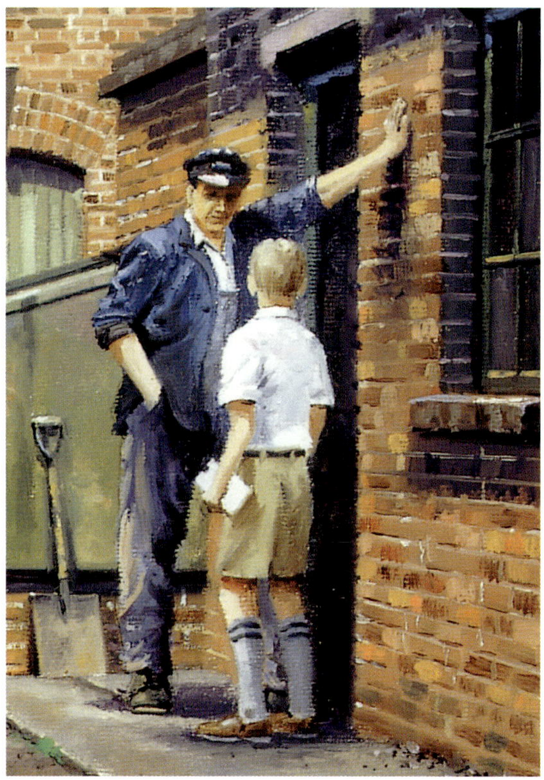

The locomotive being refreshed is an ex-GER 0-6-0 J68 class tank engine designed by AJ Hill and introduced in 1912. They weighed about 42.5 tons, and developed 19 090lbs tractive effort. The one in Malcolm's picture has probably been in service for 45 years at least, and will continue faithfully almost to the end of steam. In all thirty of the class were built, and they were the largest 0-6-0 tank engines used on the old Great Eastern Railway.

However, change is on the way, radical change. Lurking in the adjacent shed is an 0-6-0 diesel shunter, built by British Railways at a number of locomotive works, and first introduced in the 1940s. It weighed about 48 tons in running order, and had a tractive effort of an astonishing 35 000lbs! (Though a maximum speed of only 20mph!). This makes an interesting comparison with a GWR Castle at 31 625lbs. Small wonder that nearly a thousand of the class were built. All the same, it was one of the least exercised locomotives on my cherished Hornby Dublo layout!

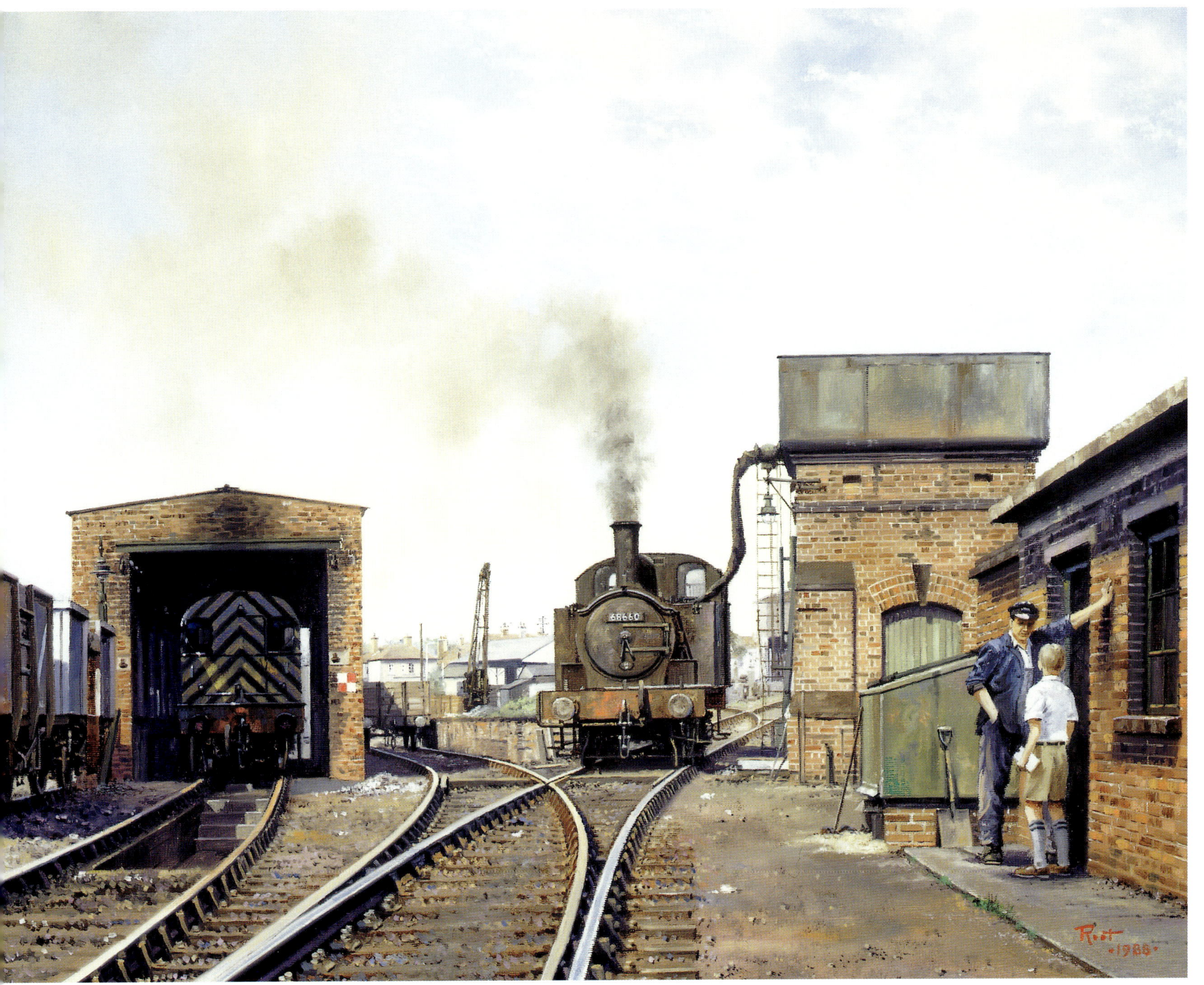
68660
Root

Coronation Scot

Painted 1998

Here we are caught up in the full culmination of the West Coast/East Coast competition for the route from London to Scotland. The race to Edinburgh of 1888 and to Aberdeen in 1895 led on to further speed records, as the railway companies discovered that passengers were prepared to pay for speed. After the main groupings in 1923, the LNER and the LMS entered into a gentleman's agreement whereby they kept one another informed of new plans for their major routes. Thus it was that the LNER gave notice of their intended Silver Jubilee London-to-Newcastle express, named to commemorate the Silver Jubilee of King George V, which in September 1935 completed the run in 4 hours. The LMS responded with the Coronation Scot in 1937. This train was hauled by the new Princess Coronation class 4-6-2 locomotive designed by Sir William Stanier. The locomotive and its train were streamlined, and painted in blue livery with silver lines stretching down the entire train. It was certainly very distinctive, if not quite as attractive as the LNER competition.

The original Coronation Scot train consisted of nine bogie coaches as shown in Malcolm's painting, with a total weight of about 297 tons. The London Euston to Glasgow journey was scheduled at 6.5 hours, but in test runs the Coronation had achieved a top speed of 114mph, which captured the world steam speed record, and had achieved an average speed of nearly 80mph. The locomotive was sufficiently powerful to haul its train over the steep gradients at Shap and Beattock without any other assistance, to heights of 1015 ft and 915 ft respectively, with a descent to sea level near Carlisle in between, yet it accomplished the whole journey on one tenderful of coal. It was a fitting tribute to its famous designer.

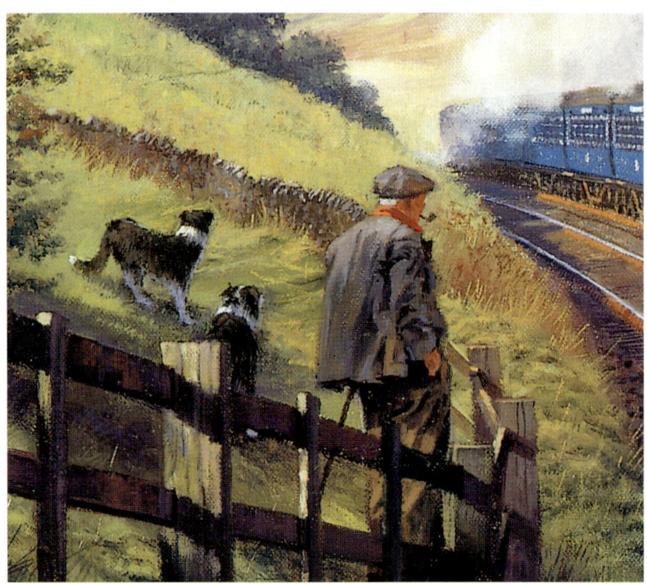

The train left its two starting points at 1.30pm and here the London bound Coronation Scot is seen crossing Dillicar Common on a fine afternoon, having had a stop at Carlisle at 3.15pm. The summit of Shap lies behind, but there was a chance to replenish water here from the water troughs (see page 16). The old Cumbrian shepherd watches the train thunder by on the track beneath him, the representative of a way of life established for centuries saluting a marvel of modern engineering.

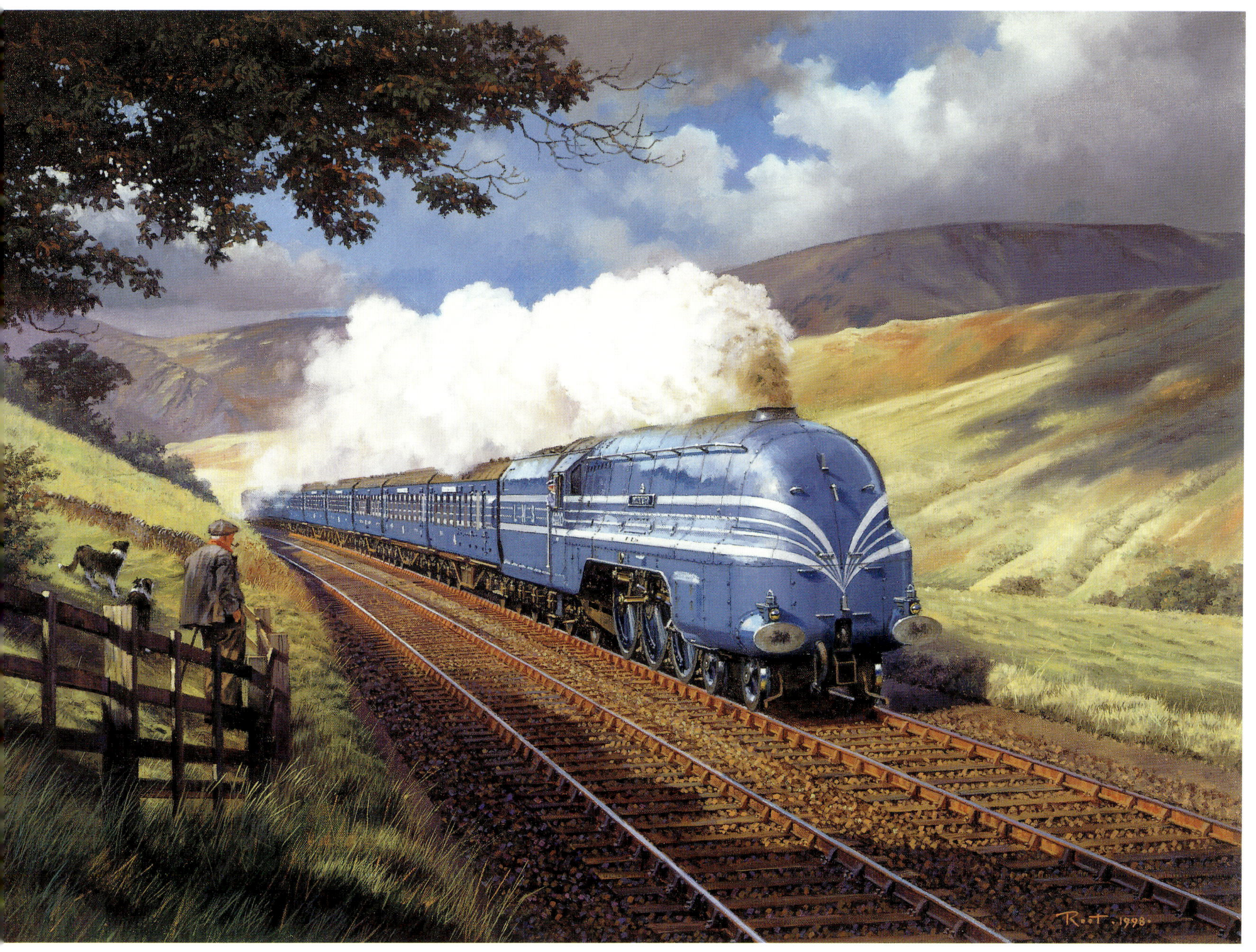

Tunnel Vision

Painted 1987

When the invading Angles established the first 'English' town in Britain, they certainly picked a good site, the lowest river crossing and some hills which could be fortified. These same hills proved something of a problem when the railway builders arrived, and were a surprise if they thought East Anglia was all flat! The line from London approaches Ipswich beside the River Orwell, but even then has to burrow through a small hill to reach the station. Even more difficult was the route to nearby Felixstowe, where the railway had to proceed north out of Ipswich, then swing in a near 180 degree curve round the hilly town, and back along the other side of the river towards its mouth. Now we are expecting the tunnel to be closed for a considerable period while the clearance is increased to permit the new higher container trucks to pass through. A number of bridges along the line have already been altered. Felixstowe, which is served by a single track line, has become one of the most important container ports in Europe.

The scene shown is Ipswich station in the late 1950s, and the fireman of the London-bound train is watching an ex-LNER B1 class locomotive emerge from the tunnel, together with a good deal of smoke. The locomotive in the foreground is Britannia class 4-6-2 70036 *Boadicea,* which is very appropriate as she was Queen of the Iceni, an East Anglian tribe which dominated the area long before the Angles arrived. The impact of the Britannia class locomotives on the London Liverpool Street to Norwich run through Ipswich was dramatic, with a 20 per cent improvement in the previous best timings.

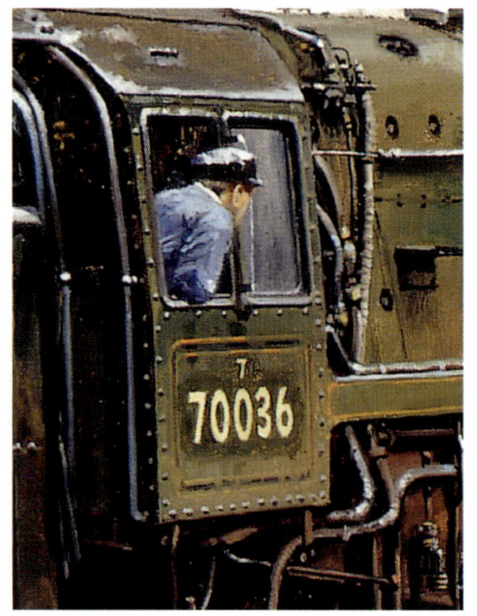

Details of the Britannia class locomotives are given on page 2. Perhaps one day *Oliver Cromwell* will again pull an express train from London to Norwich! The B1 class locomotives were designed by Edward Thompson, and introduced in 1942 with the intention that they should replace a number of older types of 4-6-0 working on the region. In all 409 of the class were built, and they were known as the Antelope class (although more affectionately known as Bongos after the sixth member of the class) because the first forty were named after species of antelope. I imagine they ran out of antelopes at that point! Number 61149 emerging from the tunnel would not have carried a name.

It is interesting to note that Dick Hardy, who has kindly written the foreword for this book, became the Shed Master at Ipswich station in March 1950 at the very early age of 26. He supervised the maintenance of 90 locomotives, and had 450 men under him at Ipswich and District.

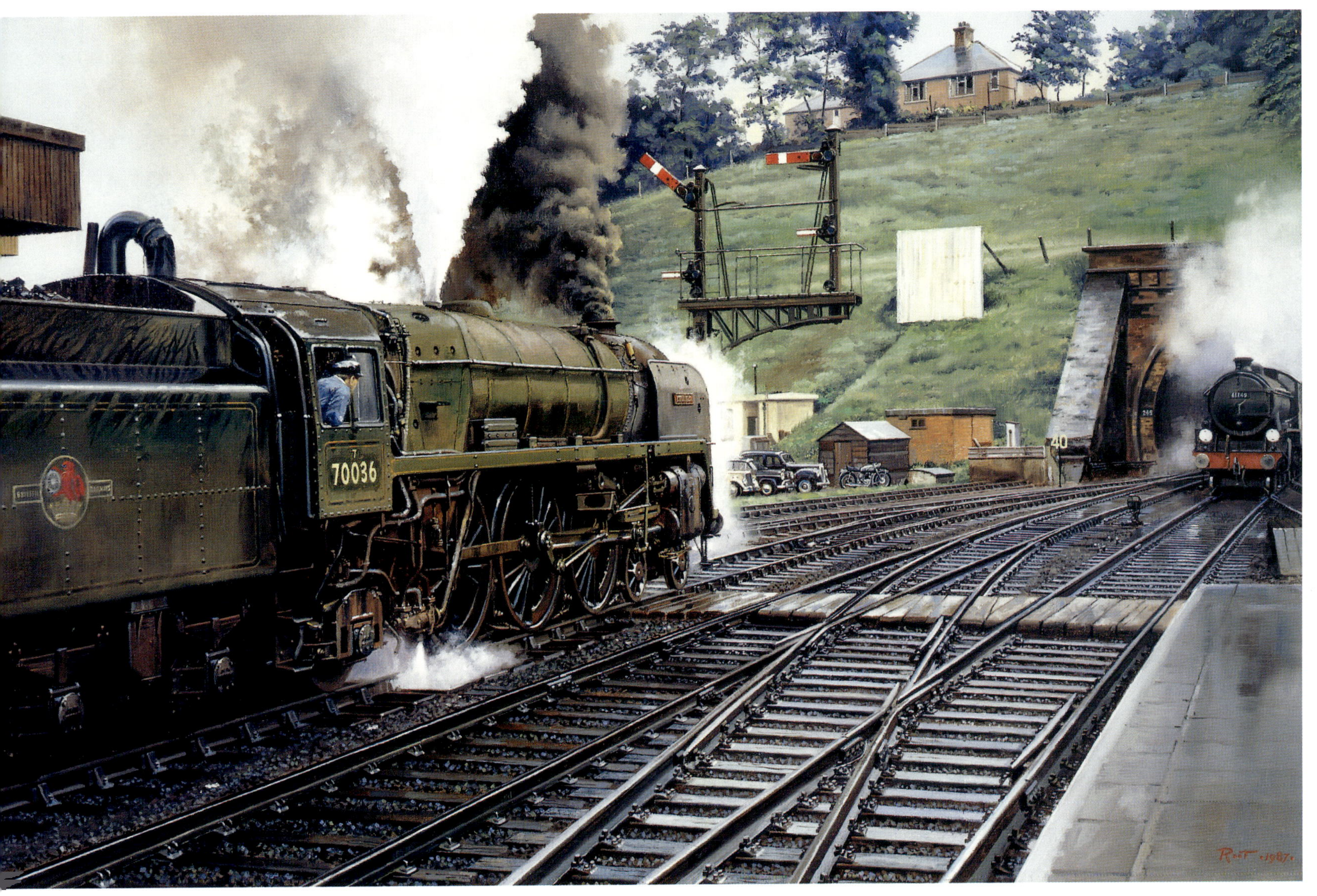
70036
40

Barmouth Bridge – Distant View

Painted 1995

Once again we are on the Cambrian branch of the Great Western Railway, and looking from the northwest to Barmouth Bridge, with the impressive mountain Cader Idris which rises to 2928 feet (893m) behind. Hills and rivers were in place a long time before railways came along, and so were ships, so the railway as the newcomer had to adapt to circumstances. In this instance the problem was the Mawddach estuary, a broad but largely shallow arm of the sea. The solution was to build three bridges in one, and create a piece of engineering history in the process. At the Barmouth end, closest to us in the picture, is a two-arch metal bridge about 110 metres long, consisting of steel plate cross and trough girders, being the result of the rebuild in 1900. The second bridge, completed in 1900 and replacing an earlier structure, consists of two girder bridges supported on steel cylinders, the northern one being a swing bridge to allow ships to pass through. The third bridge is the 113-span timber trestle viaduct, first built in 1867 and rebuilt between 1906 and 1909.

This is the longest timber structure in the country, and Baltic lumber was used in its construction, the timber being brought by ship to the site. Mr Henry Coneybeare wrote a paper in 1871 for the Institution of Civil Engineers in which he commented that 'Barmouth Harbour was free from worms'. However, he was proved wrong when in the early 1980s the viaduct was visited by a species of marine worm which nearly spelt the death knell for the line. Fortunately the necessary finance was forthcoming to save this engineering marvel.

This whole area of west Wales is magnificent, and in his *Rambles around the Cambrian Coast* written by Hugh Page and published by the GWR in 1936, the author gives details of several walks in the area, and viewing points for the magnificent viaduct. He also writes 'there is the possibility of obtaining refreshment at one of the farms, at least I did at Maes-coch, and was shown an interesting and effective home-made water wheel, used for churning butter, and consisting of a number of ordinary pails fastened to an old cart wheel. Verily necessity is the mother of invention.' I wonder if it is still in use?

The two-coach local train which has left Barmouth is heading south over the trestle viaduct and is hauled by a GWR 'Mogul'. This 2-6-0 locomotive was a mixed-traffic locomotive designed by GJ Churchward, and introduced in 1911. In all 342 of the class were built, and as they only weighed about 105 tons with tender they were ideal for lines like the Cambrian Coast where lighter loadings were demanded.

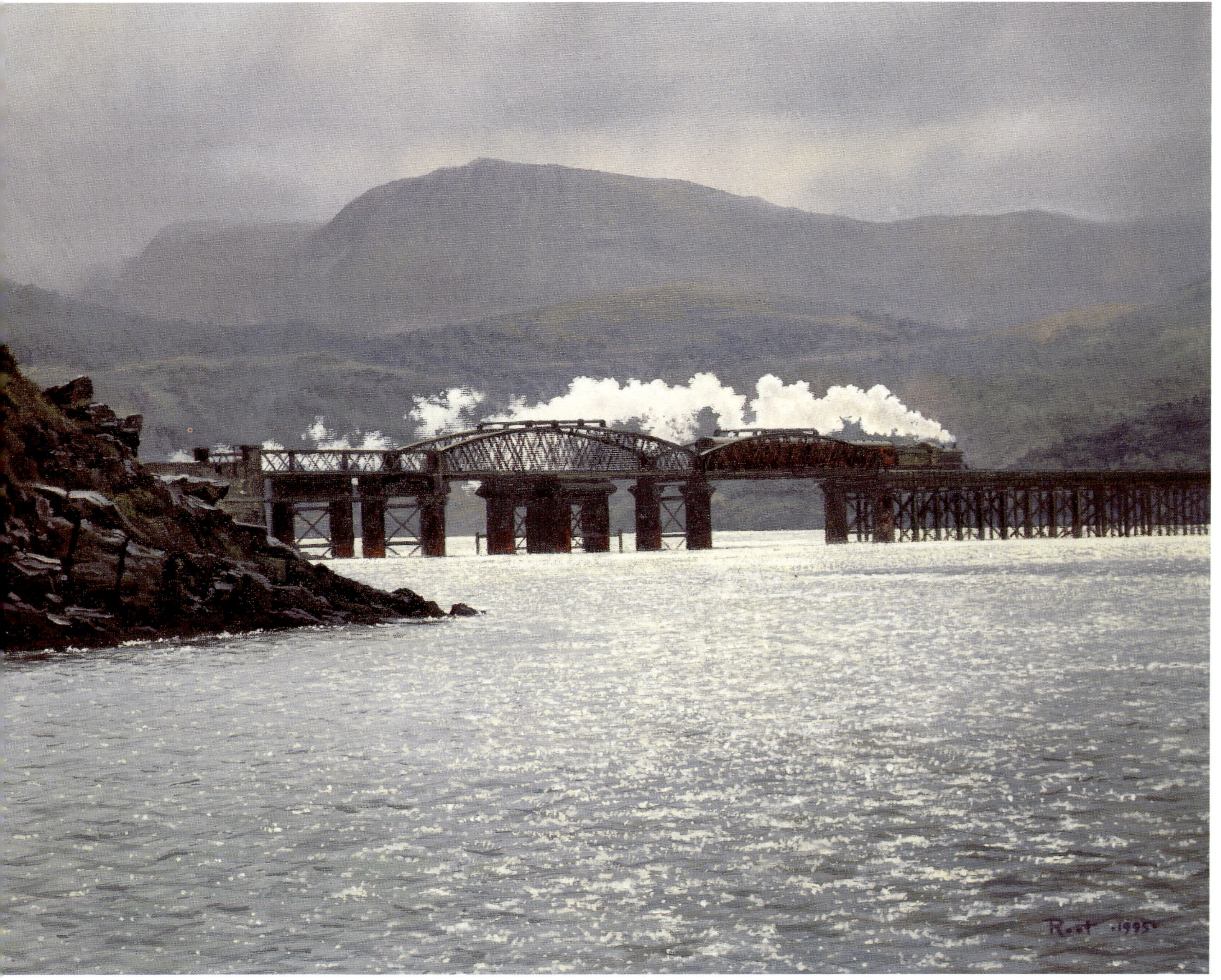
Root 1995

Lifting the Arrow

Painted 1991

Below the bridge it is just on slack water, with the boat's painters almost trailing in the water. Above the bridge nothing is slack, just the opposite as the three tank engines strain to pull the empty stock of the Golden Arrow. The train has just left Folkestone Harbour station on the tough climb to Folkestone Junction about a mile away. The front locomotive in the picture is just reaching the bottom of the steep gradient, visible to the naked eye, and as there has been no opportunity to take a run at the hill it will take full power and eighteen driving wheels to pull the heavy Pullman coaches up. The gradient on this short stretch is 1-in-30, the steepest on the entire Southern Railway, and at least two and often three 0-6-0 tank engines were needed. Once the train reached the junction, the Bulleid Pacific locomotive was coupled to the appropriate end of the train before continuing on to Dover, where the passengers from the return ferry would be picked up. The Golden Arrow would then set off for London Victoria.

The Golden Arrow came into being in 1929 when it was decided to offer a first class Pullman car service linking London and Paris using a new steamer, the *Canterbury.* The train would leave London at 11am, reach Dover at 12.38pm, allow 17 minutes to embark, and 75 minutes for the channel crossing. The French 'Fleche d'Or' would arrive in Paris at 5.35 pm. The inclusive fare was £5! In May 1931 economic depression dictated that the boat train carry second and third class passengers as well, and the coaches were arranged accordingly. After suspension during the war, the 'Arrow' took 92 minutes to run from Victoria to Dover Marine. In autumn 1952 a radical change was made, and the 'Arrow' left Victoria at 2pm, crossing to Calais from Folkestone. This lengthened the journey time to 7 hours 34 minutes. The return journey, leaving Paris at 12.30pm went via Calais and Dover and took the same time as before. Thus the pre-war routine was exactly reversed.

The three locomotives working their hearts out are ex-South Eastern Railway R1 class 0-6-0 tank engines designed by J Stirling and first introduced in 1888. At the time of the painting ten of the class were in service. The different coloured smoke indicates the different combination of steam and smoke that a locomotive produced when the footplate team were working flat out. Anyone in a boat downwind would have received the full benefit! The three locomotives between them produced the necessary 56 000lbs of tractive effort to haul the heavy train up the hill.

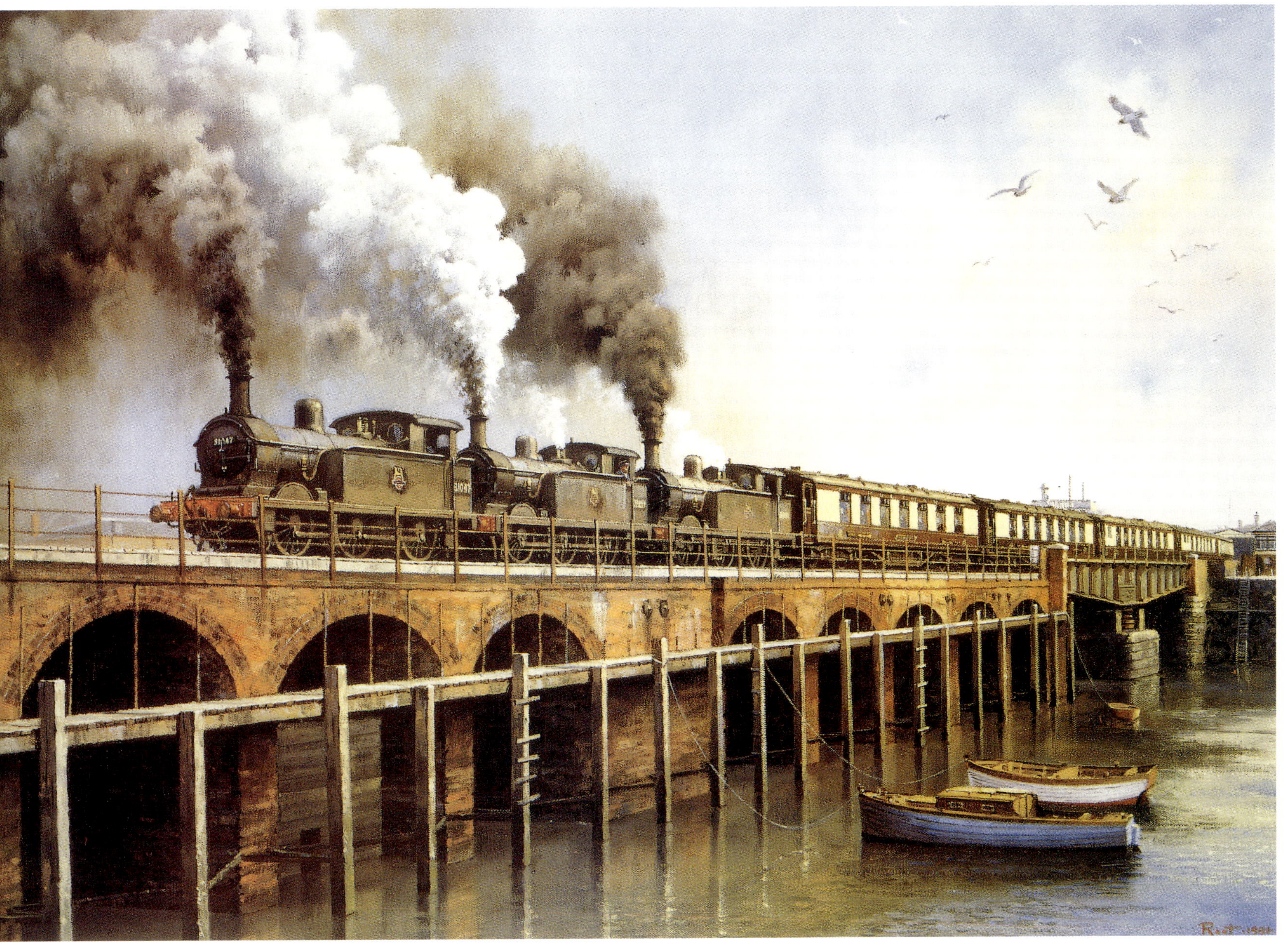

East London Fog

Painted 2001

This is a scene on the Great Eastern Railway at Stratford, east London, prior to the amalgamation of 1923. Stratford was and still is the gateway to London from the east. The main motive power depot for the railway was located here, and now two underground lines, the Central and the Jubilee, and also the Docklands Light Railway connect at Stratford. The A11 trunk road passes nearby. The huge signal gantry indicates the complexity of the railway system at this point. It spans many tracks, and has the word 'Through' above the fast lines in the centre. Stratford housed the locomotive works for the Great Eastern Railway, and it was here that James Holden and his son SD Holden presided as Locomotive Superintendents.

In 1911 a more powerful locomotive than the Claud Hamilton (see page 36) was required for the runs to Harwich and Norwich. Because of the axle weight requirement on the GER a 4-6-0 type was needed, and the first of the 1500 class was built, designed by SD Holden. These locomotives were to be renamed B12s in later LNER days. Although in appearance a large locomotive, the boiler was deceptively small and very modest for a 4-6-0. From 1932 the class was rebuilt with a round-topped boiler by Gresley.

Malcolm has painted this scene in 'mild fog'. Had it been a real London 'pea souper' the train would have been invisible! Fog was a great problem for the safe running of the railways in those days, as a railway book of 1948 testifies. 'Fog is the great enemy of all enginemen and signalmen, and to date the most commonly used method of fighting it has been the laying of detonators on the tracks; when the engine wheels pass over them the detonators explode, thereby giving a warning of danger, and the driver is ready to stop the train if necessary.' Remembering how some trains were blown off the tracks during two previous wars, drivers could well have got a bit jumpy when they proceeded down the line accompanied by a series of explosions! I have never placed a detonator on the track, but perhaps this is the moment to confess that we did put pennies on the track to be flattened by a passing train. I now realise we not only trespassed on railway property to do so, but also defaced the coin of the realm, but I have a cherished and very flat coin that the Cornish Riviera passed over, without being derailed, and I hope I am forgiven!

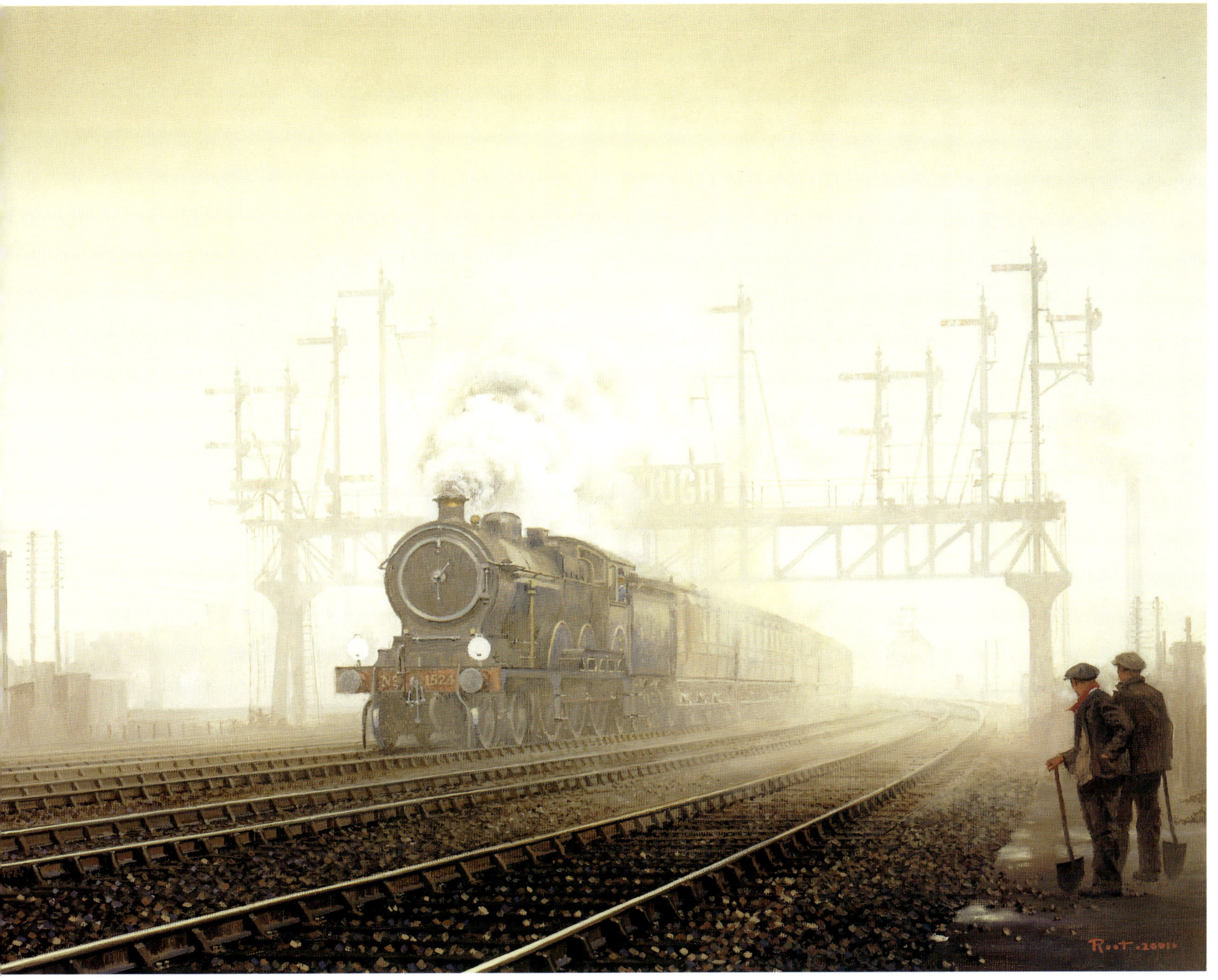
ROOT.2001

Hepworth Hall Bridge

Painted 1984

When railway mania struck Britain in the middle of the nineteenth century, building railways was perceived as the perfect way to quick riches, and an amazing number of railway schemes were put before the public with invitations to invest. As is usually the case with such investment offers, the financial returns were too optimistic, and the cost of building the railways was invariably underestimated. Railway planners would all too easily visualise a railway running straight from terminus to destination, while underestimating the cost of embankments, cuttings, tunnels and bridges. In East Anglia the flatter country reduced much of the earth moving, and rock blasting was kept to a minimum. Where railways followed the river valleys, as with the Colne Valley Railway (see page 48) there would need to be a lot of bridges, as the slow-running rivers meandered to and fro across their valleys. Hepworth Hall Bridge, seen in this painting, is called after the hall which stands on a low hill half a mile to the north of the railway. The bridge is on the line north-west of Halstead, and the view is from a field near to the Halstead to Sible Hedingham road which also crosses the railway nearby. It was the financial constraints of the railway builders which led them to construct bridges using a light timber construction. This was quite adequate for the trains of the time, but as the years went by traffic increased, and so therefore did the weight of the trains, and of the locomotives needed to pull them. Axle weights of locomotives became an important part of the equation, and all railway lines had to be classified with a 'route availability' according to the maximum weight the bridges would safely carry. This was strictly adhered to in order to avoid a disaster.

The Colne Valley Railway became especially important in the Second World War when munitions trains passed along it to the nearby American base at Ridgewell, and others in the area. The Worsdell designed J15 shown crossing the bridge was an ideal locomotive for this line, as it had an axle weight of only 13.5 tons (see page 48). Even so it is likely that some of the wartime trains, even when double-headed, were very close to the weight limit for the line.

As with so many country railways, much of the time the trains are a small diversion from a quiet rural scene, and the grazing cows hardly bother to look up from their lush pasture as the train wanders by on its way to Haverhill.

A characteristic of the branch lines of East Anglia was the wooden trestle bridge exemplified here on the Colne Valley Railway. This route was classified RA2 due to the light construction of the bridges, and only the lightest axle weight locomotives were permitted to work the line. The bridge holds fond memories for me, for as seemingly fraught with danger as it was, it was one of our 'play areas' when children. Nowadays parents would be rightly horrified if their children played near a railway line, but in those days we were more afraid of being told off than of the dangers.

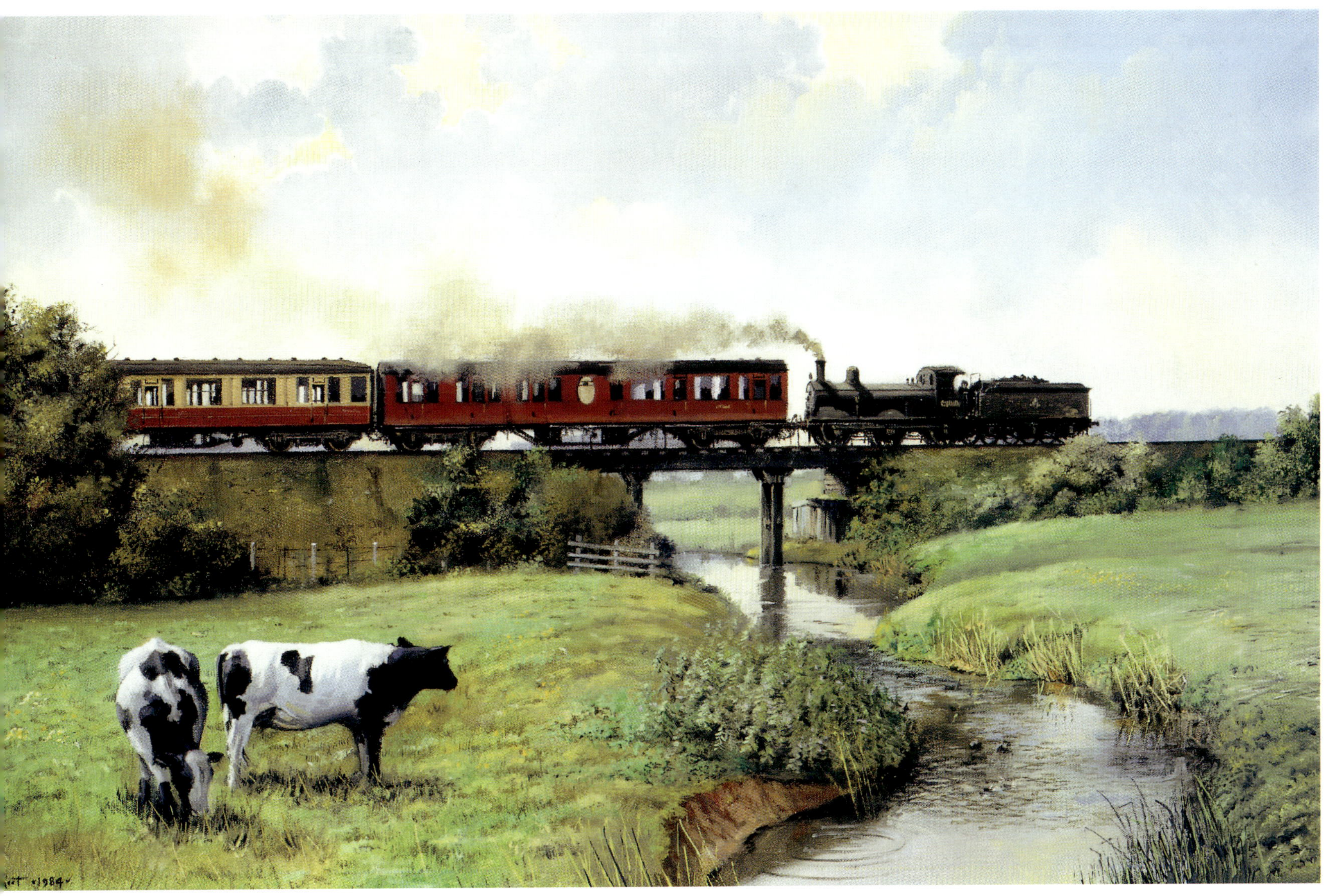

Resting on Shed

Painted 1982

This is a most evocative painting, and quite different from a gentle country branch line or a mighty express thundering along beside the sea. Here all is damp, with the warm moisture of confined steam, and the ground is covered with shallow puddles of oily water. The smell is that curious blend of smoke, steam and oil, which was so unmistakable. The shed may not have been a very glamorous place, but it was vital to the whole running of the railway system. The scene here is Eastleigh shed on the Southern Region of British Railways, situated to the north of Southampton. From the railway point of view Southampton had always been an important hub. Here two main lines from London, one via Winchester and one via Guildford, joined the coastal route, and also served the important ports of Portsmouth and Southampton. A line also ran north-west to join the London to Exeter main line at Salisbury. Eastleigh was both the main Running Shed for the area, and the main locomotive building works for the old London & South Western Railway, and the subsequent Southern Railway. Oliver Bulleid, the Chief Mechanical Engineer of the Southern Railway appointed in 1937, had learnt his craft under Sir Nigel Gresley on the LNER, but he was perhaps unfortunate to be a little late on the scene for his innovative ideas. Somehow Bulleid managed to persuade the authorities to allow him to build twenty of his revolutionary Merchant Navy class Pacifics between 1941 and 1945, despite the constraints of war. These engines, with thermic syphon, chain driven valve gear and air smoothed casing were most distinctive, and although designated mixed-traffic locomotives were in fact express passenger engines. The lighter West Country class appeared in 1945 (see page 10) and two of these locomotives are resting in the Eastleigh shed in the picture.

All the Merchant Navy class locomotives were rebuilt beginning in 1956, and their streamlined outer casing was removed as part of the process. Many people felt they looked much better without it. Of the West Country/Battle of Britain class, just over half of the total number of 110 were rebuilt. The scene here at Eastleigh, set in the early 1960s, shows the two alternatives. All these Pacific locomotives continued in service well into the 1960s, and many of them to the end of steam on the Southern in 1967. Bulleid's Pacifics are well represented in railway preservation. Oliver Vaughan Snell Bulleid, went on to produce other remarkable locomotives (see pages 82 and 128). He ended his career as CME of Coras Iompair Eireann in Ireland.

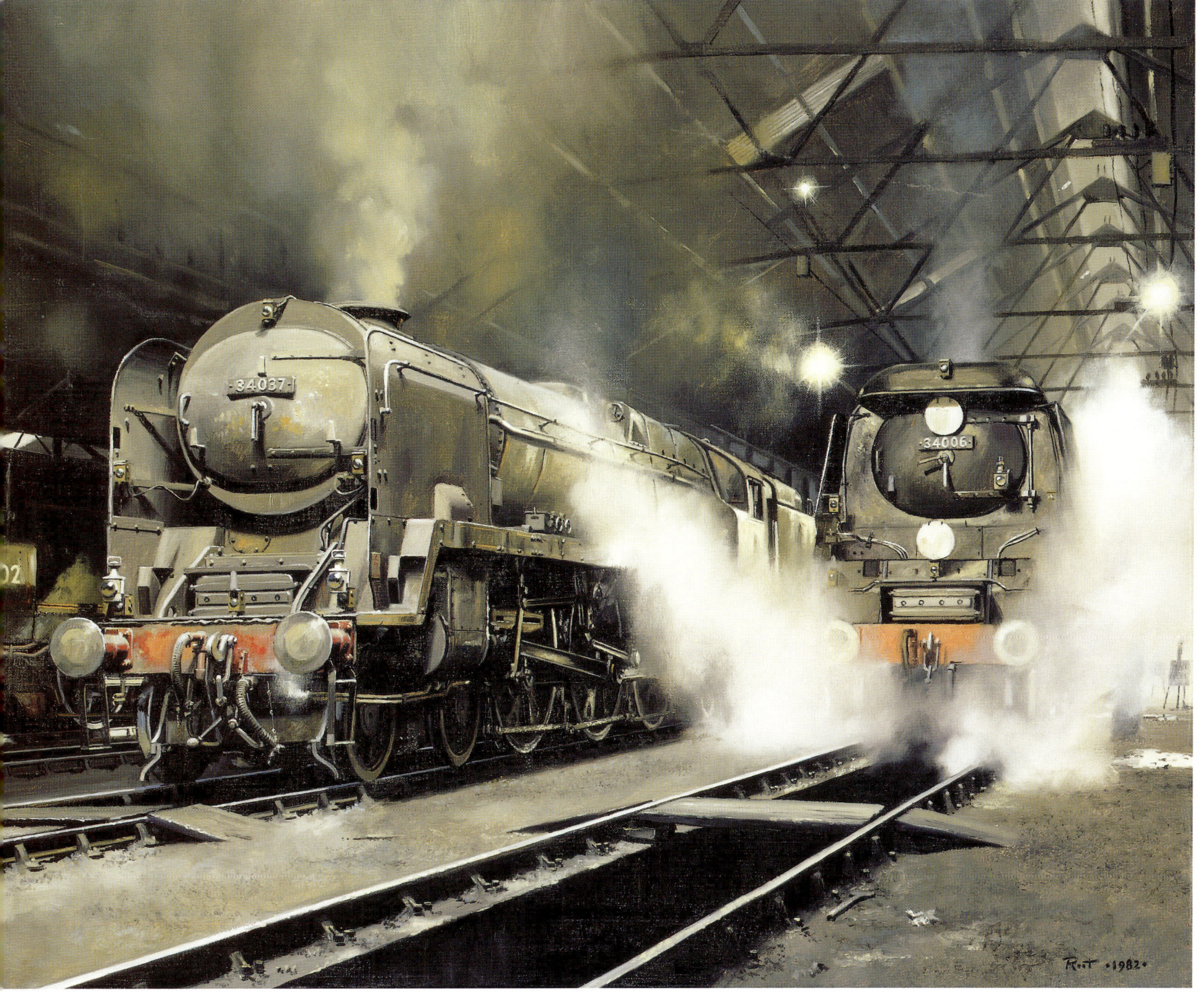
34037
34006
Root ·1982·

Beside the Sea

Painted 1999

This distinctive piece of track is one of the best known railway scenes in the British Isles, partly due to the excellent work of the GWR publicity department. In the book *Brunel and After* published in 1925, the chapter Into the Far West declares: 'As long ago as the closing years of the eighteenth century the attractions of Devonshire as a popular holiday ground had created considerable traffic on the Exeter Road. Early in the railway era Devonians began to demand the conveniences of railway travel. Brunel was called upon, while still busy with the London–Bristol line, to establish a route from Exeter to Plymouth. Brunel decided to follow the right bank of the Exe to Starcross, and then the coast-line past Dawlish to Teignmouth. Beyond that town the track would run along the left bank of the river Teign and cross it just before reaching Newton Abbot.' That was the easy bit, and this was also to become a section of Brunel's 'Atmospheric Railway' (see page 28).

Because of the attractiveness of Starcross, Dawlish and Teignmouth, the addition of a railway passing the beaches and darting in and out of tunnels produced an extra romance for the area. One could almost alight from the train at Dawlish straight on to the beach, with buckets and spades at the ready. Passing trains were always an extra attraction for the holidaymakers, as Malcolm's picture shows. The scenic views appeared in books and leaflets and on several jigsaw puzzles.

The Cornish Riviera Limited is one of the most famous trains in the world, and when it was pioneered in 1904 had the longest non-stop run in the world of 247.7 miles from Paddington to Plymouth. In its heyday it also dropped off three slip coaches on the way. This was a help when the steep gradients in South Devon had to be tackled, and it needed all the power of Castles and Kings to do this, as the train could weigh 500 tons when it left Paddington. The train would pass Dawlish, as seen in the picture, at lunch time, having left Paddington at 10.30am, and would arrive at its final destination of Penzance at about 5pm. Here we see the train being hauled by perhaps the most famous of all GWR locomotives, King class 6000 4-6-0 *King George V*. These locomotives were designed by CB Collett, and represented the ultimate in GWR 4-6-0 design as pioneered by GJ Churchward (see page 28). She is now preserved and is located at the GWR Museum at Swindon.

I am not sure of the make of the pram, but it too is certainly a vintage model!

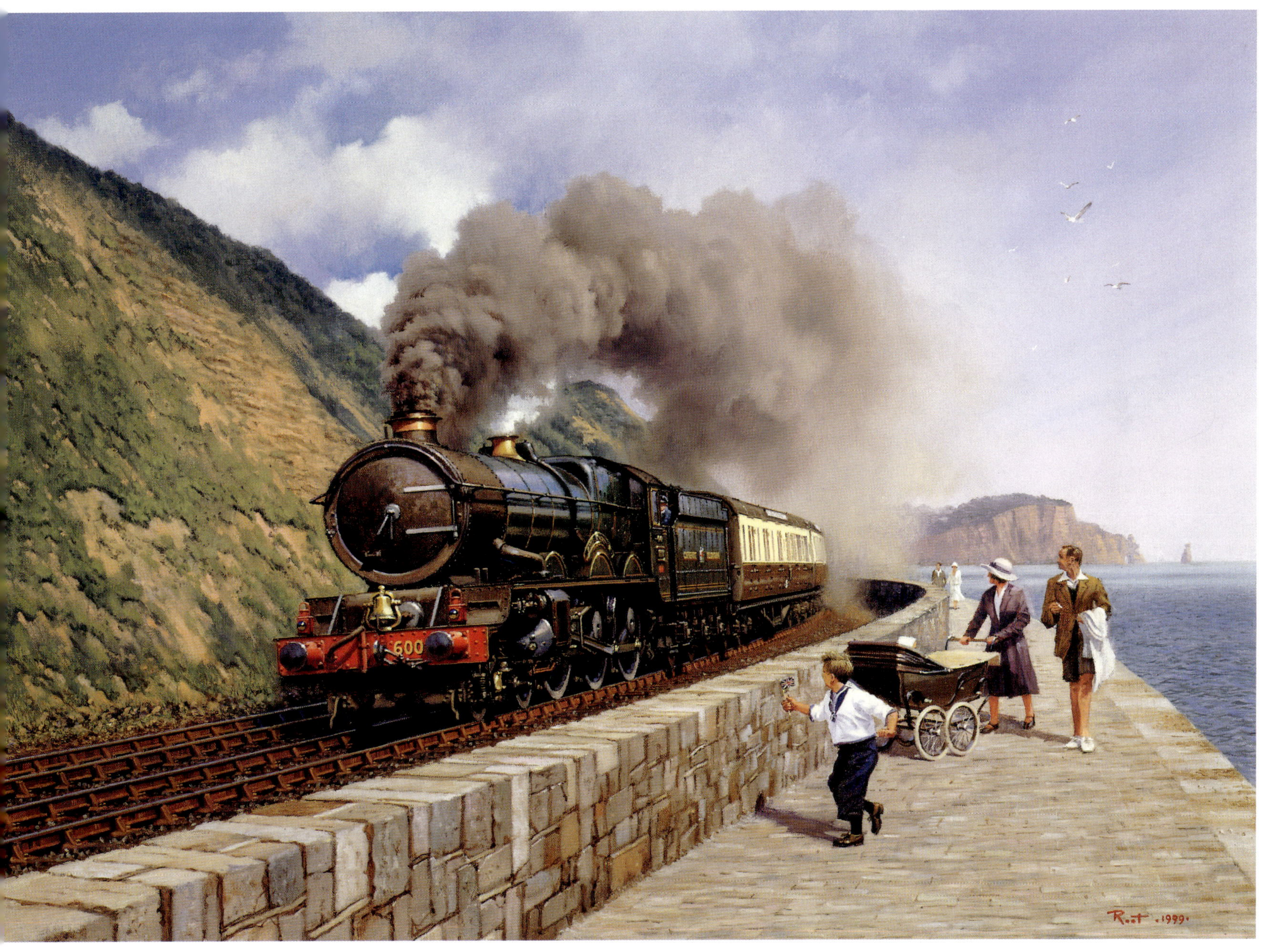
600
Root .1999.

Partick West

Painted 1997

We move now from the playground beaches of the south coast to the industrial north. Glasgow, because of its strategic position on the river Clyde, has long been an important port and centre for shipbuilding and other industries. Partick West station was situated west of the city centre and north of the river. The huge cranes used for shipbuilding can be seen on the right, beside the river, and the scene is set in the early 1960s. The four trains indicate that this is a period of changeover for railway traction. Partick West station finally closed in October 1964, and much of the site is now beneath a new road scheme, which says it all!

On the left a British Railways standard 2-6-4 tank pulls away heading east with a local passenger train. The design origin of this locomotive can be traced back to the design of Sir Henry Fowler for the LMS in the 1920s. The RA Riddles design was adopted as one of the standard designs for British Railways, and 155 were built between 1951 and 1957. This has to be regarded as one of the most successful tank locomotive designs.

At the platform a Cravens diesel multiple unit has stopped to disembark its passengers. These units, powered by the equivalent of bus engines, were ideal for urban areas like Glasgow with a large number of stations in short distances. They were efficient, economical and comfortable, if a bit noisy. It was the Great Western Railway that had introduced Diesel Railcars in 1933, building on their experience with steam-powered rail motors first seen thirty years before. These cars had a rather limited ability and speed, but they continued in service until the early 1960s, by which time technical developments had made the diesel multiple unit a sure winner for the future.

Coming west out of Glasgow is a freight train hauled by WD class 2-8-0 90468, one of the 'austerity' engines built during the war for the Ministry of Supply and designed by RA Riddles, and purchased by British Railways in 1948. Over nine hundred of this class were built in three years. These locomotives had a total weight of 125 tons, and a tractive effort of 34 125lbs. They were intended for freight duties, and gave invaluable service during the war. Only one has survived in preservation, and that travelled via Holland and Sweden before returning to Yorkshire! This empty train will be loaded with ingots, slabs or strip at Rothesay Dock on the Clyde.

On the right hand side is a 0-4-0 diesel shunter on the siding connecting with the shipyard. This is a diesel hydraulic locomotive, first introduced in 1953 and built by the North British Locomotive Co. These little locomotives were ideal for short-haul work on freight trains on industrial sites, and this one has come off the Clydeside Tramway with a trip freight from Whiteinch Riverside yard. Finally, the car at far right is a Ford Anglia, as introduced in 1955.

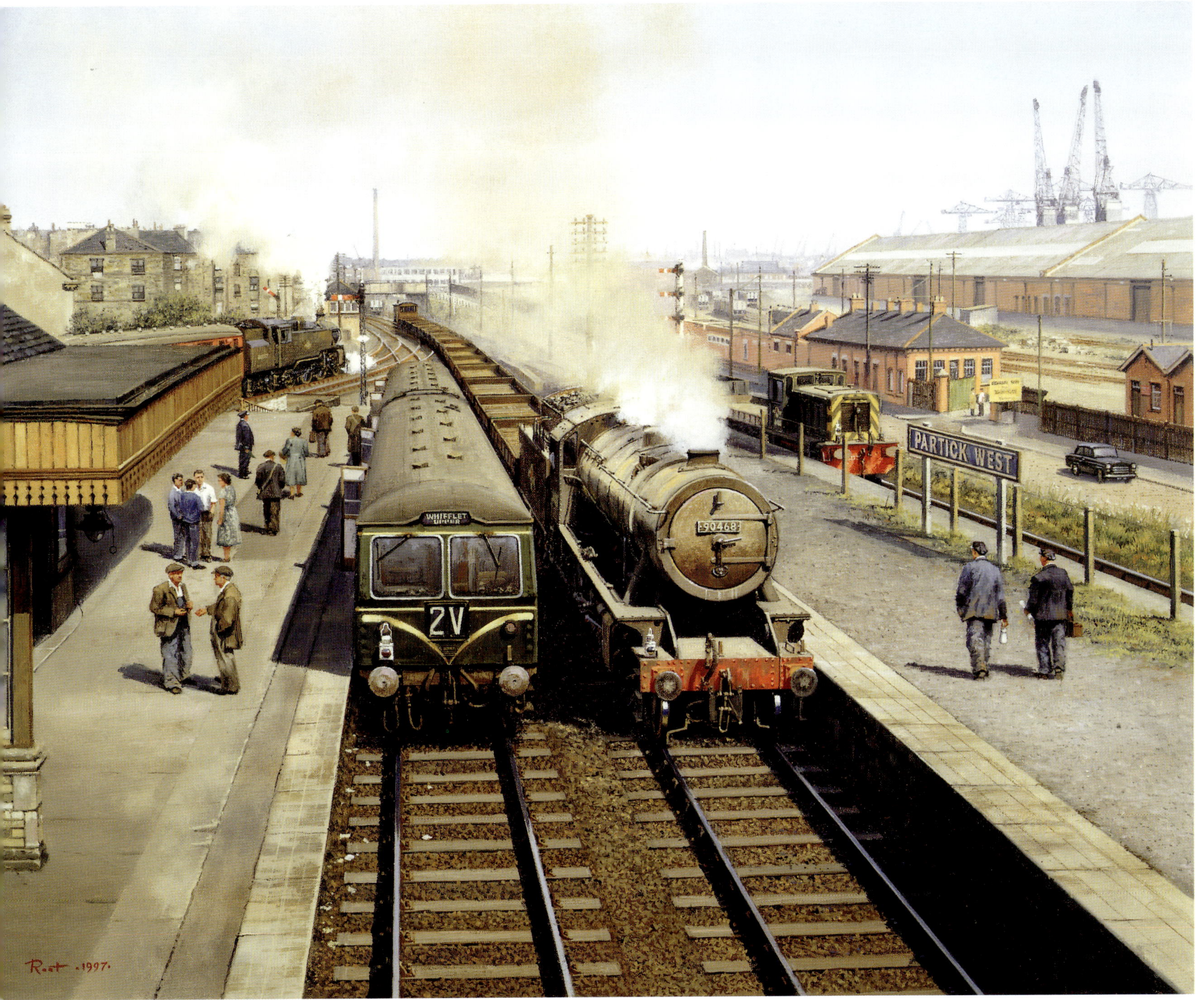
PARTICK WEST
WHIFFLET UPPER
2V
90468
Root 1997

Camden Night

Painted 1997

One might almost feel that this is a great beast resting in its lair during the hours of darkness. However, even if the locomotive was resting, albeit with a good steam pressure maintained, those around it were not, as work went on through the night watering and coaling, greasing and cleaning, and checking mechanical parts ready for the day's work ahead. The scene is Camden coaling plant, and the two ingredients of power for the steam locomotive are seen behind; a huge water tank and the automatic coaling machinery, whereby loaded trucks full of coal could be hoisted up and tipped bodily so that the load was emptied into a gigantic bunker from which the tenders of locomotives beneath could be filled in a few minutes. The scene is set in the later 1930s, and the locomotive being refreshed is an old friend, the LMS Princess Coronation class, *Duchess of Sutherland* (see page 22).

On the left of the picture another engine is resting, a streamlined member of the same class (see page 56). During these pre-war years the LMS ran both versions of the locomotive together. However after the war the LMS abandoned the streamlined casings. Maintenance was made very much easier, but two other factors influenced the decision. Firstly, tests showed that the streamlining really had no effect on the locomotives' performance at speeds below 90mph. Secondly, the locomotives were undoubtedly very ugly. Even though the ground had been prepared two years earlier by the introduction of Gresley's A4s, the LMS version just looked all wrong. No amount of silver stripes could conceal a bulbous front end and flat featureless sides.

However, these locomotives, the culmination of Sir William Stanier's design genius, proved marvellous and long-lived express engines on the West Coast route. The doyen of the class, 6220 *Coronation* attained a speed of 114mph near Crewe in 1937 with the press run of the Coronation Scot, capturing the speed record for a short period until it was decisively taken by *Mallard*. Another pulled a train weighing 610 tons over the stretch from Crewe to Carlisle, which included Shap summit, covering the 102 miles in 118 minutes.

Both the locomotives in the picture will soon be dropping down the hill to Euston, and the start of another day of streaking through the British countryside on their way to the North.

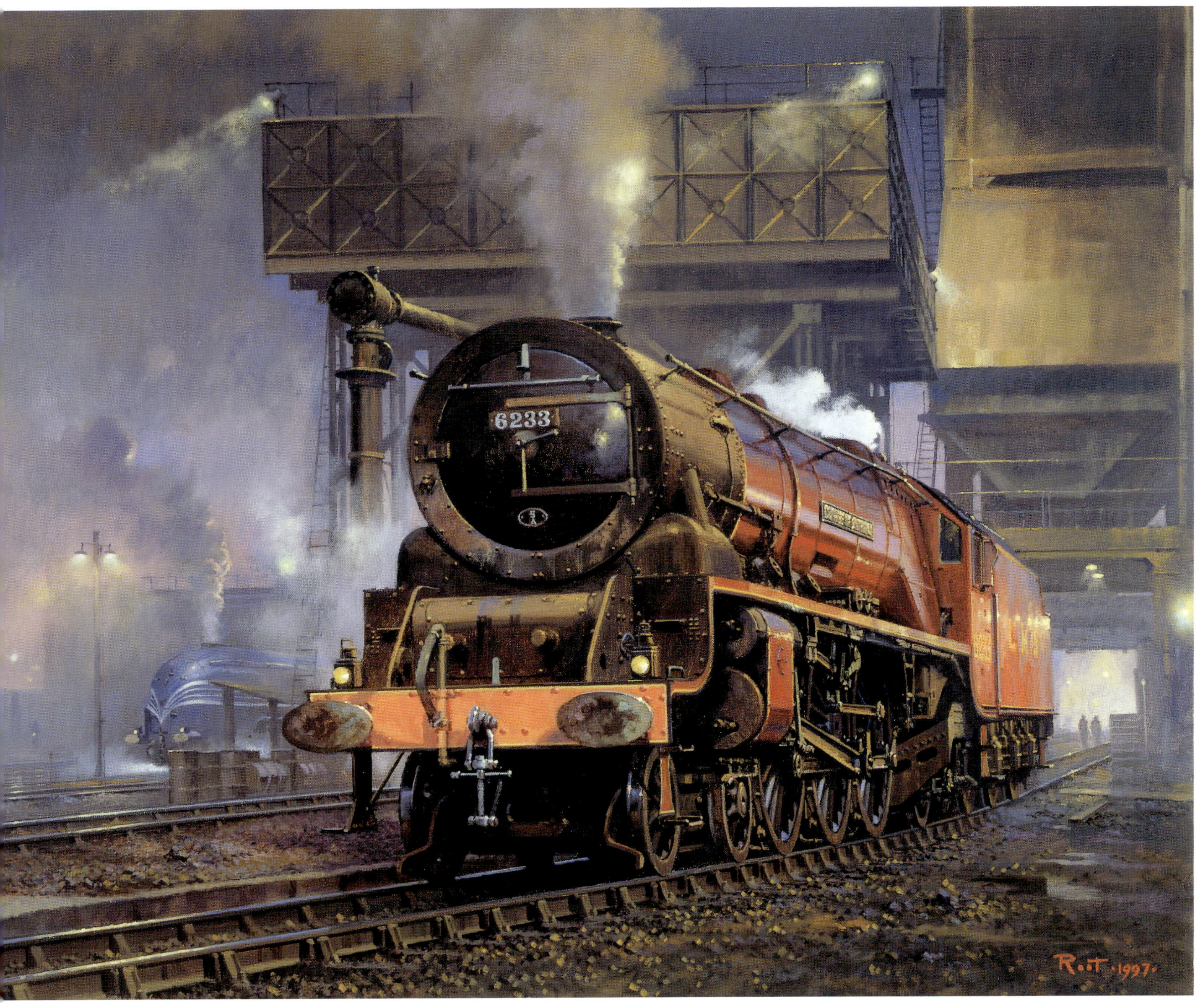
6233
Root ·1997·

Spanning Time

Painted 1989

The area east and north-east of Norwich in Norfolk is the Broadlands, and between Norwich and the coastal towns of Lowestoft and Yarmouth you could easily imagine from the map that it was all marshes. But roughly half way between the towns there is a very important junction, Reedham, which is the setting for this painting. Reedham, which is situated on the river Yare, is surrounded by no less than seven large marshes. It is a road junction where the only notable road in the area crosses the river by means of a chain ferry. Close by, the 'new cut' canal links the river Waveney with the Yare, and here also the railway from Norwich divides, one fork going to Yarmouth, and one to Lowestoft, both notable holiday resorts. We see in the painting Reedham Junction signal box, where two trains are meeting. We are travelling with a train signalled for Lowestoft, while another train comes up in the opposite direction from the same town. Beyond the signal box is a handsome brick bridge carrying a track occupied by two onlookers and a Fordson tractor.

In this painting Malcolm has shown the wonderful view that the driver would have leaning out of the cab of the Claud Hamilton locomotive. This reminds us that on most steam locomotives this was the way the driver obtained the best view of the road ahead. Forward-facing cab windows were usually obstructed by the boiler in front. The GER D16 class were known as Claud Hamiltons after the chairman of the Great Eastern Railway (see page 36). The view we have gives a very good impression of the exhaust blast from the chimney and the Westinghouse steam brake pump near the cab. The locomotive approaching with the Lowestoft train is a B12 class 4-6-0 61572, the engine now preserved on the North Norfolk Railway. Although designed and built for the main Great Eastern routes, some were transferred to Scotland from 1931. These locomotives were notable for having two inside cylinders only, and the rear driving wheels almost entirely beneath the cab. Weighing 108 tons, they were available for most routes, and many had a long life in service.

The apparatus beside the line on the right-hand side of the picture is designed so that the necessary token required for running could be placed on the arm by the signalman, and picked up by a slowly passing train.

By the 1980s when this picture was painted much of the railway infrastructure in this country had changed dramatically from the period covered by this book. This corner of Norfolk held on to its past, bucking the trend, and in so doing provided me with a backdrop for a painting, complete with semaphores, signal box and telegraph poles. Having taken photographs from the front of a DMU, and sketched details of the Westinghouse brake pump on the preserved N7, the picture was duly completed. The preserved B12 No 61572 was incorporated not only for pictorial reasons, but also as a tribute to the late Bill Harvey.

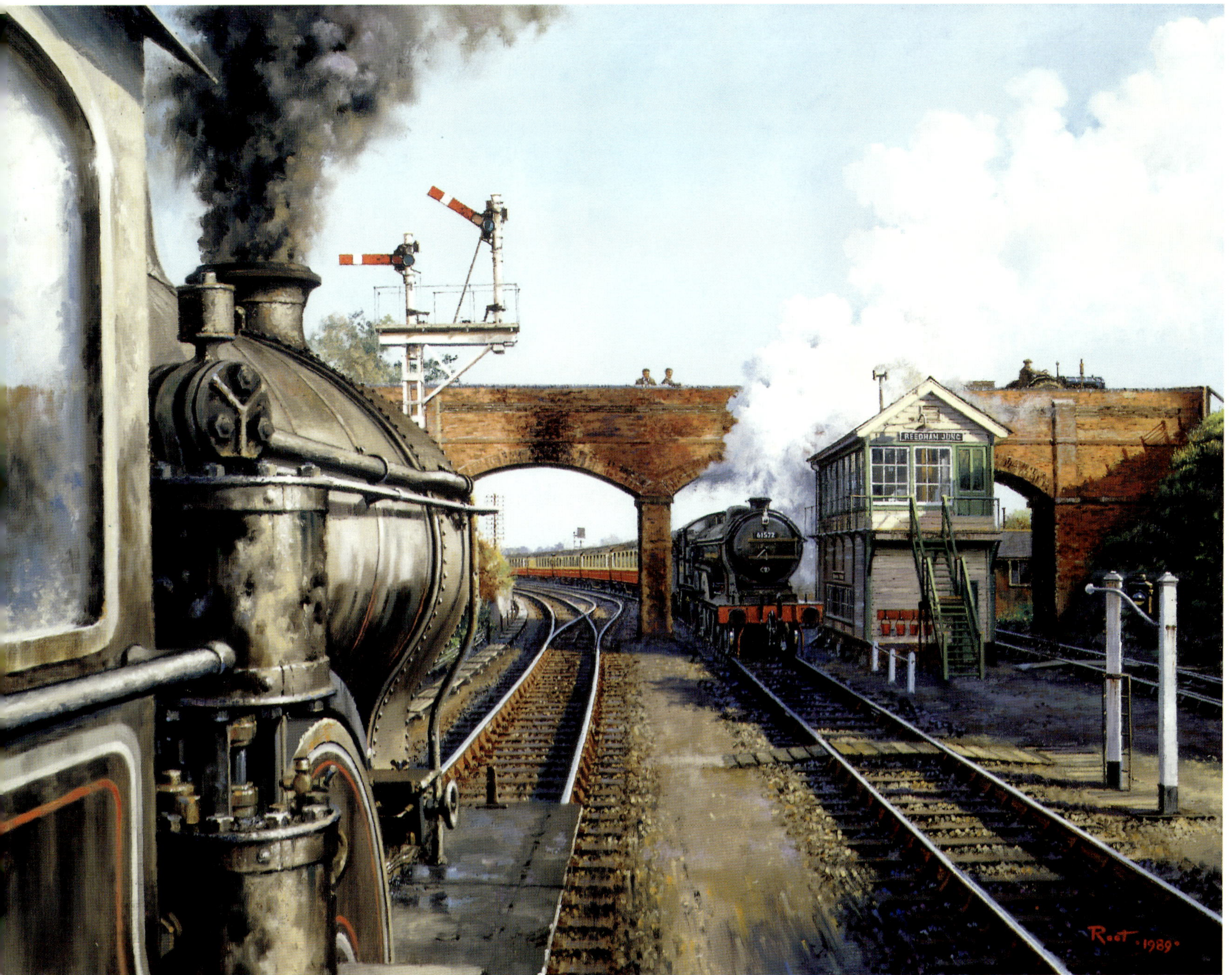
REEDHAM JUNC
61572
Root 1989

Travelling Post Office

Painted 1989

In 1700 it would take about a week to travel by road from London to York, mud or snow permitting. When the rich wanted to communicate they would send a letter via a post boy on horseback. The poor did not communicate at all. By 1800, surprisingly, the roads had improved very little despite huge advances in carriage design. Coaches often overturned, even the royal coach, throwing the occupants into the mud. However, a mail service was growing fast, and where turnpike roads were better maintained, the mail coaches were beginning to operate a service across the country. This was a service at once eyed with interest by the new railways, for they could offer greater speed, greater dependability in bad weather, and the mails were easily transported and paid well. As early as 1838 the Grand Junction Railway converted a horsebox to make a Travelling Post Office which could be used for sorting letters while on the move. In the same year the automatic pick up of mailbags from the lineside was introduced (see page 98).

The first Travelling Post Office was such a success that others quickly followed. The special carriages were provided by the respective railway companies at the request of the Post Office, and each company tended to adapt its ordinary passenger stock for this special use. Windows would be smaller, and perhaps glazed with frosted glass, and doors would be larger and of sliding design. As the volume of mail built up in the mid 1800s, it became desirable to have separate but adjacent coaches for sorting and storage of letters respectively. This led to the suggestion that the coaches should be connected by a gangway with doors. This was such a success that it was soon adopted for ordinary passenger coaches as well. However, the mail coaches had gangways offset to one side, to make best use of the space in the TPO.

The Travelling Post Office became a memorable feature of the railways. Inside, as shown in the painting, they had bags hanging down one side of the carriage, and sorting pigeon holes covering the other side of the carriage. A staff of about half a dozen postal workers per coach would staff the TPO. The lamps shown were replaced by fluorescent lights later on. Sorting mail on a long journey was quite an arduous task for the workers. One other feature of the TPO was a posting box set in the side of the coach, so that other passengers could post letters from the station platform.

This painting of the interior of the North West TPO was a challenging one and a departure from my usual subjects. One group of postal workers would work the shift from London to Carlisle to be replaced by another who would work the Carlisle to Scotland leg. The following day the process was reversed. The gentleman in the foreground is Mr Colin Langley who served on the North West TPO during the 1960s. This train was the unfortunate victim of the Great Train Robbery at Sears Green in 1963. Fortunately Mr Langley was not on duty on that historic night.

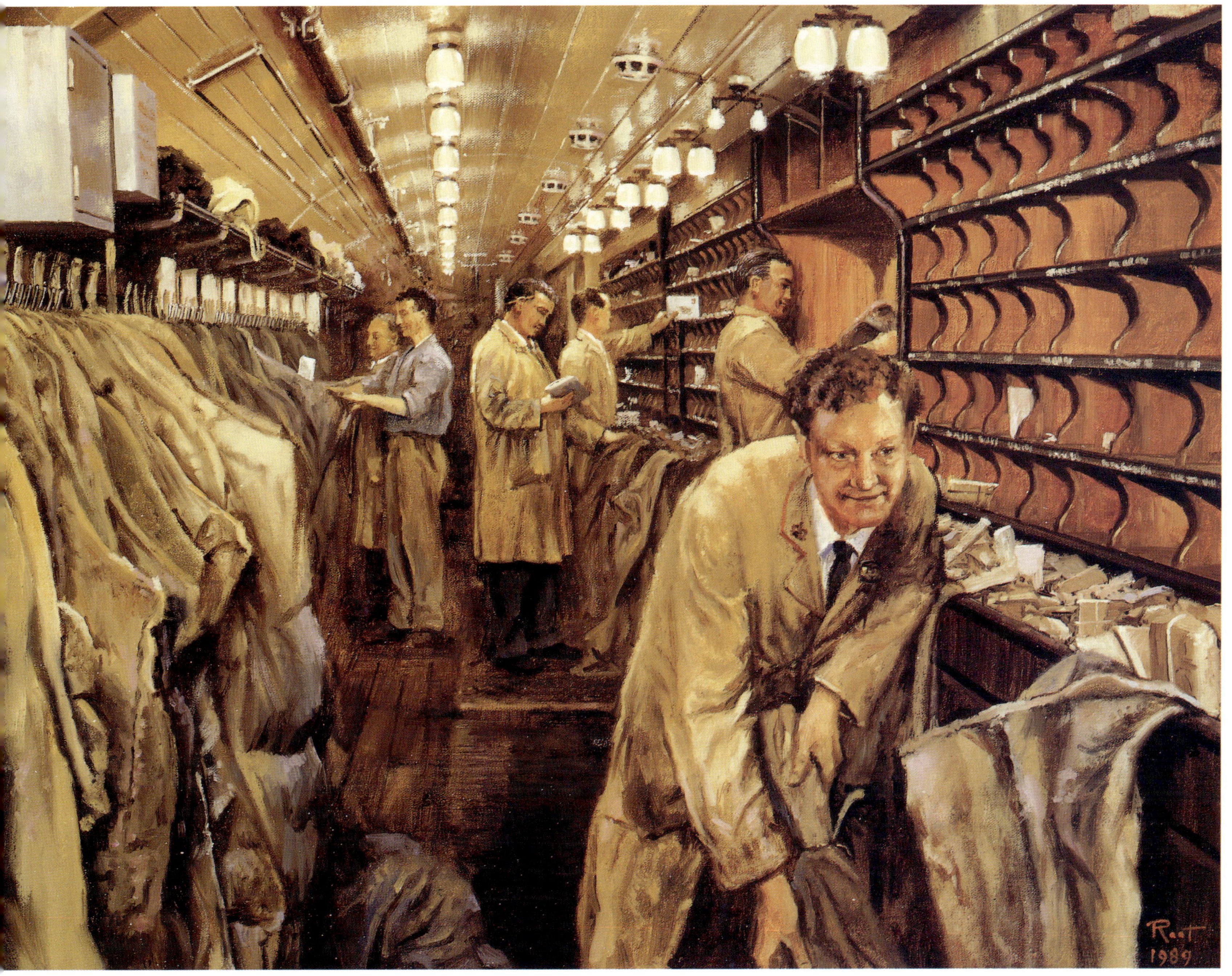
Root
1989

Dovey Junction

Painted 2003

Once again we are back on the GWR Cambrian Coast railway, and it is a wet day at Dovey Junction. The station is situated at the head of the River Dovey estuary, on the west Wales coast, and remarkably there is no main road to the station. The A487 trunk road passes close by, but the passengers on the platform will all be changing trains, and only aware of the remoteness of the sea level location, and the silence when no train is present. On occasion very high tides have covered the tracks and washed ballast away. Prior to local government re-organisation in 1974, the station stood at the junction of three counties, so that the platform was in Montgomeryshire, the up distant signal in Cardiganshire, and the stationmaster's house in Merionethshire!

Station arrangements at the junction were often complicated, as the Cambrian Coast Express divided here, one part taking the northern coast route to Pwllheli, while the remainder took the southern route to Aberystwyth. As the track layout was basic, a game of railway 'musical chairs' could be required! In the painting we see the up express which has paused to have the additional portion added before resuming its journey to Shrewsbury, where a more powerful Castle will probably complete the journey to Paddington. The train is in the care of GWR Manor class 4-6-0 7820 *Dinmore Manor*. This class was designed by CB Collett, and was part of the stable of famous 4-6-0 locomotives. Weighing in at 109 tons they could be used for mixed-traffic on secondary lines, and were ideal for the Cambrian Coast. The class was first introduced in 1938, and thirty were built, but this one has been in service for only ten years and still looks very smart.

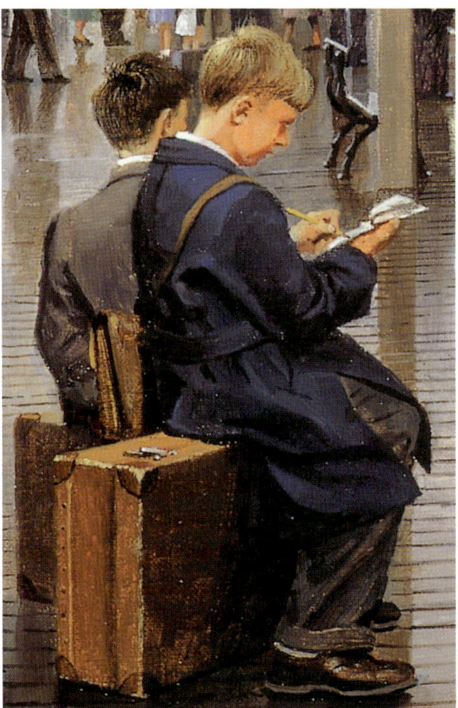

The painting beautifully captures all the detail of the station on a wet morning, down to the ardent train spotter sitting on his long-suffering suitcase! I noticed the pile of redundant railway sleepers beside the line, and was reminded of all the former railway property scattered round the countryside. Sleepers are ideal for small bridges over culverts, or for raised gardens. Trucks made excellent henhouses or storage containers. But the most fascinating thing I came across was a house in Woodmancote in Sussex. The front was a wooden bungalow type building, of modest size, but I did not realise until I went in that the back was a railway carriage, minus its wheels and up on a foundation, providing the living room and kitchen for the house!

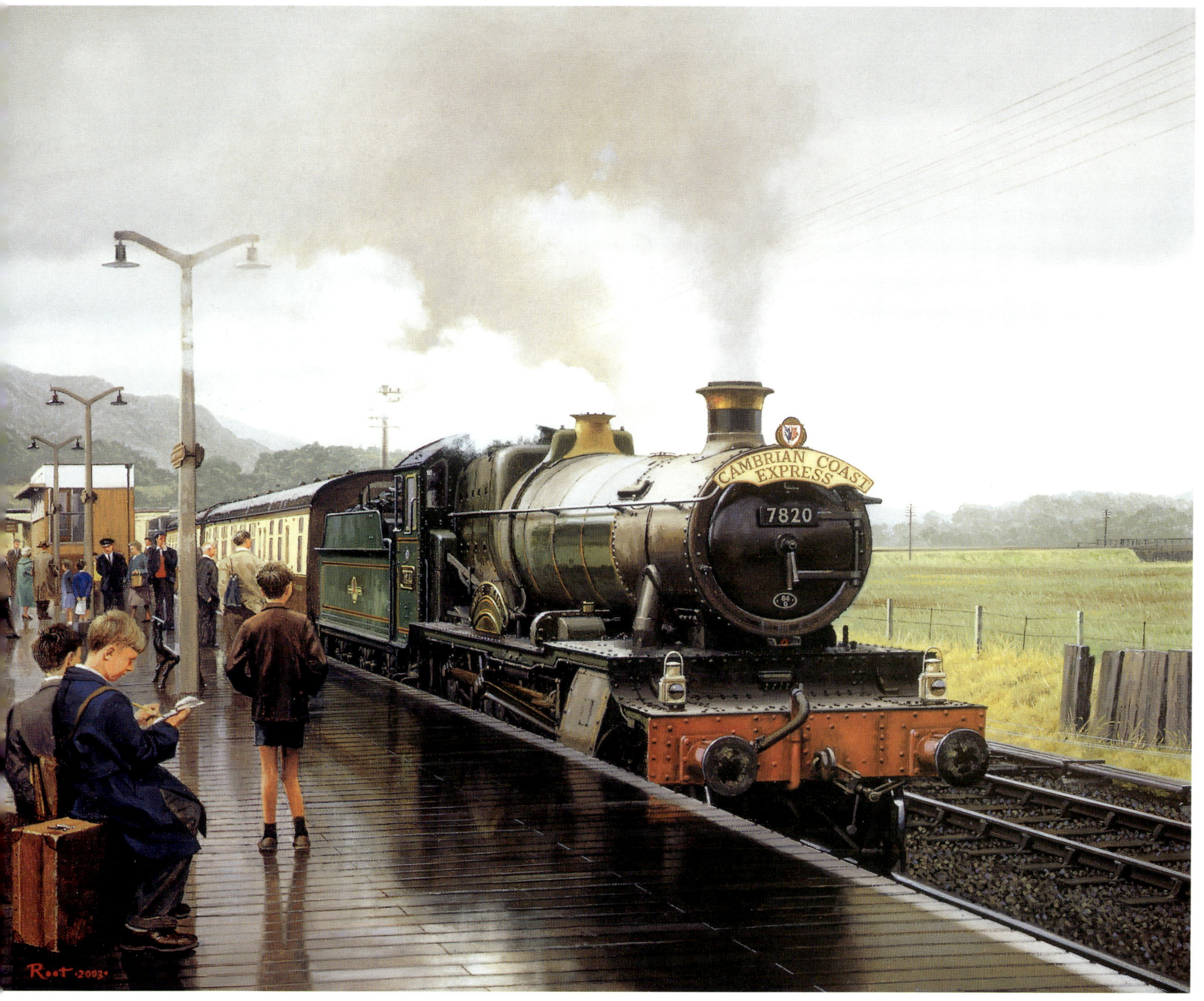
CAMBRIAN COAST EXPRESS
7820
Root 2003

Q1 at Guildford

Painted 1982

On a grey October afternoon in 1939, a German Luftwaffe pilot held for a moment the Forth Bridge in his bomb sights. Aware that Spitfires were darting in to attack him, he hastily released his bombs and turned for Germany. A column of smoke rose from a cruiser moored beside the bridge. The cruiser was important, but the objective had been the vital rail link between Scotland and the South. Down below, railwaymen heaved sighs of relief at the escape of the great bridge. During the Second World War the railways in Britain rose to the occasion magnificently. They had to cope with major bomb damage, directly aimed at disrupting and destroying the railway network. At 5am one morning the Coburn Road Bridge received a direct hit. Seventeen hours later an Ipswich to Liverpool Street train was able to pass over it, though in the photograph recording the occasion the driver does look a little anxious! At the time of the evacuation from Dunkirk, the railways amassed 186 locomotives and 2000 coaches in the corner of Kent, and 320 000 exhausted troops were transported round London to bases and homes in every part of Britain. The control offices for the railways were moved underground, and blackout requirements meant tarpaulins had to shield the glare of a firebox when the fireman refuelled it. Signal boxes operated in the dark, and the glass roofs of great stations were removed. Children with labels tied to their coat lapels were evacuated to safe areas all over the country.

To help with this challenge the railways needed new locomotives, with an emphasis on utility and economy. With this in mind Oliver Bulleid designed the Q1 class. Described as perhaps the ugliest locomotive ever to run on Britain's railways, it served its purpose admirably, with minimum weight, maximum power and wide route availability. It eliminated the need for double-heading on many secondary lines. It had no running plate or splashers, and sported the BFB (Bulleid Firth Brown) wheels so familiar on the SR Pacifics. Introduced at the height of the war in 1942 it weighed only 89 tons but had a tractive effort of over 30 000lbs. Forty of the class were built, and one has fortunately survived in preservation.

In the picture Q1 33027 is seen in the heart of Southern Railway territory, at Guildford (see page 50). Later in the war the railways in southern England played a huge part in the build up for the invasion of Normandy, and doubtless the Q1s made their contribution to this great enterprise.

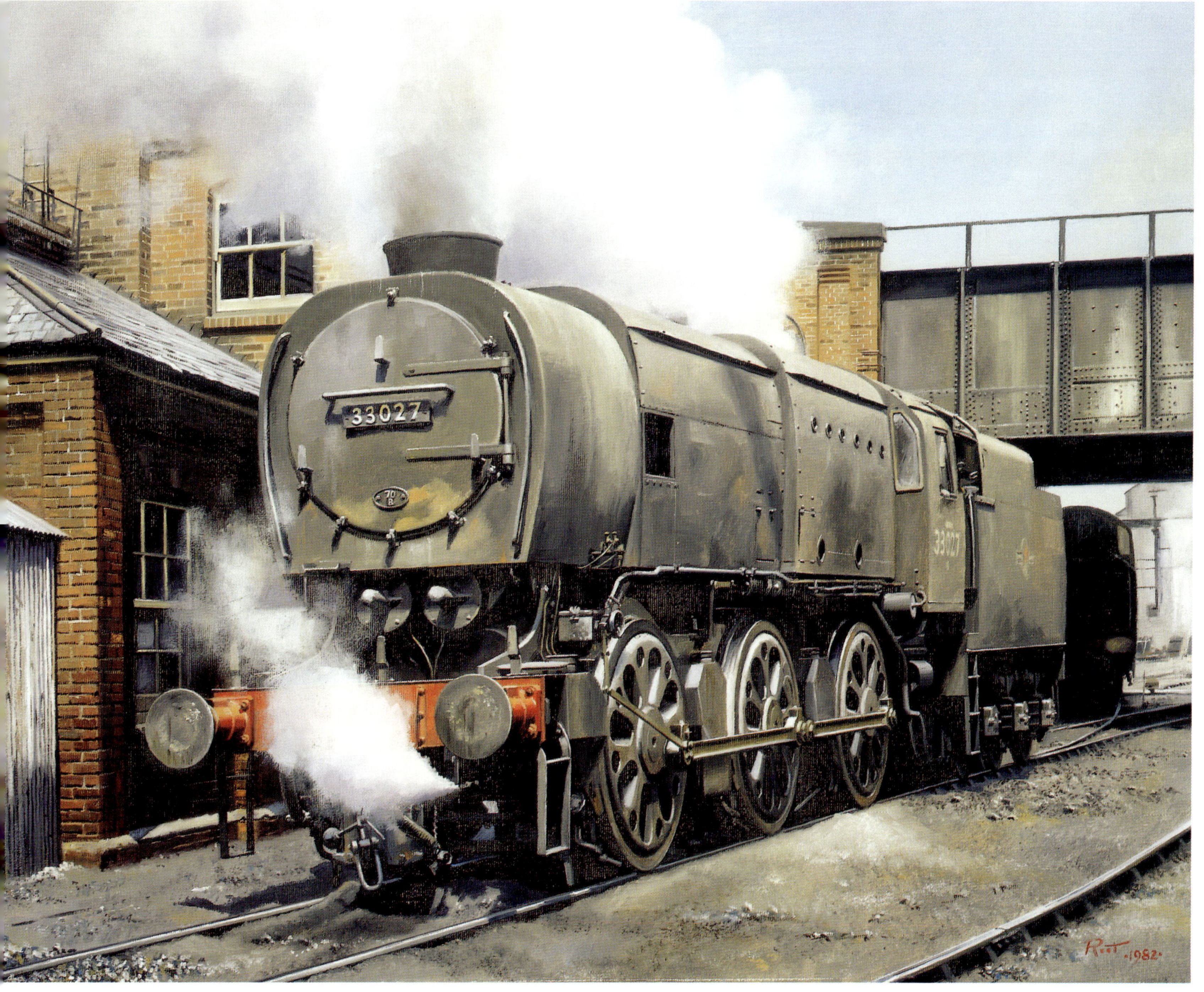
33027
33027
Root .1982.

Approaching Dent

Painted 2003

High up in the North Pennines in west Yorkshire is one of the highest sections of railway line in the British Isles, where the route passes Dentdale on the way from Settle to Carlisle. Dent is the highest station in England, and the railway engineers had to construct a line which taxed all their skills, with the huge viaduct at Ribblehead, and two long tunnels along with many embankments and cuttings. Up on these high moors there is very little noise, just the bleating of sheep, the croak of a raven and the musical whistle of the curlew. If you are beside the railway line, and upwind of an approaching train with the regulator shut off, it can coast down without giving any advanced warning. But for trains breasting the steep gradient it is a very different matter, and the beat of the locomotive exhaust can be heard long before the train itself is in sight. Real railway experts can identify the type of locomotive by the sound, the rhythm relating to the number of the cylinders. If the train is double-headed however this can easily confuse the issue. I can remember being able to distinguish between a King and a Castle coming up Dainton Bank, where because of a wooded curve you do not see the climbing trains until they are a hundred yards away.

In the painting ex-London, Midland & Scottish Jubilee class 4-6-0 45608 *Gibraltar* is having a successful climb up to Dent. In 1923 the GWR introduced the Castle class 4-6-0 locomotive, and in 1926 the LMS finding itself short of powerful express engines borrowed *Launceston Castle* from the GWR to test its effectiveness on the steep West Coast Route. It was so successful that the directors at once required CME Sir Henry Fowler to produce a similar 4-6-0, and the result was the Royal Scot class. When Sir William Stanier took over as CME he introduced the Black Five mixed-traffic class, along with the Jubilee class, an express passenger type. Stanier had been at the GWR locomotive works at Swindon under Collett, and brought a number of GWR design features with him to the LMS. The tapered boiler on these handsome engines is a typical and very obvious example. It is interesting to note that although the big four railway companies were in competition with one another, there was a lot of co-operation, cross-fertilisation of ideas, and exchange trials of locomotives took place.

I always feel it is necessary to have 'space' for the train to run into. I have seen too many pictures where the train has been cropped too near the buffers. In order to retain the space and include the viaduct the train has just passed, the canvas selected was wider in relation to height than I would normally choose. Because the locomotive has been positioned more to the left, necessary balancing techniques have been employed. While the countryside in the left of the picture bathes in sunlight, the viaduct and fells beyond lie in shadow under a dark cloud, thus moving the weight of tone to the right.

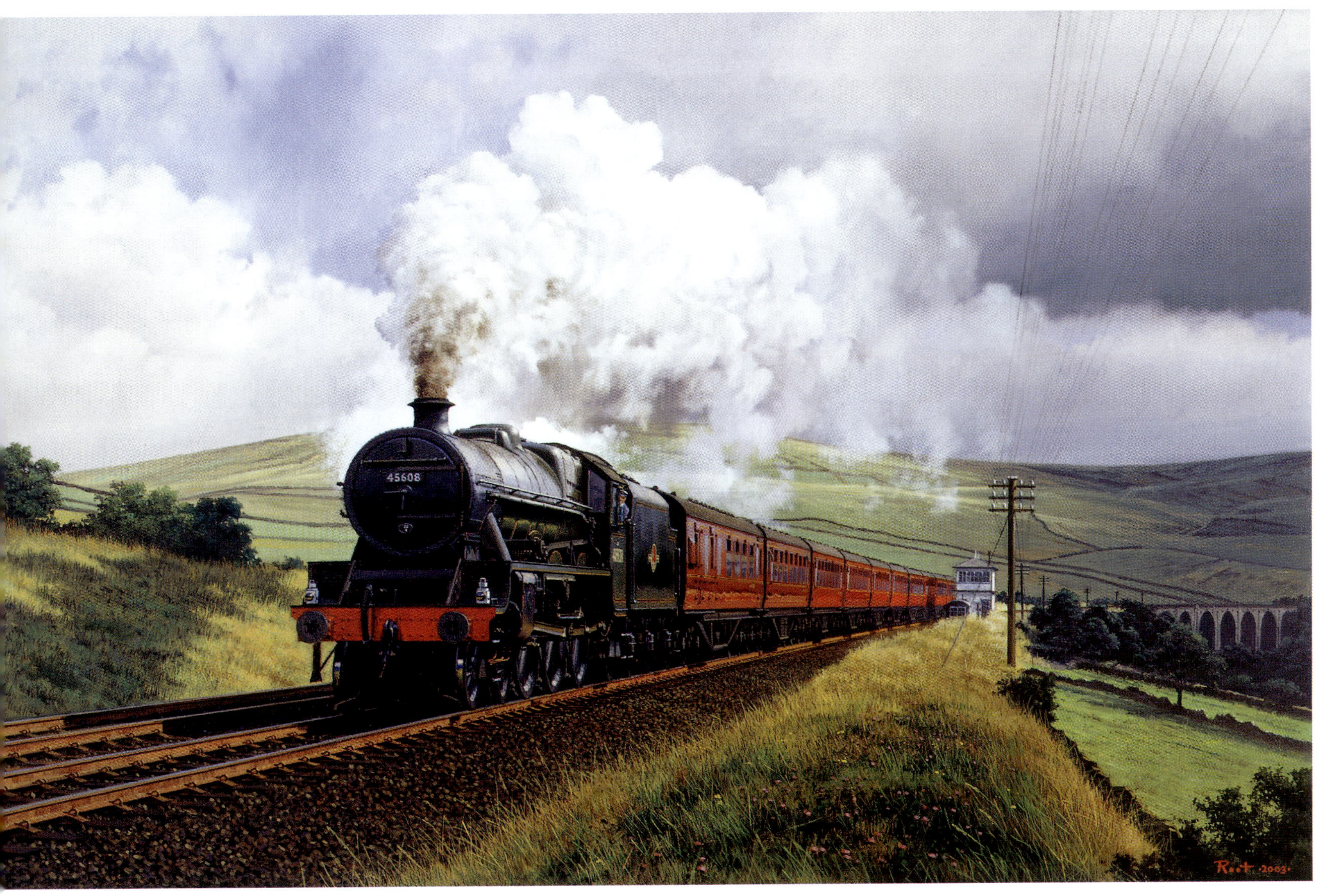
45608
Root 2003.

Night Ferry

Painted 1999

In the early years of the twentieth century it was the dream that a railway service could be provided to enable one to go to sleep in London and wake up ready for a day's work in Paris, or vice versa. An early attempt to dig a Channel Tunnel was abandoned, but during the First World War through trains were arranged, using train ferries on two routes. These, and a later service from Harwich to Zeebrugge in 1924, were for the carriage of freight only. It was not until 1936 that a train ferry terminal was opened at Dover, and on 14 October of that year the first London-Paris Night Ferry travelled between the two cities, using a cross-channel route from Dover to Dunkerque. Those booked into sleeping car accommodation alone travelled through, the passengers in 1st and 2nd class carriages had to change at the ferry terminals. I can remember the excitement as a child of feeling the carriage going on to the ship, and then the strange motion of the sea crossing. I don't think I slept very much!

The inaugural Night Ferry left London Victoria at 10pm and reached Paris at 9am. In the painting we see the very first up Night Ferry travelling along the coast of Kent between Dover and Folkestone having crossed by ferry overnight. The dawn is breaking and the white chalk cliffs and the calm sea provide a beautiful backdrop. The train consists of the Pullman-style Wagon-lits sleeping cars, with their distinctive livery and crests.

Pulling the train is the Southern Railway 4-6-0 Lord Nelson class locomotive 855 *Robert Blake*. The sixteen locomotives of the class were all named after Sea Lords, Nelson being the first. Robert Blake was the English admiral in the sea wars against the Dutch in the late seventeenth century. These locomotives were designed by REL Maunsell, and introduced in 1926. For a year they were the most powerful engines in the country, with a tractive effort of 33 510lbs, until superseded by the GWR Kings the next year. The locomotive had an unusual feature in that the cranks of the engine were set to give eight power impulses to the driving wheels per revolution, instead of the usual four. This also resulted in a very soft and smooth exhaust beat.

The postman and two other early morning workers cannot resist pausing to admire such a magnificent train.

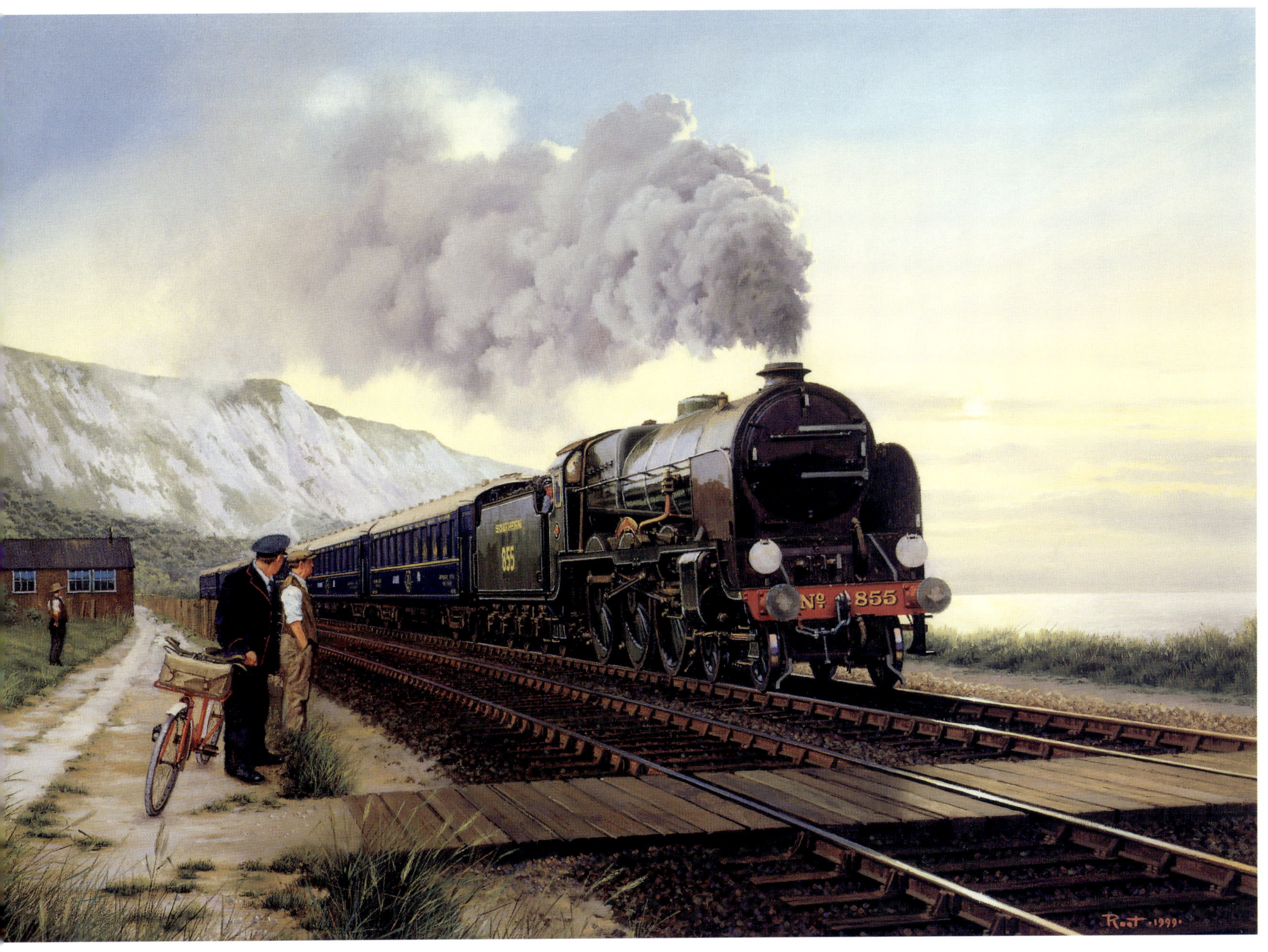
SOUTHERN
855
Nº 855
Root ·1999·

Le Shuttle

Painted 1997

The first attempt to dig a tunnel beneath the English Channel was abandoned in 1882, when the Prime Minister, William Gladstone, was persuaded it could be a risk to national security. In 1975 a new attempt was discontinued when talks failed, but at last in 1986 the Treaty of Canterbury was signed by the English and French governments, and the work began in 1987. The actual tunnel took 3.5 years to build, is 31 miles long, and descends to a maximum depth of 75 metres below the seabed. When the tunnellers from the two sides met, they were only a few centimetres out in their calculations! The bore consists of two railway tunnels with a service tunnel between them. The tunnel was officially opened by HM Queen Elizabeth and President Mitterand on 6 May 1994.

Le Shuttle, shown in the painting, is not actually steam-powered, but we like to put in a picture like this to show how up to date we are! There are 38 locomotives in service for the Shuttle trains, and two locomotives can pull a train of 2400 tonnes at 140kph and also tackle a gradient of 1-in-90. Atmospheric conditions can vary a lot, with freezing temperatures outside, yet hot inside with 100 per cent humidity. Road vehicles are carried in special double-decker wagons, with decks which run the entire length of the train. Cars will enter by one of two doors, to either the upper or lower decks, and at the end of the journey drive off at the further end of the train. During the trip car occupants are free to leave their cars, but there are security doors between the wagons, with a shutter also, and each wagon is able to be sealed off in the event of a fire. Vehicles over 1.8 metres high have to be accommodated in single storey wagons, which have excellent clearance for large vehicles. Vehicles are embarked at Folkestone, and leave the train at Coquelles, near Calais, after a journey taking 35 minutes.

The Eurostar trains, for foot passengers only, leave from the international terminal at London Waterloo, and go through the tunnel to either Brussels or Paris. Drivers on all the trains have to speak both English and French.

Competition with the airlines is likely to be much keener when the high-speed link on the English side of the channel is complete, and journey times are much reduced as a result.

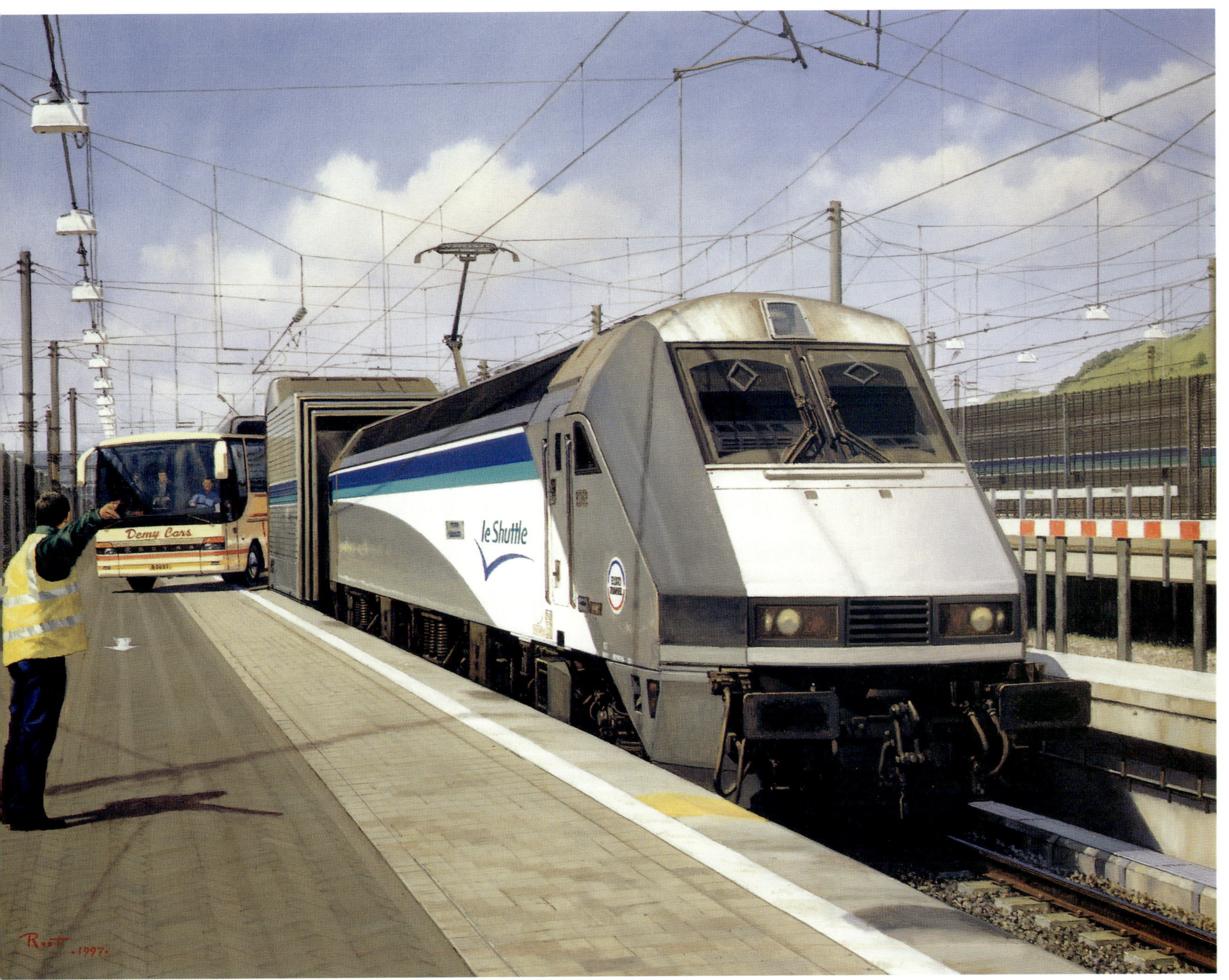
le Shuttle
Demy Cars

Ice and Steam

Painted 2002

We move away from the south coast of England and as often happens into a different climate! It is winter, icy and dark, though the rising smoke and steam indicates that for once East Anglia isn't windy as well! The scene is set at Marks Tey, on the old Great Eastern Railway between Chelmsford and Colchester, and a hundred years ago the village boasted an inn and a smithy and not very much else, except the railway station. However this was also a railway junction, and from here a single line branch began facing back towards London, and then swung north, forking again beyond the Chappel Viaduct with one line going to the old Suffolk market town of Sudbury, and the other becoming the Colne Valley Railway (see page 48). Here on the branch line platform there has been an attempt to clear away the snow, or perhaps some salt has been put down to make the edge of the platform safe, but it still needs careful navigation.

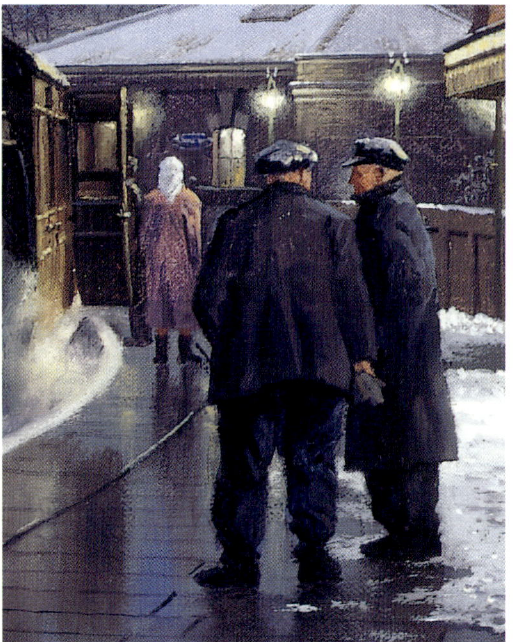

Waiting at the platform is a local train, perhaps the last of the evening, hauled by an ex-Great Eastern Railway E4 class 2-4-0 locomotive, which has such a full head of steam that the safety valves have lifted. By the early 1950s, which is the period shown in the painting, these faithful old workhorses had been in service for over 60 years, having been designed by J Holden and first introduced in 1891. They were designated light mixed-traffic locomotives. In 1923 one hundred of this type were in service, but by the time of this picture only eighteen remained. They were ideal for the lightly constructed branch lines of Essex and Suffolk as they weighed only 70 tons complete with tender. They were distinctive little engines with a tall chimney, and the dome close to it at the front of the boiler. The locomotive would have originally been painted in royal blue, and lined out in vermilion red, but sadly by the time of this scene BR black is the order of the day, and it is a pretty grubby black as well.

I hope that someone will shut that carriage door very soon, or there is going to be one very cold railway compartment!

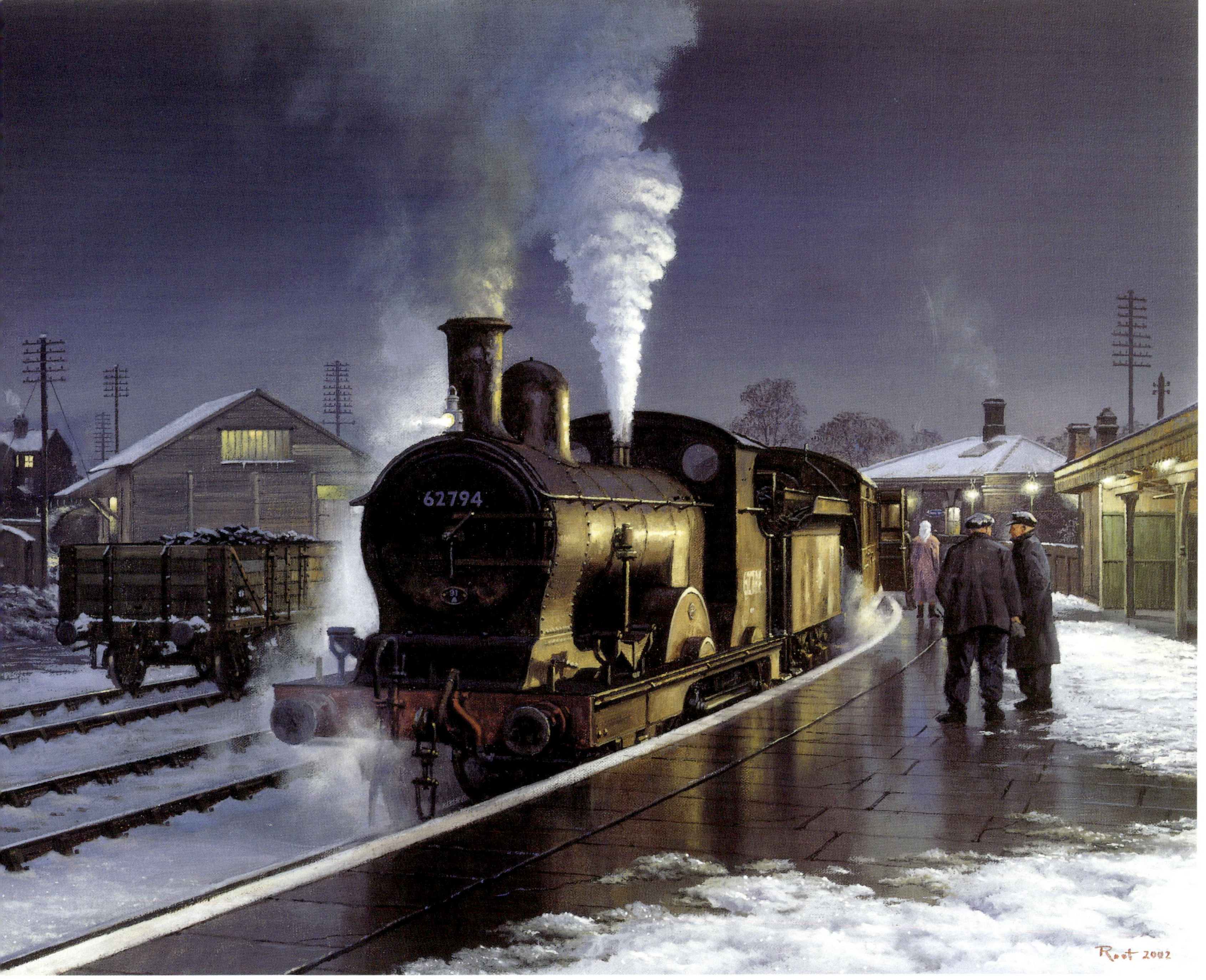
62794
Root 2002

Steam – Road and Rail

Painted 2000

In this painting we move a few miles up the main line from the setting of the last picture, in the direction of London, and Witham station provides a mouthwatering scene partly because the painting has a secret connection with a well-known maker of chocolate! In fact one parent seems to be withholding a box of the same chocolates to the obvious distress of her offspring. The period is the early years of the twentieth century, the heyday of the Great Eastern Railway, and the train passing through the station bound for London is hauled by one of the famous Claud Hamilton class locomotives, first introduced in 1900 (see page 36). The interesting variety of costumes shown would confirm a date well before the First World War, as would the steam-powered double-decker omnibus.

The picture is interesting as it contrasts the older method of travel by rail with the new public transport, the steam-powered omnibus, which is following the tradition of the stage coaches which the railways put out of business. By 1900 travel on an express train was for the first-class passenger really quite luxurious, with plenty of space and comfortable upholstery. There were porters and other staff to assist the traveller at stations, and heavy luggage would be taken care of. In winter the carriages were steam heated, and reasonably draught free. Even on a fairly warm day the driver of the omnibus is wearing an Ulster, and the passengers on the top deck look well wrapped up. A heavy shower of rain must have been a very dampening experience! Yet within a few years battle was well and truly joined between road and rail, as depicted in the splendid film 'The Titfield Thunderbolt'. By the 1960s, with the closing of so many of the feeder lines, the railways acknowledged defeat, and since have only been able to hang on to commuter and long-distance traffic. Buses and coaches carried a large proportion of the local and excursion traffic.

Two other details are of interest. The tank engine standing in the station is a Great Eastern Railway 2-4-2 designed by Worsdell and later to become LNER class F4. This type, with over 100 in service at the time of the grouping, were the mainstay of the London suburban services before the introduction of the N7s.

The firm of Cadbury was founded by John Cadbury in 1831, and handed over to his sons Richard and George, who like their father were members of the Society of Friends, and it was due to their vision that in 1878 fourteen acres of land south of Birmingham were purchased, and the Bourneville factory and community were built. The firm set new standards of care for their workforce which were an excellent example to others. I think Malcolm may have a particular weakness for chocolate!

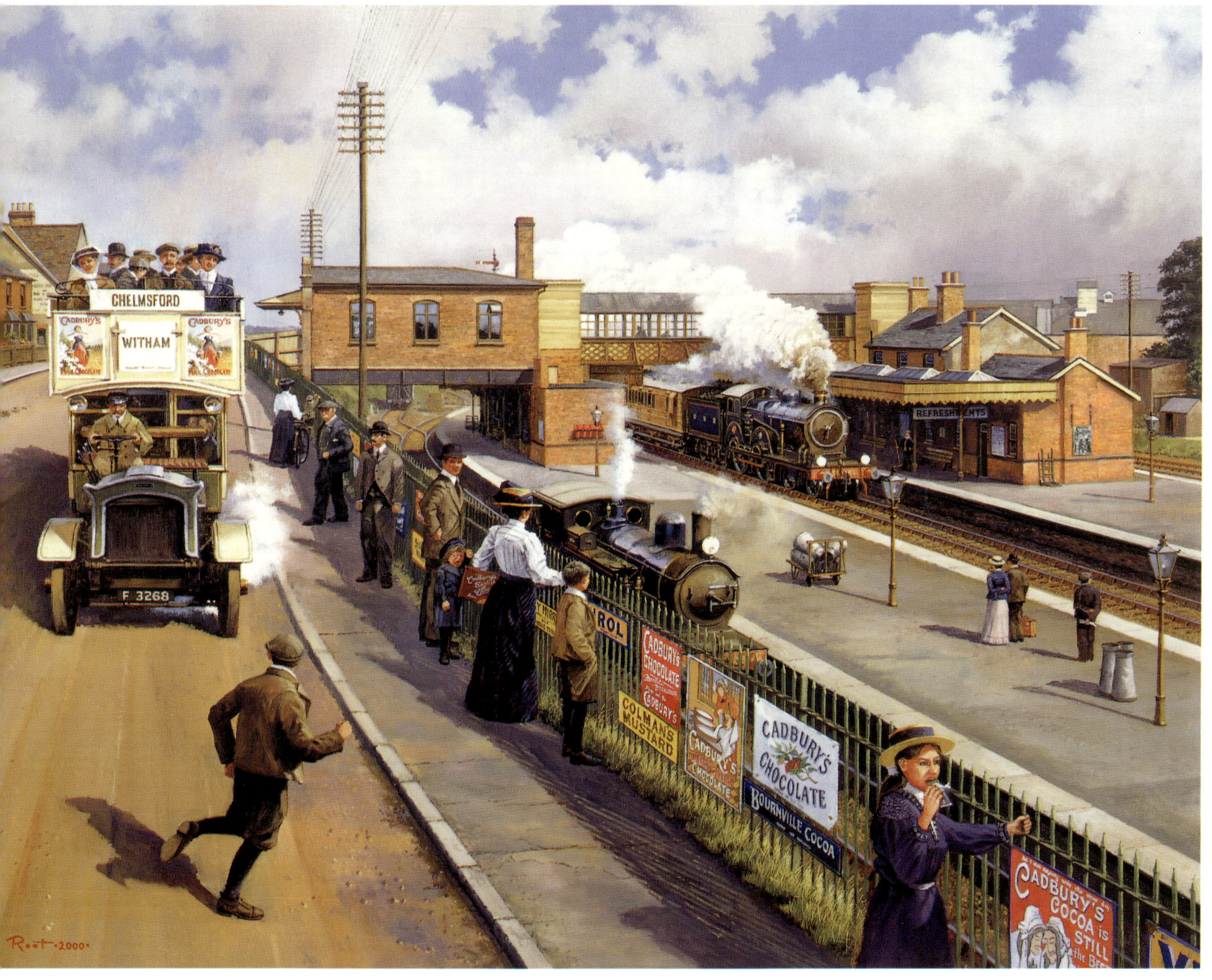
CHELMSFORD
CADBURY'S
WITHAM
F 3268
REFRESHMENTS
CADBURY'S CHOCOLATE
COLMAN'S MUSTARD
CADBURY'S CHOCOLATE
BOURNVILLE COCOA
CADBURY'S COCOA IS STILL
Root 2000

The Climb to Copy Pit

Painted 1993

Our scene shifts dramatically to the Burnley to Todmorden route in north-east Lancashire, near Nelson and Colne, and an area that abounded with coal mines. The monks of nearby Bolton Abbey began mining coal from Trawden Moor as early as 1300. Each monk was permitted a small fire in his cell for warmth in deepest winter. Over the centuries an enormous number of workings came into being, some 'bell pits' which were just single shaft mines, and some open cast where there were outcrops of the precious coal. It is amazing to remember that fifty years ago our country still largely ran on coal, apart from a quantity of diesel and petrol. Today all these pits are closed, and Copy Colliery does not even appear on the map. Some names are left in the area however, such as Foulridge, Blacko, Elslack and Roughlee which may date back to the mining days.

The two requirements for a successful colliery were coal and transport. Men would migrate to the work, however arduous and dangerous it was. Unattractive villages of tenement houses would be quickly built to house them. Transport was more of a problem until the coming of the railways, although in places canals could be utilised, and in fact the Leeds and Liverpool Canal passes close to this area. Railways provided relatively cheap and efficient movement for the bulky coal, and trucks could be filled on sidings, using narrow gauge tramways from the actual workings. Later conveyor belts came into use, depositing the coal into the waiting trucks. From the mines coal could be ferried to destinations all over the country.

Coal was a heavy product as well as a bulky one, and coal trains fifty years ago were very heavy to haul, especially up gradients, which accounts for all the smoke and steam in this painting. Originally trains would require two locomotives to haul them, but Sir William Stanier introduced a new 2-8-0 in 1935, a heavy freight locomotive known as the 8F. With a driving wheel of 4ft 8.5 inches diameter, compared to the 6ft 9 inches of the Coronation and Jubilee class locomotives, this engine had considerable power and excellent traction. It was the premier freight locomotive on the LMS and later the BR Midland Region, and was built in large numbers. They were so successful that during the war they were built by all the four railway companies. Many were sent abroad, and number 48773 built by the North British Locomotive Co became No. 41-109 on the Iranian State Railways. In 1946 it was sent on loan to the Egyptian State Railways as WD 70307, and returned to the UK in 1952. In June 1957 it was purchased by BR as number 48773, and is now preserved on the Severn Valley Railway as LMS number 8233. It was in fine form when I saw it a few years ago.

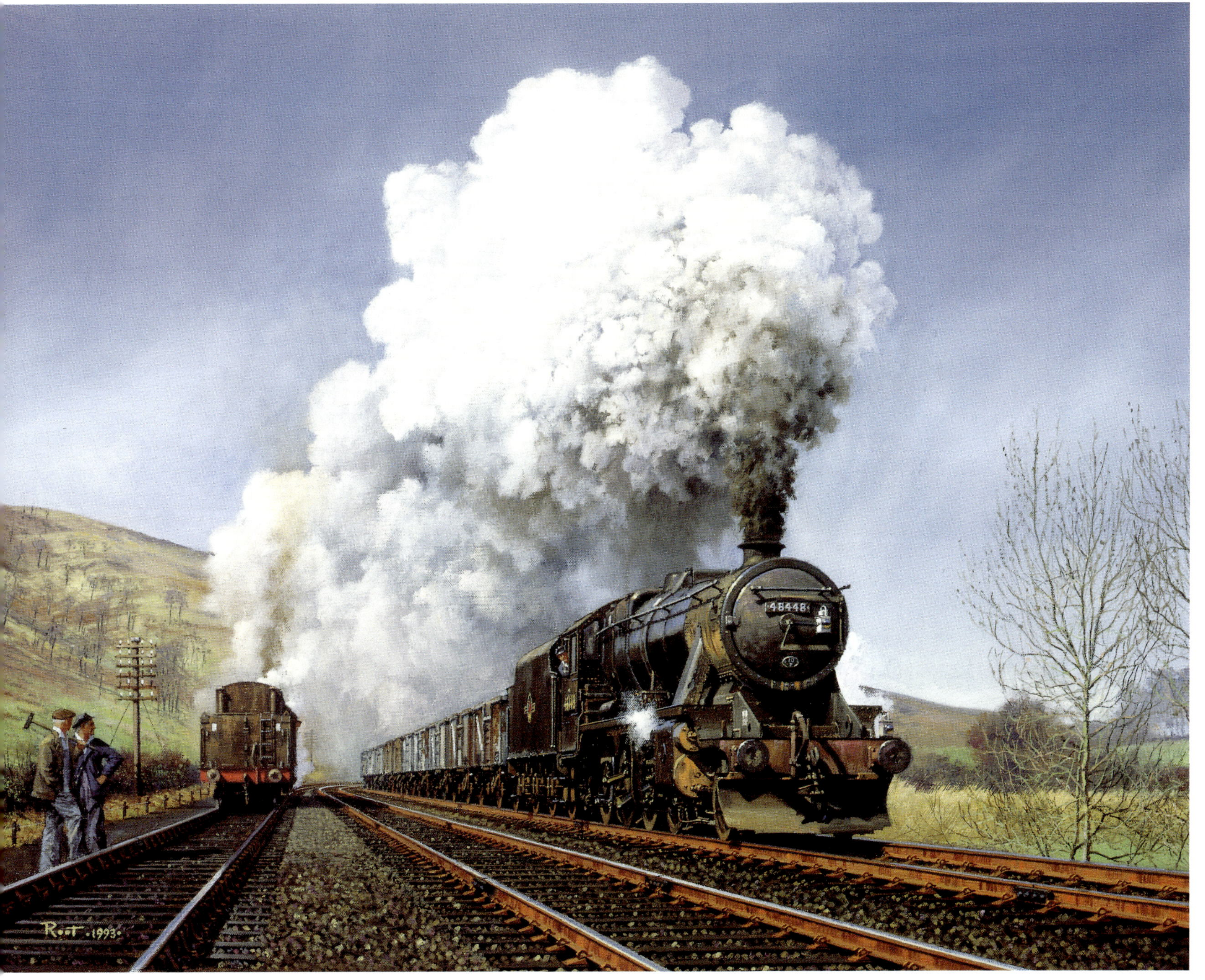
48448
Root .1993.

Britannias at Ely

Painted 1984

Once again the scene is a powerful one. It is now late in the age of steam on British Railways, and the Britannia class were supposedly the final successors to those great express engines of the 1920s and 30s like the Castles and Kings, A4s and Princess Coronations. Built under the supervision of RA Riddles, and introduced in 1951, they acquitted themselves well during a relatively short working life, despite early criticism (see page 2). In 1949 with the formation of British Railways no-one visualised that within about fifteen years steam would be phased out on Britain's railways, and it was planned to produce twelve standard designs of locomotive to run the railways. Much had been learned over the years, and the new locomotives were of traditional design, yet incorporating the many improvements which had been developed as a result of years of experience in design and operation. Again we have a painting which shows the interesting detail of a particular locomotive, and especially the unusual siting of the steam chime whistle on the Britannia, moved forward from its traditional position just in front of the cab roof. The approaching locomotive is Britannia 70042, *Lord Roberts*. The class was named after great figures in English history from Hereward the Wake to Earl Haig, and also after stars and heavenly bodies, with a few exceptions thrown in such as *Lightning* and *Tornado*, perhaps to suggest power.

The sight of two massive steam locomotives about to pass one another at speed reminds me of a delightful 78rpm record of my childhood, called simply 'Trains', and consisting of imitations of railways noises done by a very clever performer. The train crossing the joints in the track made a gentle 'fiddley-dee' sound, lulling one into a false sense of security, for suddenly without any warning it would change to a very loud 'hulley duh hulley duh' as a train rushed past in the opposite direction.

The setting for this painting is Ely Dock Junction. Ely was an important railway centre, as six different lines converged there. The Dock Junction, where the line for Newmarket left the Cambridge and London line, ran close to the River Great Ouse, which wound its way round the Isle of Ely (see page 32). The picture shows good examples of the different types of signal to be found at a typical junction, with danger and caution signals for both the lines involved.

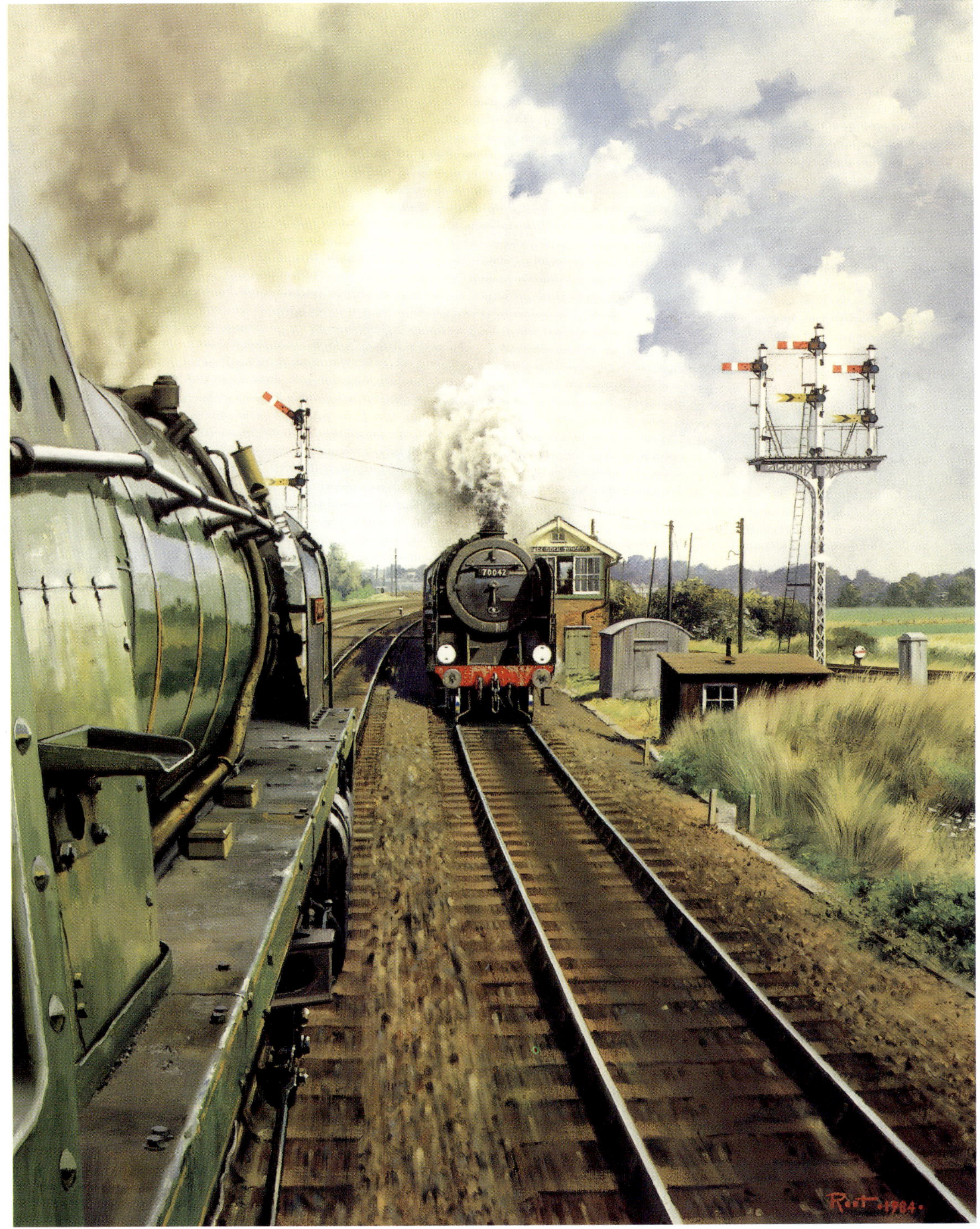

Waiting for the Night Mail

Painted 1991

The first Travelling Post Office was introduced on the Grand Junction Railway in 1838, after considerable negotiations between the GPO and the railway companies (see page 78). Payment from the Post Office for the use of trains in 1838 was £1743. By 1860 the figure had risen to £490 223, and to £1million by 1896, showing how important this service had become to both sides of the partnership. At once a problem arose with regard to transferring mails at smaller stations where the train was not scheduled to stop. The answer was to throw the mailbags out on to the platform, but even at 25mph this could do considerable damage and bowl over waiting passengers like ninepins! Meanwhile, Nathanial Worsdell, Superintendent of the Grand Junction Railway carriage works had built an apparatus for exchanging mails with a moving train. He obtained a patent as early as January 1838, but failed to agree a price with the Post Office. Meanwhile the GPO encouraged one of its employees, John Ramsey, to build another apparatus, but this gave a lot of trouble under working conditions. Eventually in 1852 a modified type was produced by an inspector called Dicker, and this was used for the next 100 years or more. Dicker received £500 for his efforts.

There were three items of equipment essential to the operation. The first item was a leather pouch with flaps that were strapped round the mails, and which could weigh anything up to 60 lbs. The second item was the standard seen in the painting, on which the mailbag was hung. When not in use the top of the standard was turned away from the track to give passing trains more clearance. On the TPO a traductor bar was swung out from the carriage with the pouch fixed to it. This was a somewhat hazardous operation for the staff, and there was only a metal bar to prevent them falling out of the fast-moving train. The third item was the collecting net. One could be deployed on the side of the train, and another would be raised into position by the postal staff at the lineside. Timing was essential, as the carriage net could foul other lineside equipment if put in position too early. The net by the lineside received the pouch from the traductor bar, and similarly the net on the TPO captured the pouch from the standard.

There was a certain fascination about this whole operation, and I still enjoy my Hornby Dublo model TPO which can propel small metal 'pouches' across the room at remarkable speeds! Sadly, on 9 January 2004 the use of TPOs was discontinued, so now we can have even more large red lorries being driven at high speeds on our congested main roads.

Coming in the opposite direction is an express hauled by Britannia class 70036 *Boadicea* (see page 58).

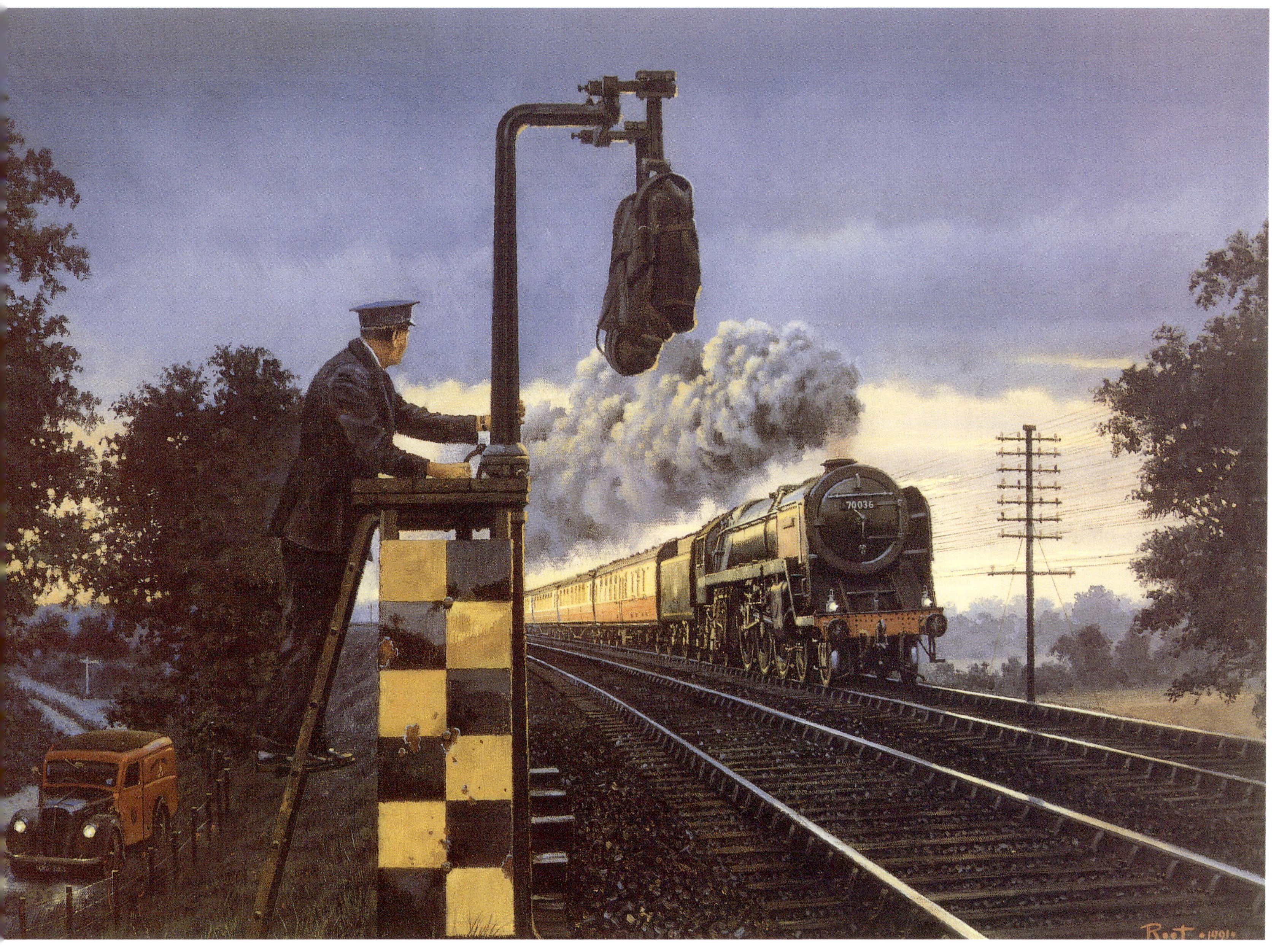
70036
Root 1991

Grantham Departure

Painted 2002

Although the 1920s and 1930s were years of economic depression, following the national exhaustion caused by the First World War, on the railways they were years of great development and activity presided over by great figures like Churchward, Gresley, Maunsell, Collett and Stanier. Of these men Churchward was the earliest, and the Great Western Railway under his pioneering leadership led the way with the Star and Saint class locomotives, forerunners of the Castle class. The latter performed favourably alongside both equivalent LMS and LNER locomotives in the 1920s, and led Stanier and Gresley to make important modifications to their designs. The result was eventually the Pacific locomotives produced for both railways, which were some of the greatest engines ever to appear, and which gave years of superb performance up to the end of the steam era. Along the way several partly experimental locomotives were built, and the 'Mikado' types designed by Sir Nigel Gresley for the LNER were among these.

Gresley designed two 'Mikado' 2-8-2 locomotives. The first was the P1 goods engine of 1925, and this was followed in 1934 by the P2. Although of similar wheel arrangement they were very different in appearance. *Cock o' the North* was the first to be built, and was followed by five other locomotives. These had smaller driving wheels than the LNER Pacifics, and were intended to operate heavy express trains between Edinburgh and Aberdeen. With a tractive effort of more than 43 000lbs they were easily the most powerful passenger locomotives in Britain, and although not designed for speed they could easily attain 85mph. They had a total weight of about 165 tons, and were striking locomotives. The first two of the class had distinctive smoke deflectors and sloping smokebox top which gave a semi-streamlined appearance, the remainder having the A4 'wedge' front.

In Malcolm's striking painting we see *Cock o' the North* leaving Grantham station heading north in charge of an East Coast express. Grantham on the London to Edinburgh main line (the East Coast Route) was the scene for much competitive rivalry with the LMS West Coast Route. It was not far from Grantham that *Mallard* achieved her speed record in 1938. The P2 class were soon to have the limelight taken from them by the A4 Pacifics, which appeared in 1935, and of which 35 were built. Notice the huge number of telephone lines on the pole shown, and the somersault type of semaphore signals on the gantry.

Gresley P2 2-8-2s were large and powerful locomotives. How then can their might be transferred to canvas? A low viewpoint helps. This not only gives a great impression of size but also allows welcome reflections along the boiler and tender. The extent of the exhaust would have been frowned upon by the loco inspector but quoting that well used phrase 'artistic licence' it suggests power and movement. The pall of smoke drifting to the left of the picture is balanced by the somersault signal almost silhouetted against the lightening sky.

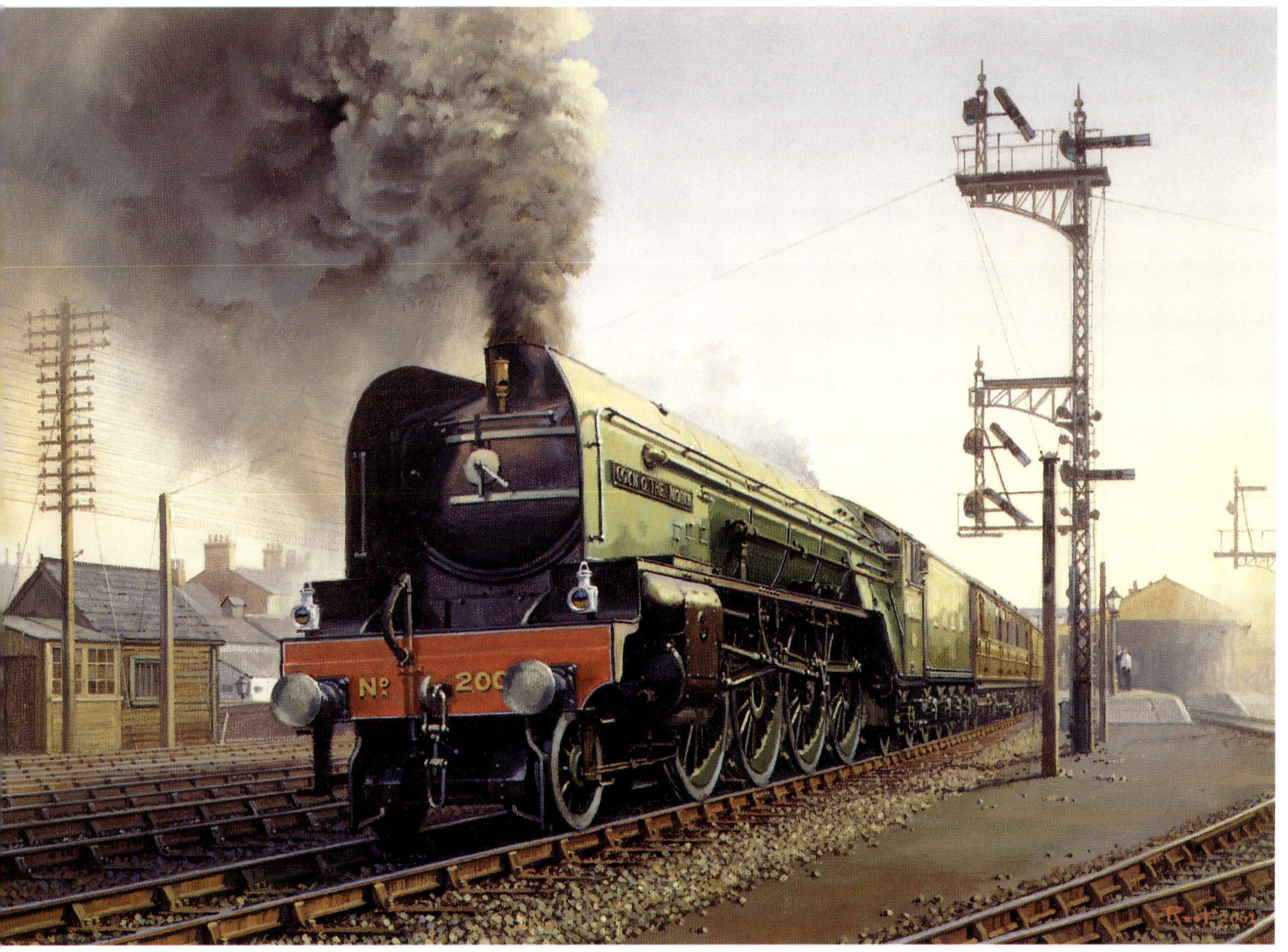

Witham Station, the Country End

Painted 1990

Once again we visit Witham station (see page 92) on the London Liverpool Street to Ipswich main line, but this time it is the other end of the station and a very different age. Witham was the junction for both the Braintree and Maldon branches. The lines swinging away to the left in the picture went via Braintree and Great Dunmow to link with the London main line at Bishop's Stortford. The branch line nowadays terminates at Braintree. The Maldon line shown on the right of the picture has now long gone. Witham is still a junction, but its main importance is now as a station from which many people commute each day, making the 30-minute journey into London. This is a classic station scene, with all the buildings and equipment to be found in the early 1950s. The platforms are neatly faced with a strip showing where one should not stand when a train is approaching. Clear white lines give warning of the platform edge. On the end of the left-hand platform is a water crane, and the large water tank that supplies it is raised up on a brick building behind it. Behind the water tank is the signal box, jutting out over the track to give the signalman a better view to the south. On the right-hand platform is a lamp with the station name in the form of the much loved totem, and a porter's trolley. The low signal gantry has three signal arms – the one nearest to the main line has a healthy coating of soot! Beyond the platform, on the right, is a maltings complete with period lorry.

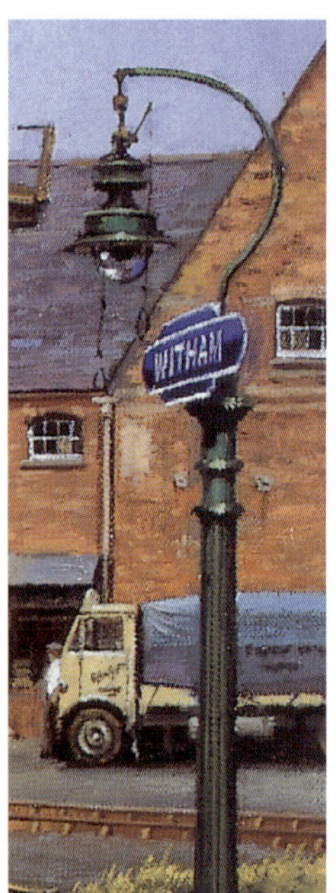

Two trains complete the scene. An ex-LNER B1 class 4-6-0 is approaching the station with an up passenger train composed of the 'blood and custard' liveried coaches of the period. The B1 was designed by Edward Thompson, and introduced in 1942. They were known as the Antelope class, and were intended to take over from the older types of 4-6-0 locomotives working on the region. They were suitable for working all but the heaviest trains, and most of the class of over 400 locomotives were built by the North British Locomotive Company at Glasgow.

The locomotive waiting on the branch line to Braintree is an F5 2-4-2 tank engine designed by SD Holden and already boasting about forty years in service. It has certainly seen some significant changes since it wore Great Eastern Railway livery. Engine cleaners were evidently in short supply as only the BR crest and number have been cleaned. These locomotives were designed for light passenger and suburban duties, and I suspect that there are a couple of vintage coaches behind, waiting for a gentle amble along the picturesque branch line.

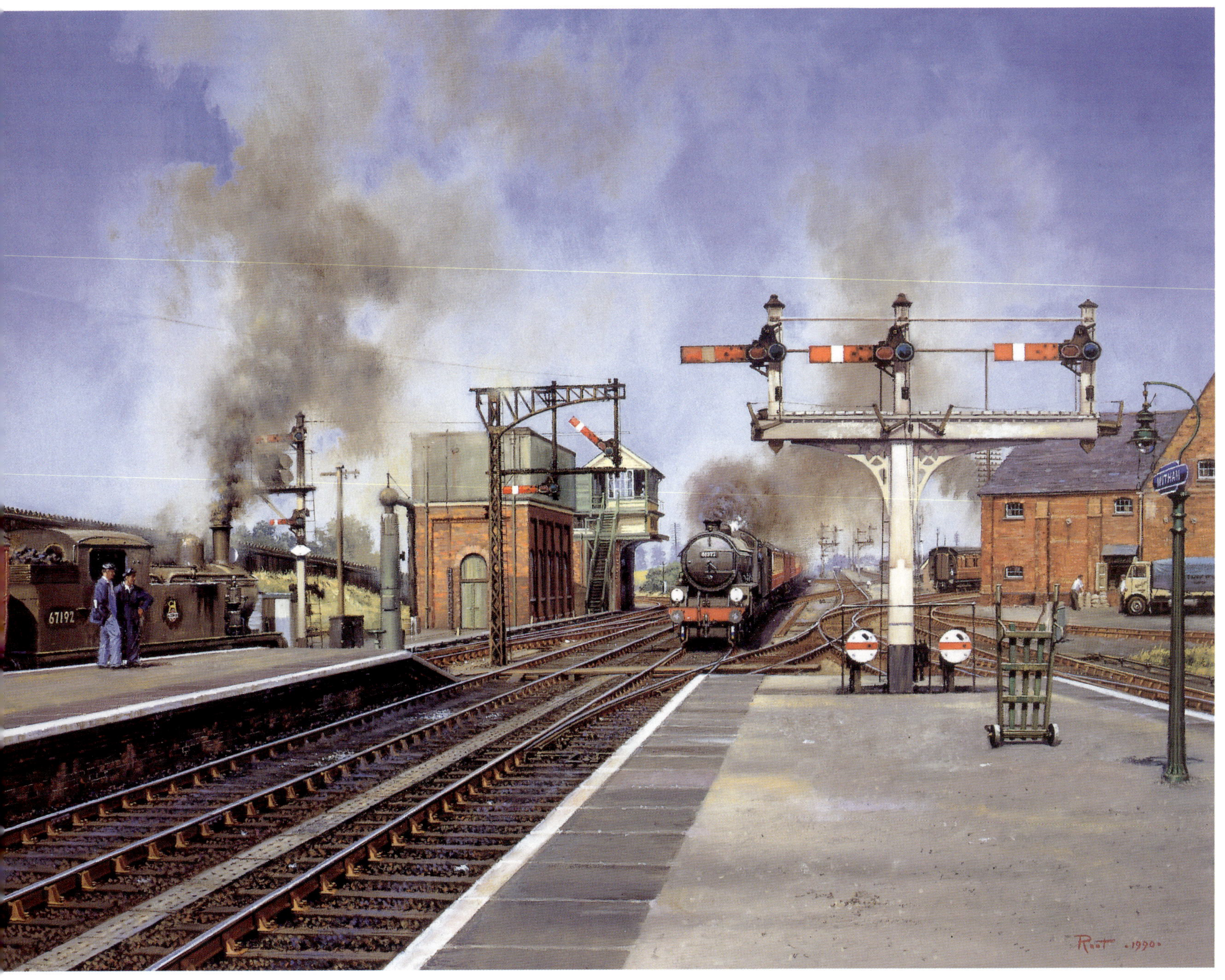
67192
Root 1990

The Royal Observer Corps

Painted 1990

This is a beautiful part of the country, and seeing it from a train is probably the best way of all. The Southern Railway leaves Southampton and curls its way through the southern part of the New Forest, before coming to the conurbation comprising Christchurch, Bournemouth and Poole. The railway then sweeps round the north side of Poole Harbour giving beautiful views, and crossing an arm of the inlet before heading to Wareham, from which the branch line went to Swanage, and may one day do so again! Our scene is the early 1960s, and the train consists of coaches painted in the distinctive green livery of the Southern Region of British Railways.

The locomotive is Battle of Britain class 34050, *Royal Observer Corps* (see pages 10 and 68). Considering these locomotives were rebuilt from the streamlined version, they turned out to be very handsome indeed, as did the Coronation Pacifics on the LMS. One of the features of Oliver Bulleid's original design had been a valve mechanism which had its primary drive by means of chains enclosed in an oil bath. This had its problems even from new, and in 1957 the locomotives were rebuilt with Walschaert's valve gear, which accounts for the significant visual difference between the engines around the driving wheels.

While researching this book it has surprised me how many locomotives were rebuilt at one time or another, sometimes just by the removal of streamlined casing, but sometimes by combining different parts of engines together, as with the GWR Dukedogs. Several locomotives like the *Great Bear* and LNER 'Mikados' were transformed. In an age

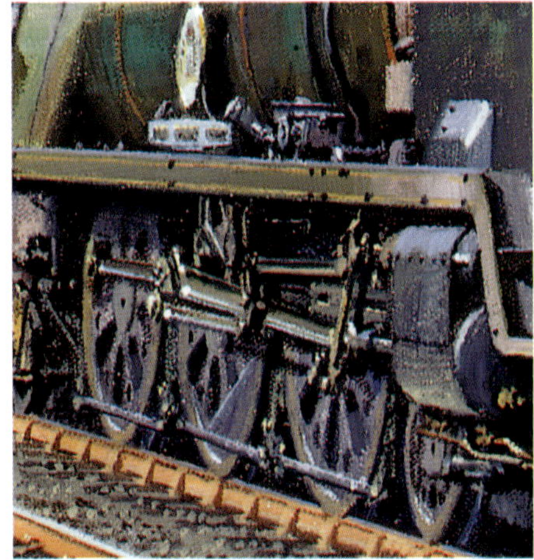

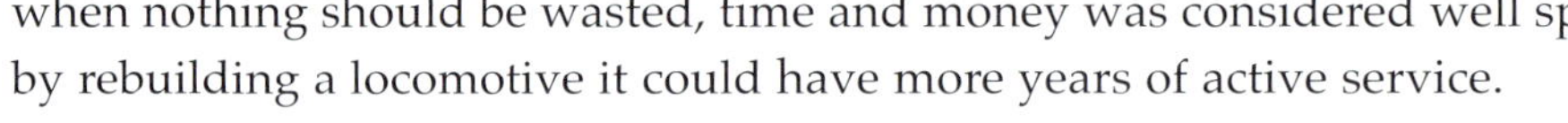

when nothing should be wasted, time and money was considered well spent if by rebuilding a locomotive it could have more years of active service.

The Southern Region of British Railways was ironically one of the last to be fully worked by steam, having been in places the first to be electrified. Right up to July 1967 steam was employed on the London to Bournemouth and Weymouth main line. It is a great tribute to the Bulleid Pacifics that they fought a magnificent rearguard action, despite sad neglect of maintenance in those closing years. In the end the changeover to electrification came in one swift operation, and another clutch of great locomotives made their last journey to the scrapyard. Fortunately examples of both rebuilt and unrebuilt Bulleid Pacifics have been preserved in working order.

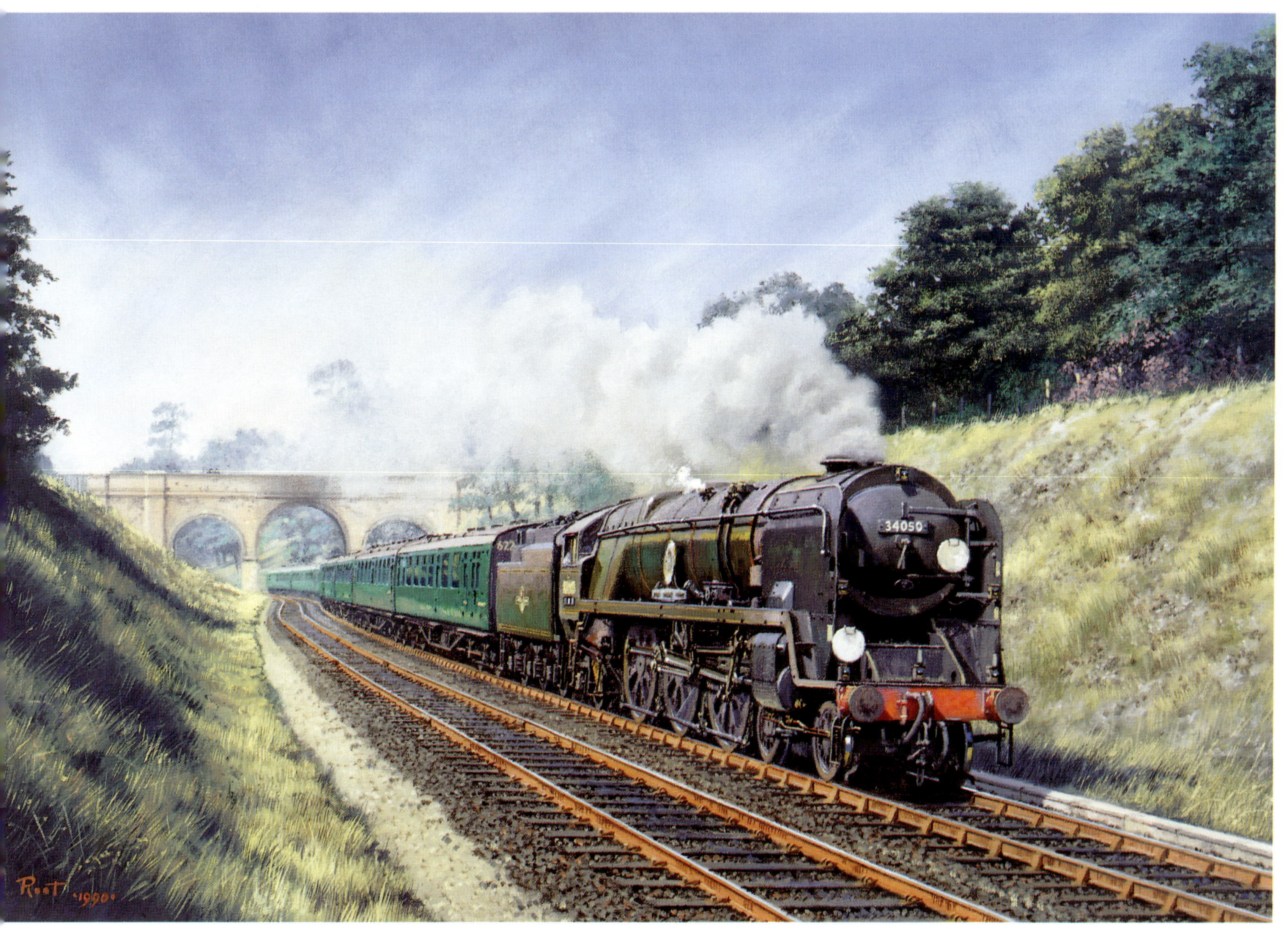
34050
Root 1990

Talerddig Crossing

Painted 1998

The hill in the background indicates that we are not in East Anglia but a lot further west! By 1852 much of England was served by the railways, but there were only two lines in Wales, one in the north to Holyhead, and one in the south to Cardiff and Swansea. The hilly nature of the country was a major factor in this situation. However, in the 1860s Brunel's original plan came into being, and the railway branched off the GWR main line at Shrewsbury, and proceeded via Welshpool and Newtown to Dovey Junction (see page 80). The scene in our picture is at Talerddig station, between Newtown and Machynlleth, where the railway crosses the road (coloured white on my map!) from Dolgadfan to Llangadfan. There are a lot of hills in the neighbourhood, rising to 1600 feet, and the railway eventually follows the river Dovey all the way down to Dovey Junction and the coast. At Shrewsbury the railway goes north-west towards Wrexham, north-east to Crewe, south-east to Birmingham and London, and south to Hereford. The Cambrian Railway, winding through the Welsh hills, thus linked up a large area, both agricultural and with a good deal of holiday traffic. Here in the late 1950s we see two typical trains of the BR steam era passing each other at the small halt. The weather is very appropriate for the Welsh hills in my experience - wet!

The two identical locomotives are BR Standard class 4 2-6-4T locomotives. Designed under the supervision of RA Riddles, these were introduced in 1951, the first batch being built at Brighton works, and the remainder at Derby and Doncaster. They were hugely successful to the end of the steam era, and many remain in preservation. The advantages of tank engines were recognised early on in railway history. They could run forwards or backwards more easily than tender locomotives, and did not require turntables. They needed less space on sidings or in engine sheds, and there were fewer parts to maintain. They could also cope with a wide variety of duties. Axle weights on the 2-6-2T and 2-6-4T were reasonable and meant that most lines could carry the locomotives. The development of the medium duty mixed-traffic tank engine can be traced back well into the 1800s, but the first obvious forerunner is the Great Western Railway 45xx class of 1906, developed in 1931 into the 61xx class, and in 1938 into the 81xx class.

The main railway companies had their own 2-6-4T designs. The Great Central was represented by the Robinson L1 locomotive, while the LMS had a succession of designs by Fowler, Stanier and Fairburn. Meanwhile on the Southern Railway Maunsell had produced his W class in 1931. It would seem that some companies favoured this type of locomotive while others were more reserved, as shown by the LNER with their sole example the Thompson L1 of 1945.

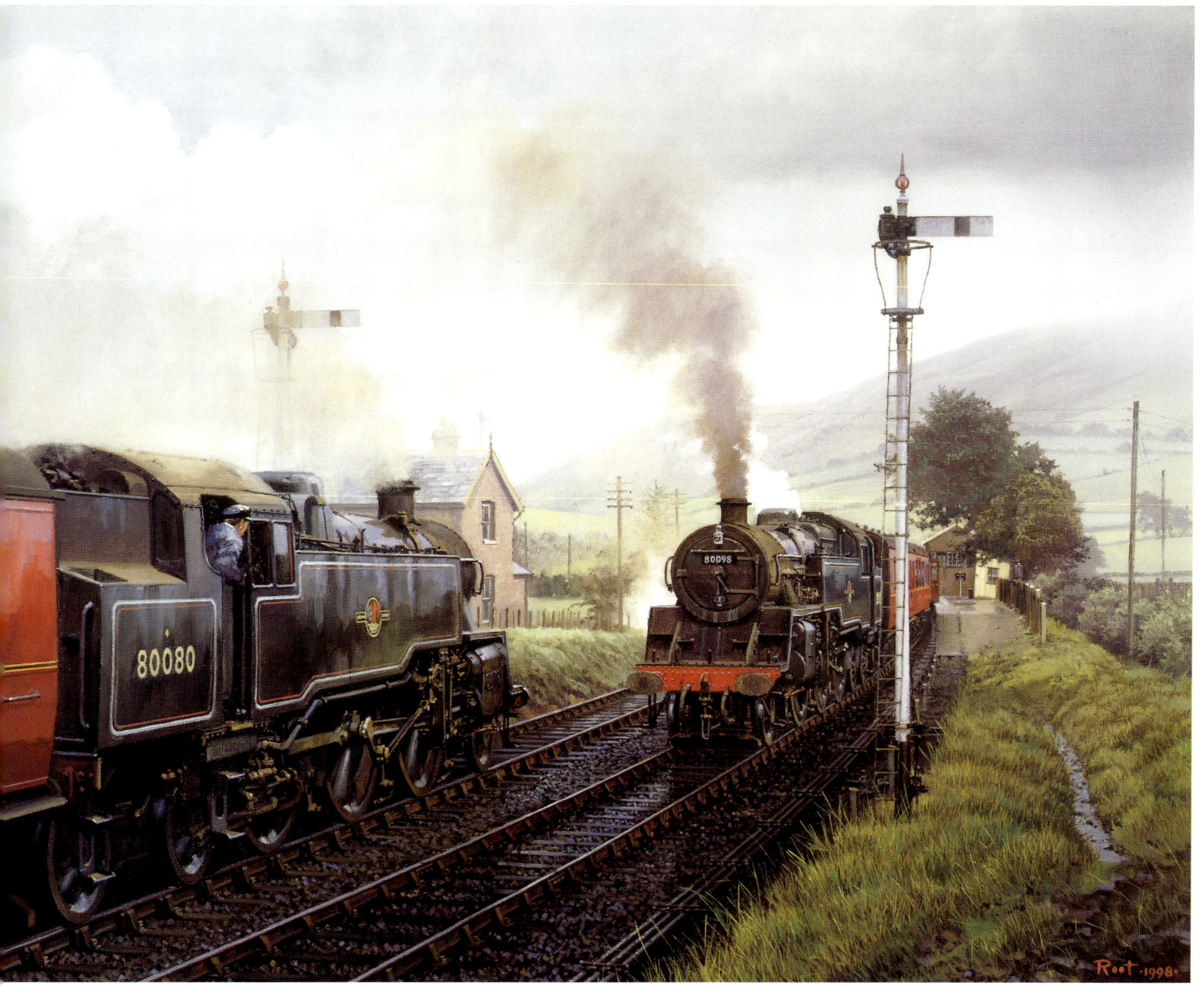
80080
80098
Root ·1998·

Blea Moor

Painted 1996

Reproduced by permission of JARVIS plc

If there was a prize for the most remote signal box in Britain then Blea Moor would be high on the list. If the presence of points for loop lines or sidings necessitated signals for safety reasons, then a signal box had to be sited nearby, for the signals were all activated using cables, and there was a definite limit to the distance which could be covered. The materials for building the box in the first place could be brought in by rail, so this proved no problem, but access would often have to be along the lineside, or by a cinder track linked to the nearest road, along which the relays of signalmen rode their bicycles from their homes, which would be as near as possible. Life in the box would be a very lonely existence, with only a bell telegraph link to the adjacent boxes up and down the line, and perhaps a telephone for use in emergency. Bags of fuel for the coke stove would be dropped off from time to time by a local maintenance train, and because the box had to be manned 24 hours a day the stove could be kept in, and the box kept reasonably warm in the bitter winter weather on the high moors. A kettle was always simmering on top of the stove, and hot tea helped keep the cold and damp at bay.

Here two platelayers stand and watch the passing train on a clear calm winter's day, beneath the high distant fells so characteristic of the Settle to Carlisle line. The steam locomotive always looks at its best when it is working hard, which means a heavy train and a steep gradient and lots of smoke and steam. Locomotives which are coasting down hills with the regulator shut off do not look nearly so impressive. The locomotive in this case facing the challenging climb is London Midland Region Jubilee class 45562 *Alberta* (see page 84). Designed by Sir William Stanier, and introduced in 1935, they were given the name as it was King George V's Silver Jubilee in that year. The names of most of the engines in the class are associated with places in the British Empire, and with the Royal Navy.

The date for this scene is the later 1950s, and in the distance behind the train can be seen Simon Fell, with Ingleborough Hill peaking at 2376 feet, and not often seen so clearly.

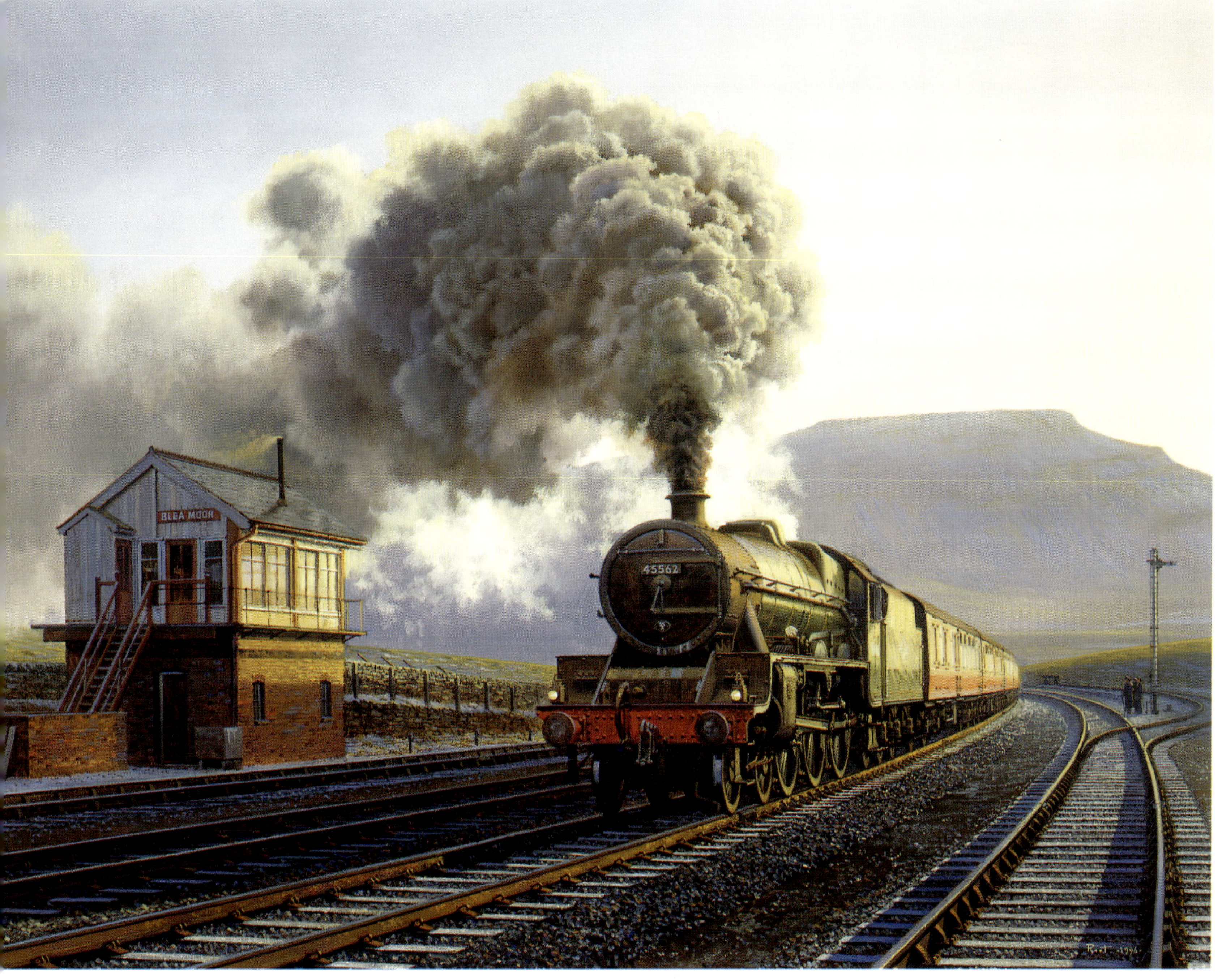
BLEA MOOR
45562

Colliery Winter

Painted 1991

There were two small consolations for coal miners in the depths of winter. Firstly, it was relatively warm underground, and one was protected from biting winds. Secondly, they received free coal to warm their houses. Here it is a very cold day in mid-winter, with the sun just set, and the temperature dropping like a stone. There is no wind, and already several inches of snow have recently fallen. The work of the colliery goes on just the same, and a train of loaded coal wagons is being shunted away from the pit head to the main line, where a suitable freight locomotive like the 2-8-0 (see page 94) will take over.

The two 0-6-0 tank engines in charge of the train are 'austerity' saddletanks, designed by the Hunslet Engine Co and chosen for the War Department, for use both at home and overseas, and built by various locomotive makers in large quantities between 1943 and 1953. Many of them were sold to private industrial concerns such as collieries after the war, and some were purchased by the LNER and classified J94. They gave many years of service, and a considerable number have survived in preservation. With a weight of only 48 tons, and a tractive effort of nearly 24 000lbs, it was a perfect locomotive for the heavy shunting duties for which it was designed.

The leading engine on the train is interesting as it has been fitted with a Giesl ejector. The chimney and blast pipe design on locomotives is of great importance. Not only does the chimney dispose of smoke and steam, but it is designed to draw a current of air through the grate and firebox to improve the all important performance of the fire. The steam being exhausted by the cylinders travels up the blast pipe to the chimney, and this creates the draught. Different designs of chimney, like the double chimneys fitted to A4s, Duchesses and Kings made a big improvement to the performance. The Giesl ejector consisted of a blast pipe split into small nozzles in line, thus increasing the force of blast and improving the draught on the fire. In order to provide a clear and unobstructed path for the exhaust a narrow oblong chimney was provided as can be seen in the picture. Because it was developed at the time when steam traction was being phased out, it was not widely used, but the design undoubtedly did increase power and reduce coal consumption, though the latter advantage would not have been quite so important if the engine worked in a colliery!

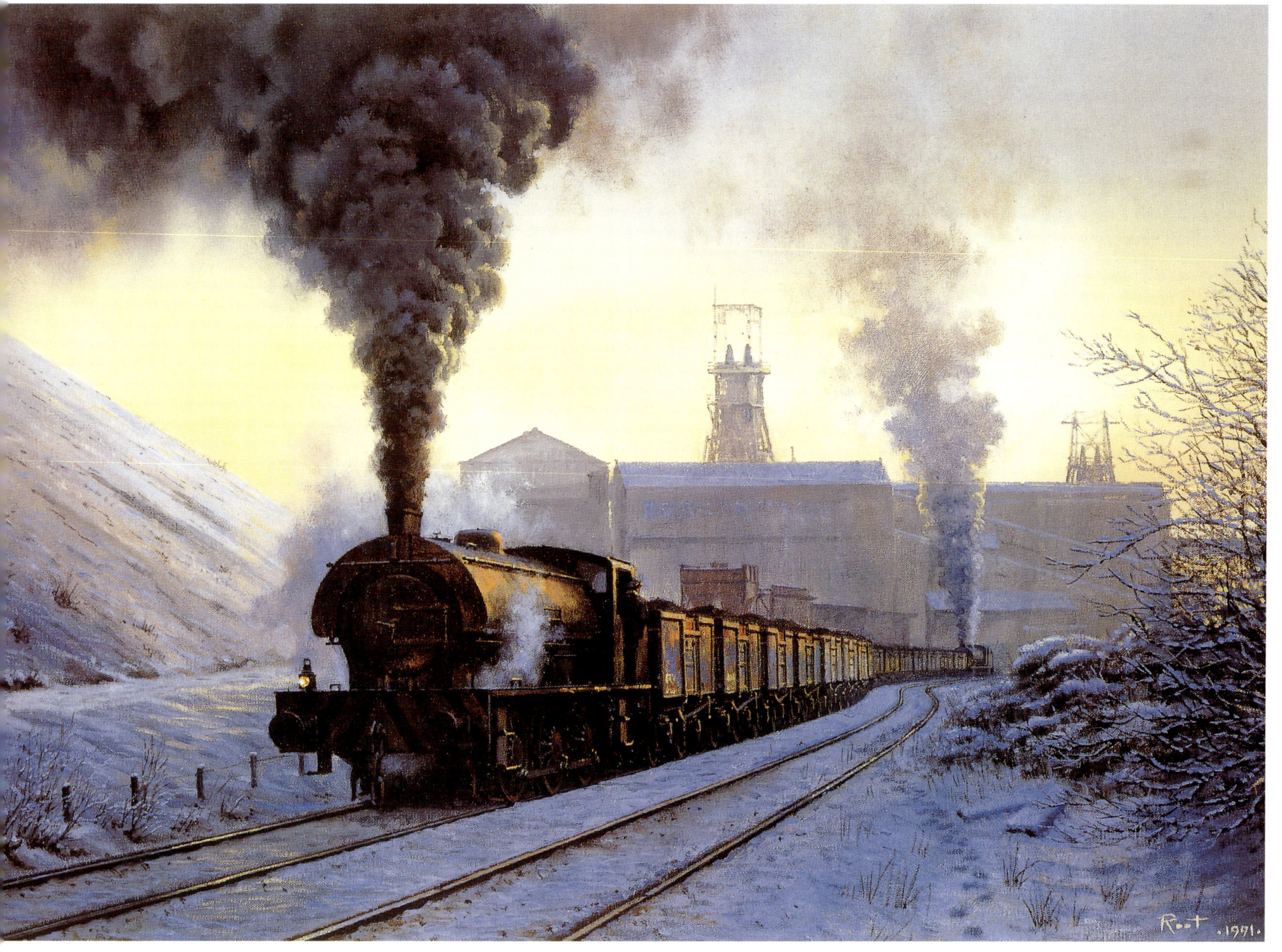
Root .1991.

Quay Departure

Painted 1985

The scene here is at Parkeston Quay, Harwich, looking across the mouth of the River Stour with Shotley Gate at the end of the Shotley peninsula in the background. The large building in the centre is the West Quay, the western extension to Parkeston Quay, which was constructed between 1931–34.

The extension, which was 1200 feet long and provided three extra steamer berths, was necessary because of increasing traffic, despite the years of economic depression. The lower floor of the new transit shed provided a new railway platform and customs facilities. On 1 November 1934 Admiral Reginald Tyrwhitt formally opened the new port extension.

At this time the Scandinavian Express left London Liverpool Street station at 4.10pm and ran non-stop to Parkeston Quay where it connected with the Harwich to Esbjerg ferry each day. The night ferry arrived at its destination early the following morning. In pre-war days the train included Pullman restaurant cars with all facilities, and was intended to rival the 'prestige' boat trains going to the south coast. By the early 1950s, which is the period of this painting, the carriage stock in use was more mundane for The Scandinavian. The locomotive hauling the boat train is an ex-Great Eastern Railway B12 class 4-6-0 61533 designed by SD Holden and first introduced as long ago as 1911 (see pages 64 and 76). Originally designed to haul the boat trains from London to Parkeston Quay they managed what was a very challenging route very well with the heavily loaded trains. Although many were rebuilt by Gresley in the early 1930s, including the one shown, they amply repaid the work done on them by continuing in service for many years.

At peak times the Parkeston Goods Junction signalman would have been extremely busy controlling troop trains, normal boat trains, branch trains and the shunting of freight traffic as shown by the little J68 on the left of the picture.

It seems appropriate with this picture to take the opportunity of thanking my good friend Bob Clow, as Parkeston Quay is very much his patch and his interest and passion for it has never waned. The interchange between rail and sea travel has always fascinated, and Parkeston is a fine example. Perhaps best known for its prestigious boat trains, the quay also handled freight and troop trains. Many a serviceman will hold mixed memories about their encounter with Parkeston Quay.

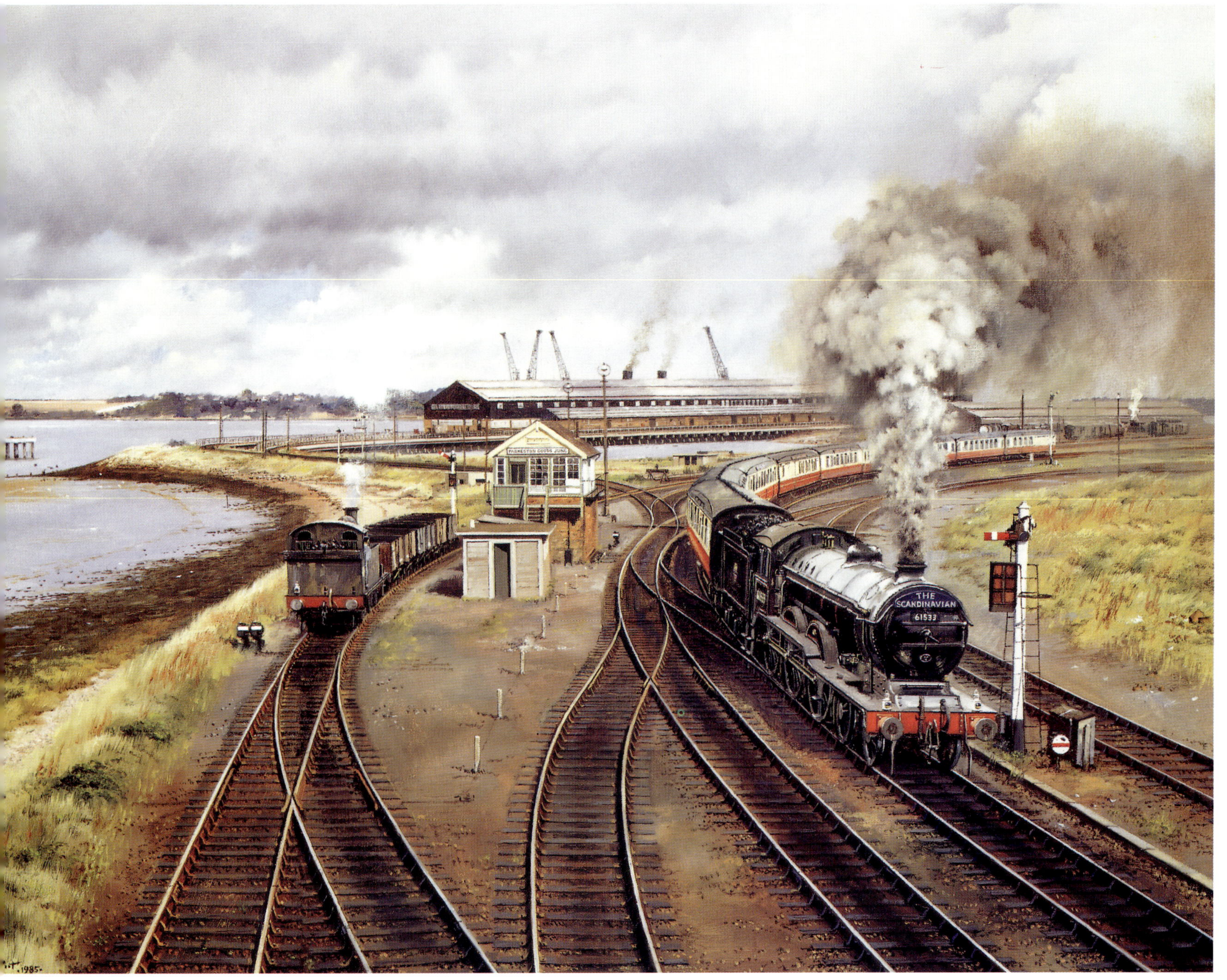
PARKESTON GOODS JUNC
THE SCANDINAVIAN
61533

Sutherland Refreshed

Painted 1996

Back to an old friend, the *Duchess of Sutherland* (pages 22, 52, and 74), and a familiar setting, the water troughs at Dillicar near Tebay, on the scenic stretch of the West Coast route. It is a typically squally day, with a north wind and sudden showers appearing from nowhere, despite the blue sky visible through breaks in the fast-moving clouds. Two hardy onlookers have set up a camp on the other side of the river (not visible in the painting), and one hopes they are well wrapped up and feel suitably rewarded by the thundering Duchess.

The couple with the dog may have been spotted by some of the passengers in the hurtling express. Some may have left their comfortable seats, reserved well before the date of the journey, and opened the sliding door of the warm compartment and walked along the corridor of the gently swaying train to the restaurant car. Here the window curtains are not yet drawn, but the table lamps already provide a warm and welcoming glow on each table, set for four people with gleaming silver and linen napkins. As the darkness closes in the feeling of being in a separate world to that outside is increased, and stewards with silver salvers move from table to table with pots of steaming tea and hot buttered teacakes. Real strawberries can be identified in the strawberry jam. Sheets of water being flung past the window indicate that the Duchess is also taking refreshment.

In days gone by such attention to the needs of the inner man did not always occur. My grandfather, returning with friends from a shooting holiday in Ireland, boarded his train at Holyhead in the early 1900s, only to find there was no restaurant car as promised. Not to be defeated, the hungry ancestor pulled out his pocket book and wrote a note on a number of pages requiring a hamper of food to be delivered to the train on its arrival at Crewe, and promising a guinea in payment. The notes were scrumpled up, and thrown out of the train every time it passed through a station. On arrival at the first stop, Crewe, Grandfather found seventeen hampers awaiting him! However, he was not a successful businessman for nothing, and having paid for them, he then went down the train selling them to hungry fellow travellers for a handsome profit!

The *Duchess of Sutherland* was saved for posterity first by Billy Butlin, who wanted locomotives for static exhibition at his holiday camps (see page 120). She was then transferred to Bressingham Hall in Norfolk, where the steam museum set up by Alan Bloom is located. For a time she was steamed regularly there. After many years of being displayed as a static exhibit in Norfolk she was finally taken under the wing of the Princess Royal Locomotive Trust in Derbyshire. Between the years 1998–2001 she was restored to main line working order with the help of a Heritage Lottery Fund grant of £342 508. With the excellent rebuild she can again be seen storming Shap.

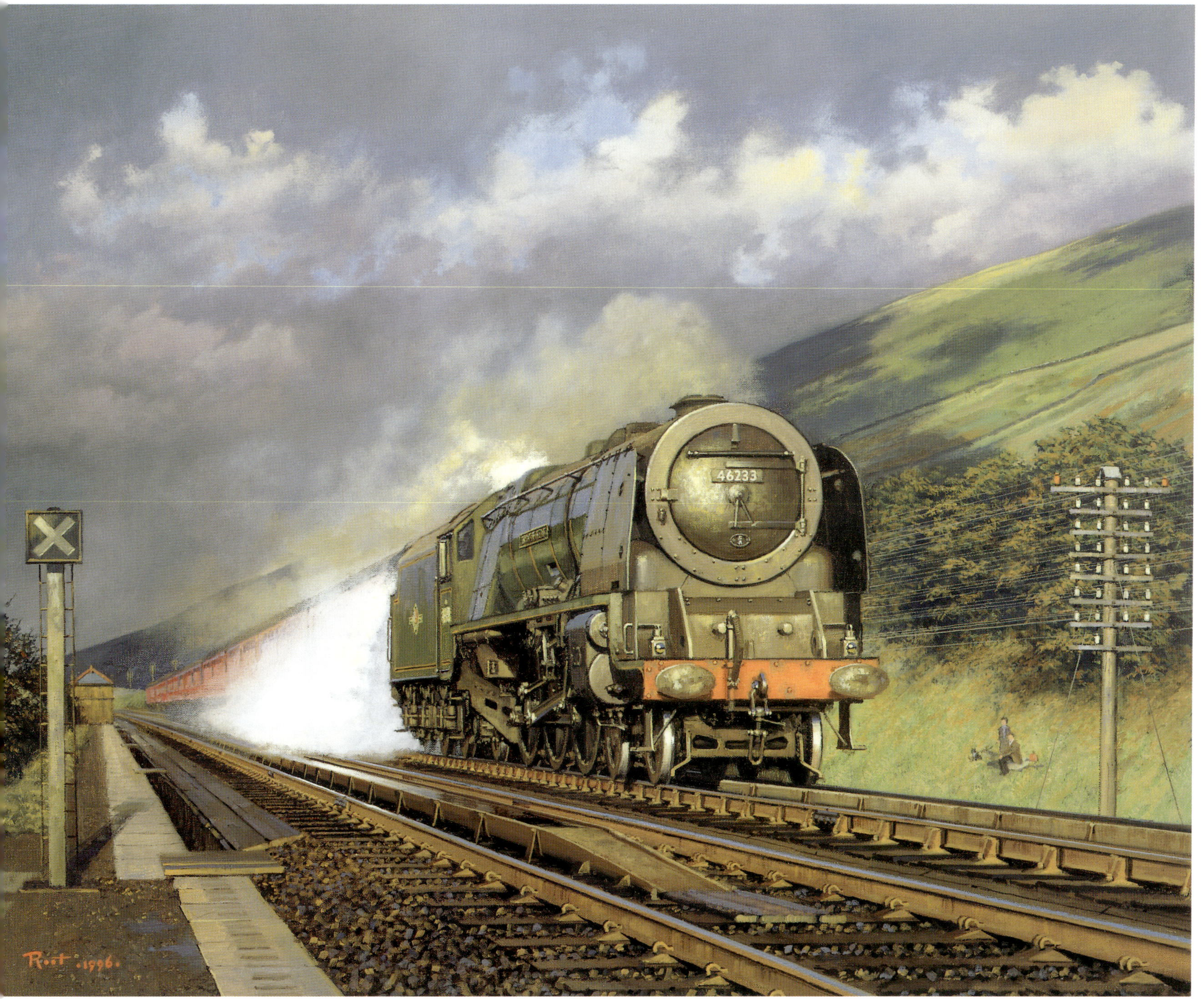
46233
Root ·1996·

Silver Jubilee

Painted 1998

This is a train well worth watching by enthusiasts of all ages! The distinctive and majestic Silver Jubilee train commissioned by the London & North Eastern Railway in 1935 to celebrate the Silver Jubilee of King George V and Queen Mary was also a fitting tribute to their Chief Mechanical Engineer, Sir Nigel Gresley. Gresley had been brought up and trained on the railways, eventually becoming Locomotive Superintendent of the Great Northern Railway in 1911. With the grouping of the railways into the 'Big Four' companies in 1923, he became CME to the LNER, where he remained until his death in 1941, a few months before he was due to retire.

Gresley had found interesting inspiration from the French locomotive engineer Chapelon, whose specialities were a more efficient exhaust system and the internal streamlining of locomotives so that the steam flowed with the maximum ease and efficiency from the boiler to the cylinders. Gresley first put these ideas into practice in the 'Mikado', *Cock o' the North*, in 1934 (see page 100). The following year, in September 1935, he unveiled the Silver Jubilee, seen in this painting hauled by the A4 Pacific 2509, *Silver Link*. This express ran between London Kings Cross and Newcastle in four hours, comprising a rake of streamlined carriages weighing about 230 tons. The silver/grey locomotive had a wedge-shaped front and whaleback top which perhaps owed something to Gresley's friend Ettore Bugatti, the Italian racing car builder and driver. The sides were smoothed and together with a deep valance concealed the boiler and much of the wheels and motion. On the press run of the new train, it ran with speeds which averaged 100mph for 43 miles and achieved a maximum of 112.5mph.

The father and son who have come to watch this passing glory have arrived in the rather more modest Ford Popular Model Y introduced in 1933, and rated at 8hp. It was advertised as the '£100 Ford Saloon' and itself achieved something of a stir, causing other companies like Morris and Austin to lower the prices of their cars in order to compete. It is interesting that Hornby, based in Liverpool, produced the Gresley A4 *Sir Nigel Gresley* as their first Dublo model locomotive in 1938, and did not produce a LMS *Duchess of Atholl* until after the war, although plans were drawn up just before hostilities began. Most of the time they gave their home railway, the LMS, the first priority!

'I know just where that is' is a statement often heard at an exhibition, and usually with a degree of smugness. 'That's funny,' comes the reply, 'the scene is totally fictitious!' Reference was made earlier in the book to people reading into pictures what they themselves can remember. I have no problem with that, in fact it can be very rewarding for the artist. While I have been as authentic as possible with the Silver Jubilee, the location for the painting is totally made up with a characteristic bridge included to help the viewer decide where it is. I recall the main problem I had with the picture was to harmonise the colours and to avoid any clashes.

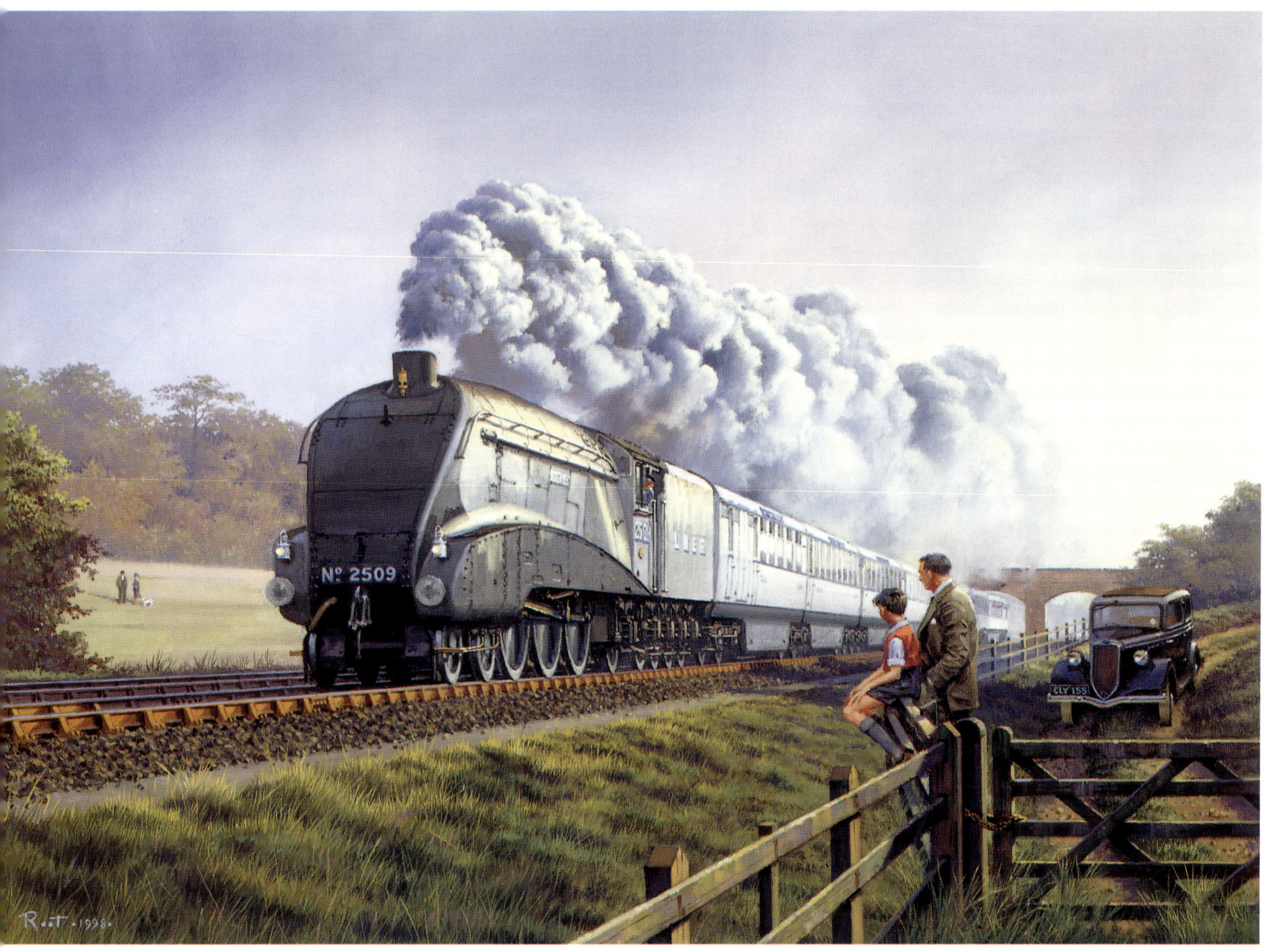
Nº 2509
CLY 155
Root . 1998.

Dovercourt Bay

Painted 1988

As an island nation, harbours and ports have always been of the greatest importance to us, and once again Malcolm has captured the atmosphere of a railway to a port - in this case again the line to Harwich passing through Dovercourt Bay, with the River Stour in the background, which divides Essex from Suffolk. It is a beautifully detailed scene. On the left is a typical wooden fence, with a tastefully painted old vehicle tyre being put to good use as a small flower bed. A regulation notice about crossing the line, the station starter signal and a telegraph pole make an interesting group. In the left foreground is a typical station lamp post of the period, with the totem name attached so that it is lit by the lamp when it is dark, and passengers can look out of carriage windows and know immediately where they have got to. It is again a wet day with a southwesterly wind, and the platforms are decidedly damp, as is the pedestrian crossing to the signal box, made from the ever-useful old wooden sleepers.

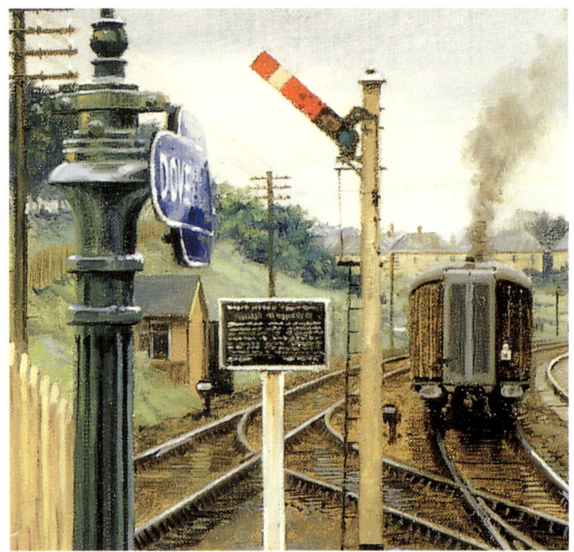

On the right is the Dovercourt Bay signal box, a very handsome timber structure that looks as if it has recently received maintenance attention. The signalman is leaning out of a window perhaps to have a word with the crew of the slowly approaching engine, but doesn't have to draw their attention to the 15mph sign! We cannot see what is at the head of a local train just leaving for Manningtree, but the one by the signal box is an ex-Great Eastern Railway J15 which was first put into service in 1883 (see pages 4 and 48). The locomotives had a neat appearance, with the front splasher combined with the sand box on the straight footplate, and the rear splasher merged with the cab sides. The dome was set forward close to the chimney in a distinctive GER manner. Inside cylinders also contributed to the aesthetic simplicity of the locomotive's design. The fact that so many of the class remained in service into the 1950s is a great tribute to their designer.

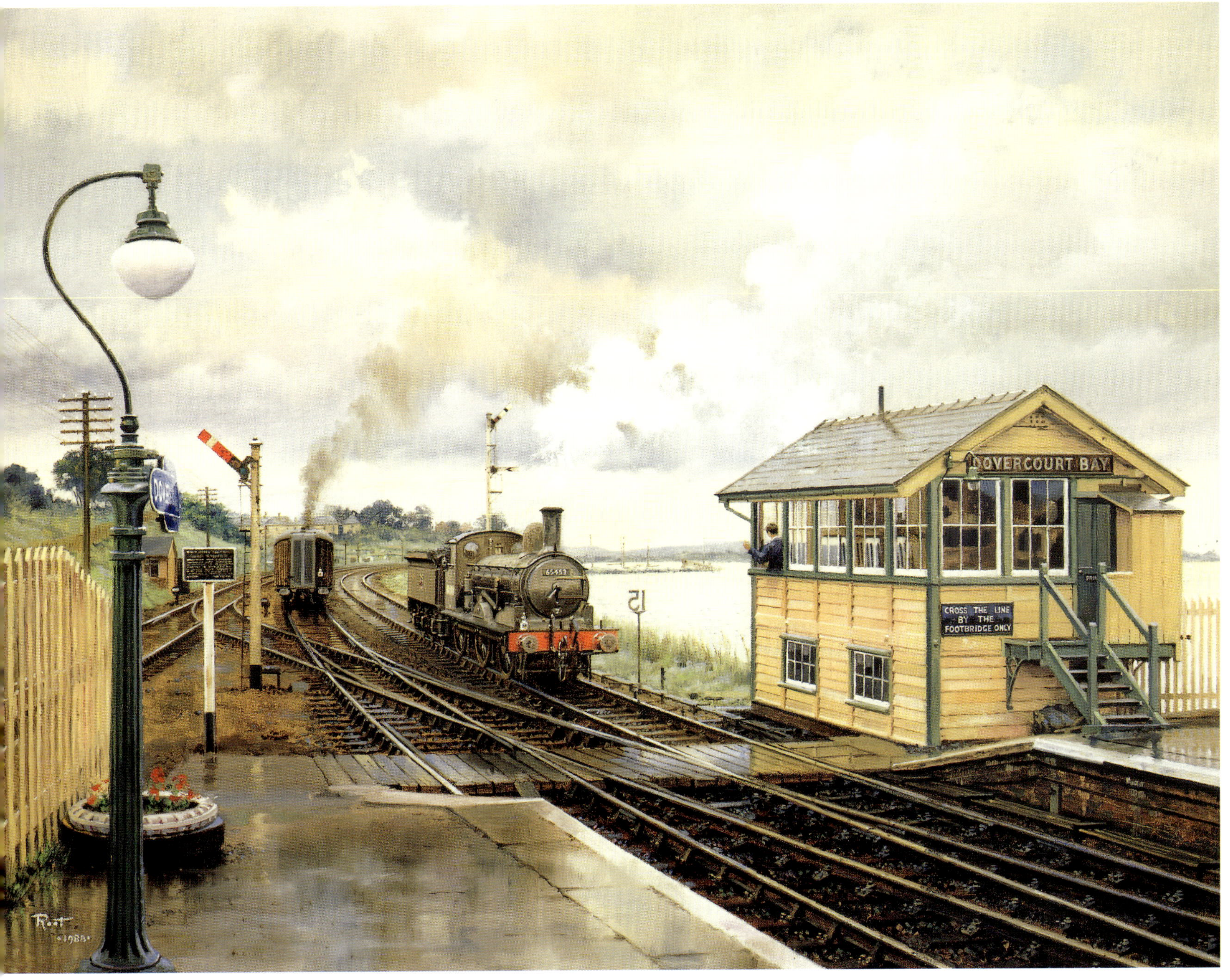
DOVERCOURT BAY
CROSS THE LINE BY THE FOOTBRIDGE ONLY
Root 1988

Butlins Express

Painted 1988

For obvious reasons, many railways in seaside towns come up against the buffers! This is true of the branch from Colchester to Clacton-on-Sea, but it will be no cause for concern to the many holidaymakers arriving on the Butlins Express from London Liverpool Street, and bound for the Butlins camp for their holiday. Billy Butlin established his first camp at Skegness in 1936, but the idea of the camp went back to the 1890s, and many had been set up before the first Butlins. Billy Butlin however was a man with flair and vision, and he transformed the concept of the camp with larger buildings, more entertainments and the legendary Redcoats, two of whom are standing on the platform to welcome passengers from the train. Butlins soon became the market leader and by the early 1960s more than a million people took their holidays in one of the nine camps that were in operation. This was more holidaymakers than were to be found in the camps of all the competitors put together! Of these nine Butlins camps, seven had miniature railways, and the one at Pwllheli ran a distance of three-quarters of a mile from the centre of the camp to the adjoining beach. Billy Butlin also spotted the opportunity in the mid 1960s to pick up some cheap full-sized locomotives for static display at his camps, and it was thanks to him that the likes of *Duchess of Sutherland*, *Duchess of Hamilton*, *Royal Scot* and *Princess Margaret Rose* were saved from the scrapyard.

The handsome locomotive hiding behind the Butlins Express headboard is an ex-London & North Eastern Railway B17 class 4-6-0, first introduced in 1928 and designed jointly by the North British Loco Company and the great Sir Nigel Gresley (see page 12). The B17s were commonly known as 'Sandringhams', and the engine shown, number 61651, had the name *Derby County* with a brass football and the Derby club colours emblazoned on the centre splasher below the nameplate. There is a small 'B17', relating to the class type, painted on the front buffer beam, and the locomotive is in British Railways livery appropriate to the 1950s. These locos were designed to work on the eastern section of the LNER, and regularly hauled the London to Norwich expresses covering the 114 miles in 135 minutes.

The second train in the station disgorging its passengers is a local headed by a 'Mogul' number 46466, designed by HG Ivatt and introduced in 1946 for the London Midland & Scottish Railway. They were modern light mixed-traffic locomotives (see page 134 for a better view) and became known affectionately as 'Mickey Mouses' – or should it be 'Mickey Mice'! As I write this it has been raining for 2½ days non-stop, a rarity in East Anglia. I hope the happy campers on the train had better luck!

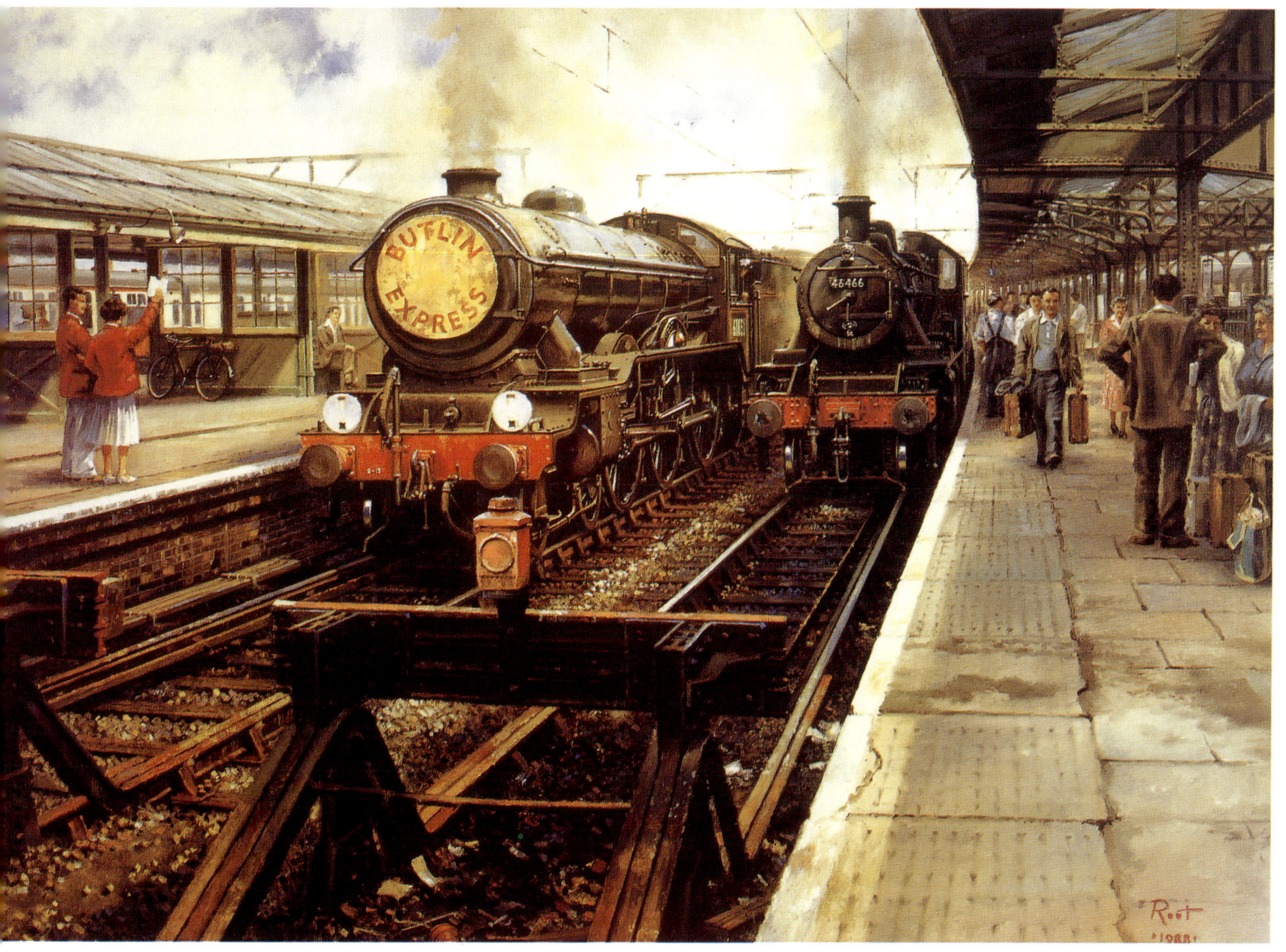
BUTLIN EXPRESS
46466
Root

Changing Tracks

Painted 1989

This painting makes an interesting comparison with that on page 5, showing Malcolm's remarkable talent as an artist. The place is the same, though one picture is painted from a spot a few yards forward of the other. The detail is the same, down to the number of telephone lines. The locomotives are the same. But one depicts high summer, and the other the depths of winter, and the contrast is wonderful. In this view of Wrabness, on the Manningtree to Harwich branch line, the scene is full of detail. The old lamp standards on the platforms, complete with the station signs, can again be illuminated conveniently at night. The four-wheeled porter's trolley is waiting in readiness for luggage or small goods items off the next train. Again we have the walkway linking the platforms. Then on the right can be seen elaborate and attractive gardens which look as though they stand a fair chance of a prize in the station gardens competition held each year. If you visit Wrabness today, you will find a striking mural painted on a wall beside the Harwich bound platform.

The siding which curls away to the right and disappears into the wood seemed originally to be a bit of a mystery. I was told by folk working in what used to be the Royal Ordnance Factory a couple of miles down the line that the siding may have served the factory. In fact it was put in place during the Second World War, and was used to facilitate a large calibre gun mounted on a special truck and located on the siding for defensive purposes. Certainly the wood shown would have been an ideal place to hide the gun from prying enemy aircraft! The gun would have covered the river in the Wrabness area, although better sites would have existed nearer the mouth of the river.

The familiar ex-Great Eastern Railway J15 class 0-6-0 is about to move forward to keep a date with a wagon or two on the siding. The J15's long service – about 70 years when this scene is set, is witnessed by its frequent appearance in this book (pages 5, 49, 67, 119, 130).

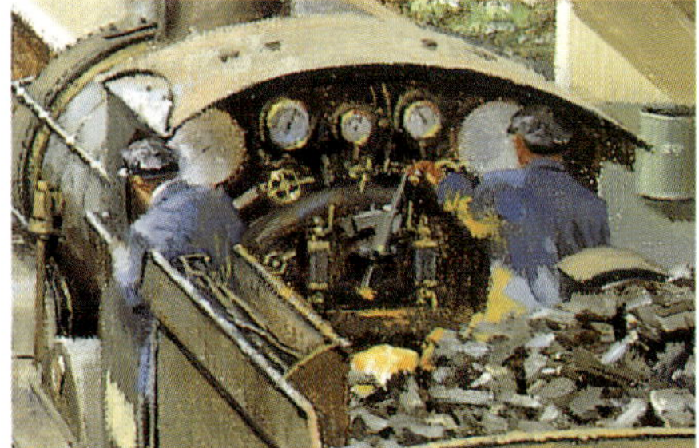

The ground signal shows that the points are set for the engine to cross the main up line onto the siding. It is interesting that points were an invention at the very beginning of railway design and engineering, and had remained virtually unchanged over the years. They were still usually controlled either by a lever in an adjacent signal box, or else by a lever by the lineside which had to be operated by one of the engine crew. The moving section of the points was simple and effective, only occasionally being hampered in its operation by ice or snow.

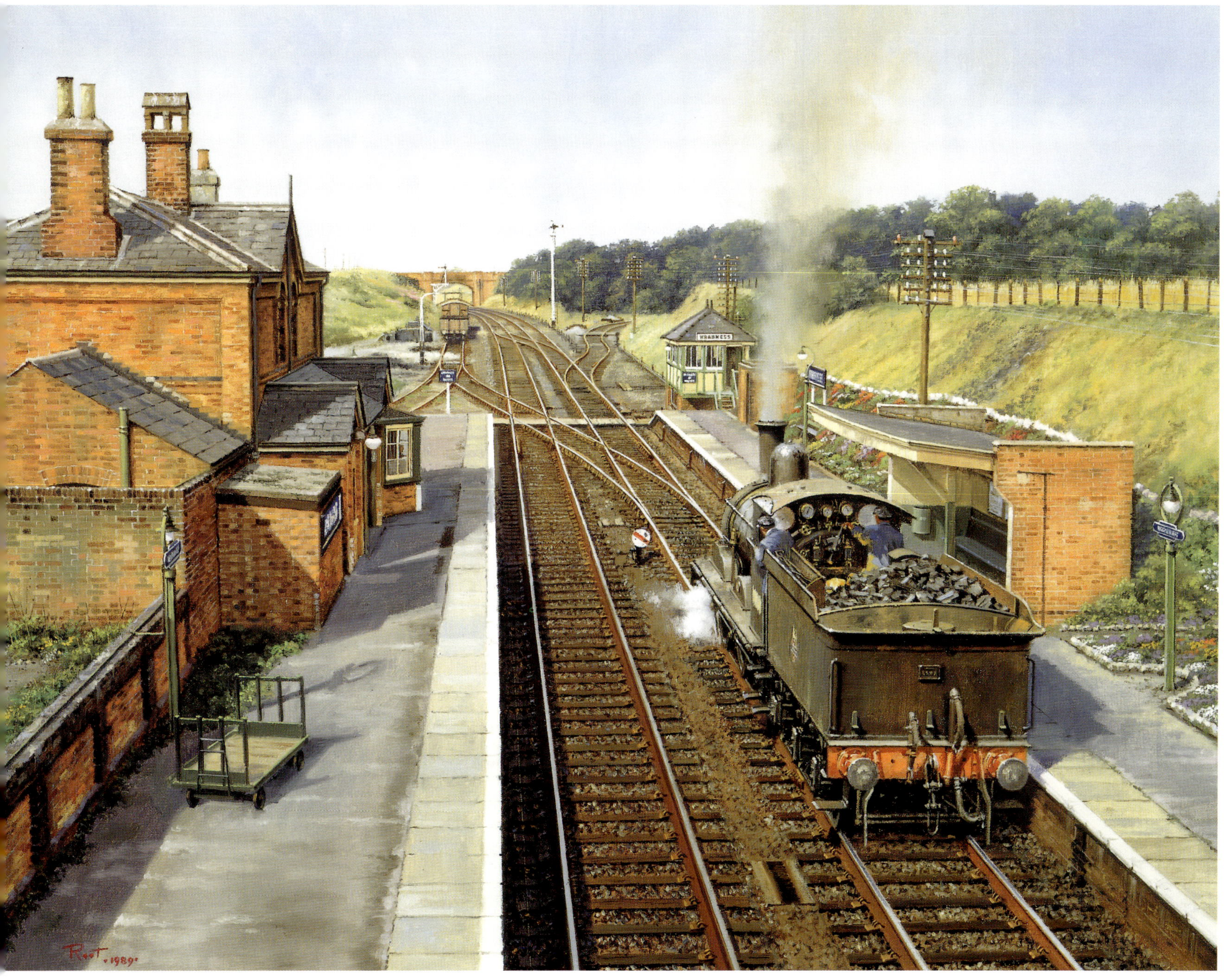
WRABNESS
Root 1989

The Level Crossing, Halstead

Painted 2001

We are again in East Anglia, and on the now familiar Colne Valley Railway, the artist's local branch line. It is early evening on a clear summer's day, and the train holding up the traffic at Halstead level crossing is on its way to Haverhill. Halstead station comprises a single platform, with a passing loop on the normally single track line. The level crossing is typical of so many on British railways. It has four gates, each hung from a substantial wooden post. From the top of each post a metal rod runs down diagonally on both sides of the gate to support it and prevent it dropping over a period of time. Each pair of gates carried a warning lamp fuelled by paraffin, with red glass to warn either motorists or train drivers if the gates were shut against them. The gates were substantial, and had wire-netting stretched across them to prevent children or animals straying on to the line. A large red disc in the middle of the shut gates also gave warning when they were closed. Today's continental-style lifting barriers are a very poor substitute from the point of view of safety.

The crossing gates could be manually opened, or as here, controlled by a wheel in the adjacent signal box. This wheel was of necessity very low geared, and needed to be spun many times to open or close the gates. Motorists in a hurry would watch the signalman to see if he was heading for the wheel. Sometimes, if there was a second train following in the opposite direction at a crossing, the signalman would walk over to his wheel and peer out to see how many cars were in the queue, and immediately all the car engines would roar into life in misplaced anticipation! Because the line here curves into the station from the east, a specially high signal was necessary so that it could be seen over the top of the station canopy by the approaching train driver. The wooden roadway across the tracks is clearly seen, and seems in very good condition. Was it also made from old railway sleepers?

Behind the level crossing are buildings well known to Malcolm in his native Halstead. The long Corn Exchange building is now the town library, and the small building on the left, behind the crossing gates, was the WH Smith bookstall.

The train comprises typical Eastern Region branch line stock. The leading vehicle is a Gresley eight-compartment all third, and hauling it is another Ivatt 2MT 2-6-0 (see page 120). Number 46466 was one of three stabled at Cambridge for Colne Valley working. Waiting patiently at the level crossing is a four-door Ford Prefect, introduced in 1954 with a maximum speed of 65mph and rather slower than the train when both were flat out!

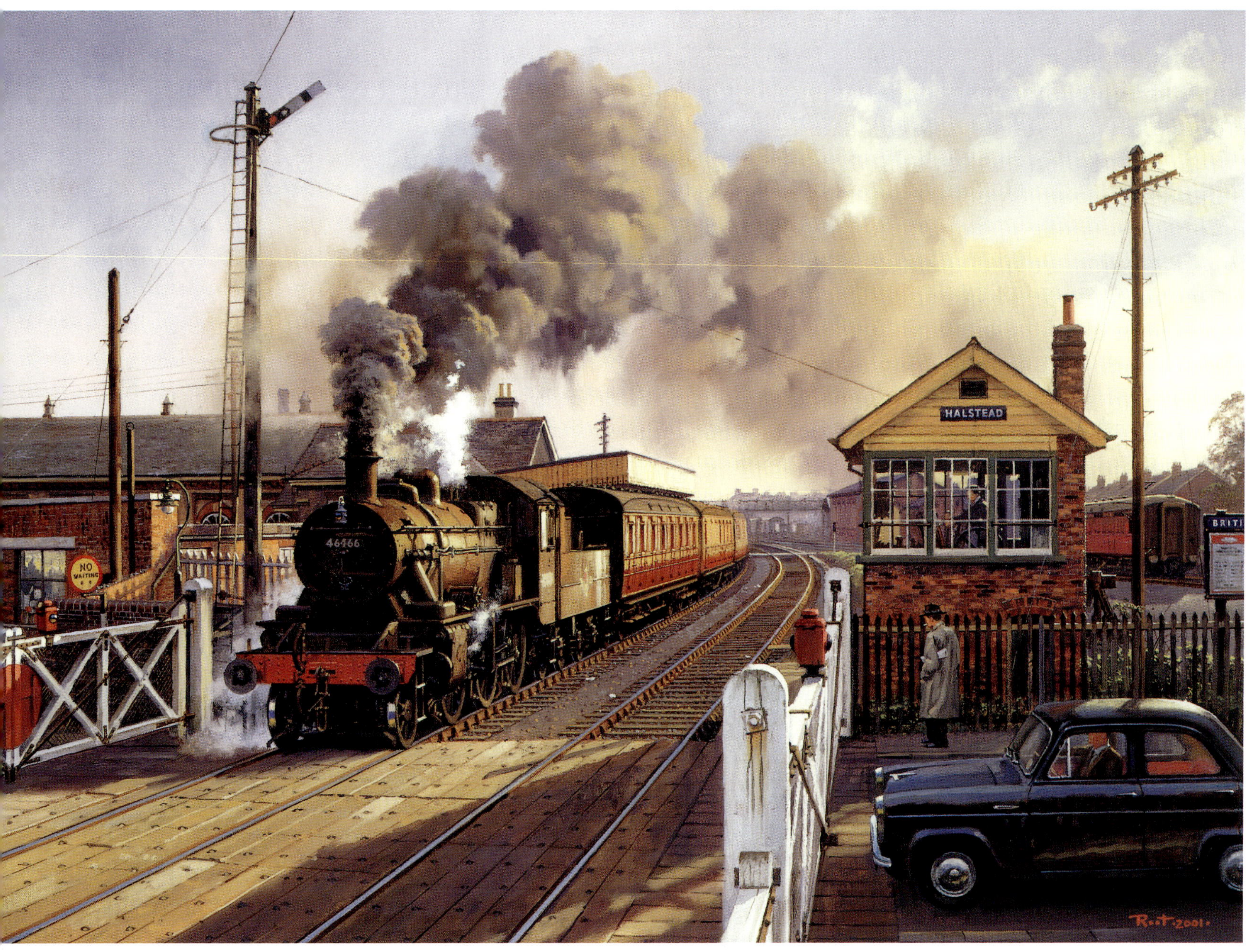
HALSTEAD
NO WAITING
46466
Root.2001.

The Essex Regiment

Painted 2003

The locomotive hauling an eight-coach express composed of Gresley and Thompson vehicles is one of Gresley's fine if sometimes rough riding B17 Sandringham class (see page 120). The train is bound for London Liverpool Street and has just restarted from Colchester. The bulk of the class were named after country houses and Association Football teams served by the LNER. Three however were named after regiments whose headquarters were also on the line – these being 61605 *The Lincolnshire Regiment*, 61645 *The Suffolk Regiment*, and the subject of our painting 61658 *The Essex Regiment*.

The Essex Regiment can be traced back to Longs Regiment which took part in the disastrous Battle of Preston Pans in 1745, where the government troops under Sir John Cope were beaten by Bonnie Prince Charlie and the Scots. In 1782 the regiment became the 44th Foot Regiment, or East Essex Regiment, and in 1881 became simply the Essex Regiment. Before then, however, its members had fought with distinction at Salamanca and Waterloo, in the Crimea, and during the Indian Mutiny. The regiment was to achieve a very distinguished war record during the First World War, taking part in many of the greatest and bloodiest battles, and again during the Second World War, fighting in several different theatres of the war. Later they were one of the regiments merged into the Royal Anglian Regiment, but at least the locomotive shown in the painting recognised their long record and tradition. The Essex Regiment has a thriving museum located in Chelmsford.

The train is passing Bakers Lane, near Colchester in Essex, and the smoke streaming back along the train suggests a gentle southwesterly breeze, or even no wind at all. The tall signal has a white sighting board to make it easier for the driver to see. This main line would have been electrified fairly soon after the period shown in our picture.

'That painting looks just like a photograph,' is the phrase often directed at a piece of artwork that has a realistic quality. I think that this is meant to be a compliment but it should have the feel of something that has been created with the brush. This is a simple and colourful image which when analysed is full of small contrivances. The skyline leads to the main subject and the whiteness of the clouds is held back to emphasise the white discs and steam. The tree highlights the yellow of the distant signal while the white sighting board for the home signal stands out from the blue sky. Manipulation is not only possible but often necessary to take the picture to a higher level.

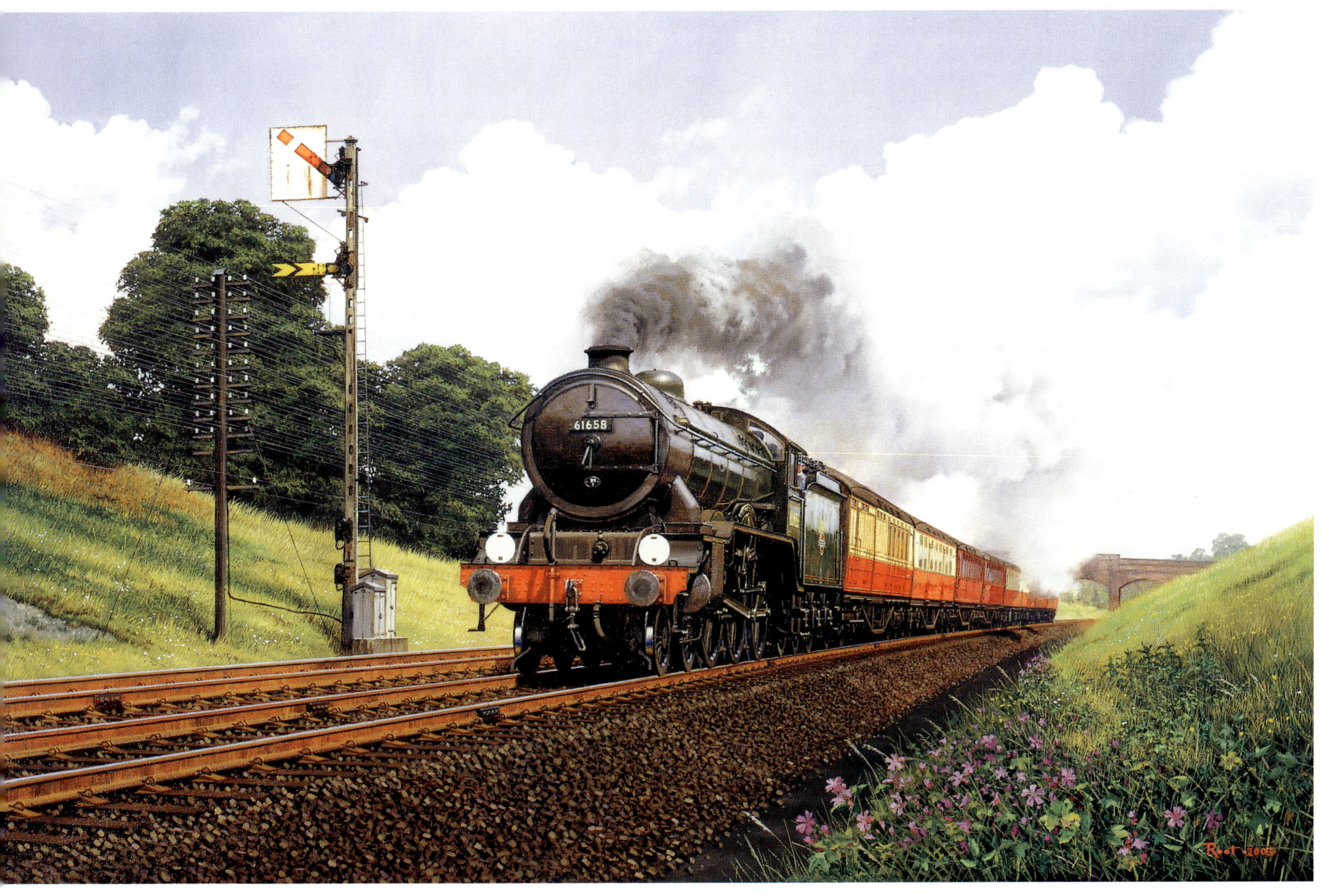
61658
Root 2003

The Leader

Painted 1982

It would be very hard to award a prize for the most innovative railway engineer, but Brunel would be up for it, and so would Oliver Vaughan Snell Bulleid. Bulleid was appointed Chief Mechanical Engineer of the Southern Railway in 1937, just at the moment when Gresley and Stanier were at the peak of their careers. Bulleid's response was to design the Merchant Navy Pacifics for the SR which were first introduced in 1941 and which gave such outstanding service on the railways over the next 25 years. However, by the end of the Second World War, one did not have to be a very notable prophet to be able to see the potential for both diesel and electric traction on the railways, and also to see how labour-intensive steam was by comparison. Bulleid was devoted to steam, and his response was to go back to the drawing board and design a locomotive which was entirely novel in its concept. He recognised that there were huge advantages in a design which allowed a locomotive to be driven equally well from either end, with excellent visibility for the driver. To achieve this, however, the boiler needed to be positioned so that the fireman could stoke the fire in the middle of the locomotive, and have access to either cab via a narrow corridor. The poor fireman thus found himself working in a badly ventilated and cramped space, at almost intolerable temperatures, which was a major problem. Other novel features included sleeve-type valves, and the coupling of the six wheels contained in each bogie by means of chains instead of coupling rods. In fact the locomotive, which would be classed as an 0-6-6-0 articulated unit looked very like the diesels of a later period in appearance.

Each bogie had a three-cylinder engine powering the middle axle, and despite various teething trials on the first prototype, it could have been successful if life for the fireman had been made easier by oil burning. Because of the upheaval caused by the nationalisation of the railways on 1 January 1948, the railway authorities had many other things to think about, without worrying about revolutionary steam locomotives. Only three of the Leader class were built, and only one actually steamed. After brief trials the project was abandoned, and after a short time the three locomotives were broken up. Bulleid went as CME to Ireland, and his last inspiration was a turf-burning locomotive rather along the lines of the Leader.

I did at one time have a remarkable model made of brass, which was supposed to have come via the Bulleid family. It comprised a small four-wheel diesel power unit, with two carriages that went either side, but which attached to the unit and had only one four-wheel bogie for each carriage. The story was that it was Bulleid's model prototype for a DMU for the Irish State Railways, but it was never adopted. Perhaps a reader can shed some light on that?

In his painting Malcolm shows the Leader as it would have appeared in service in the early 1950s, in British Railways livery, hauling a train of mixed coaching stock beside the sea at Folkestone Warren.

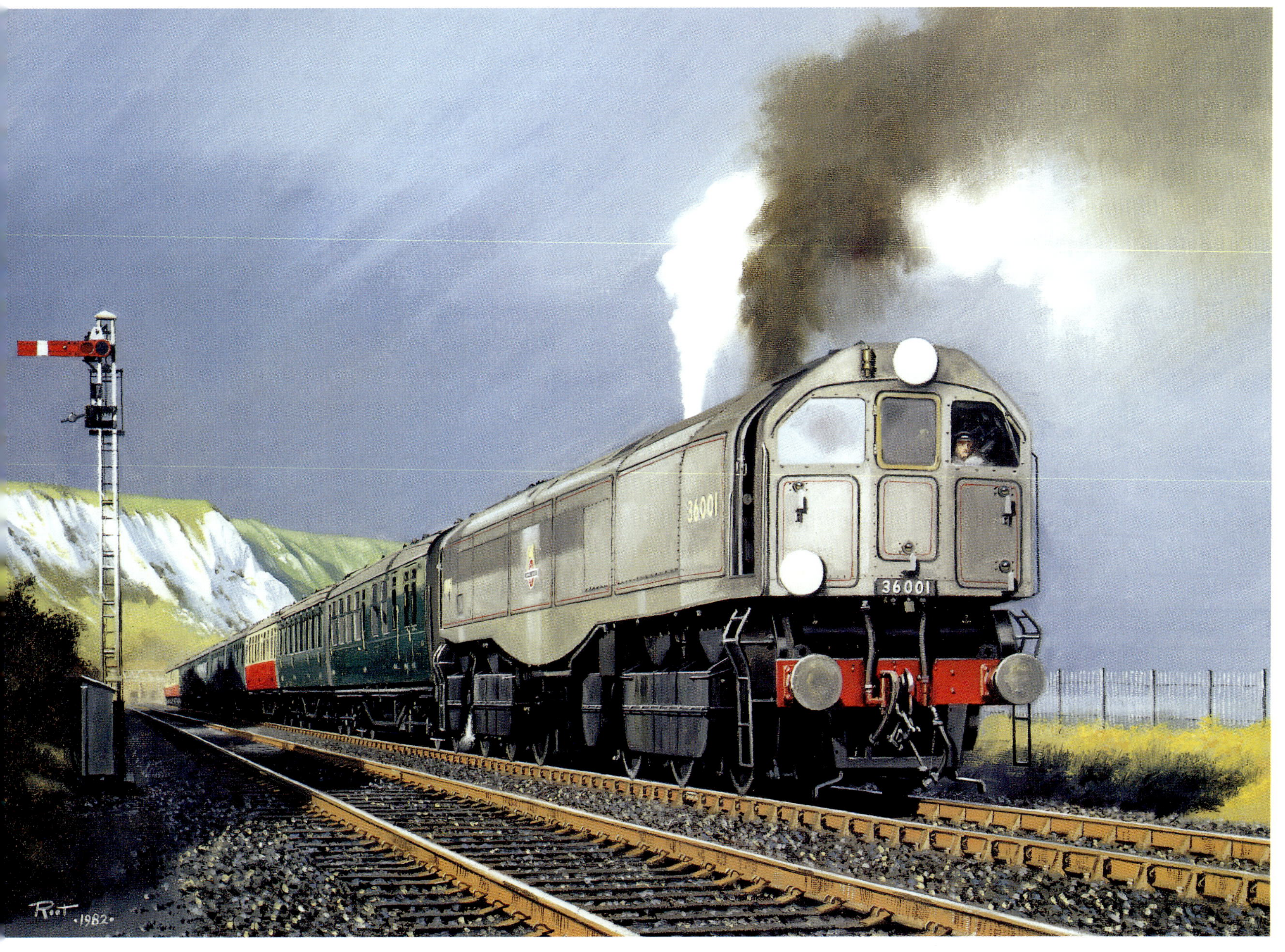
36001
36001
Root .1982.

Steam Dream

Painted 2002

The setting for this scene is the coaling plant at Norwich in 1960. Two locomotives, both very familiar to us by now, are resting between duties, while two members of the crews have a chat together. Behind on the left a third locomotive is also waiting a turn of duty, and its crew take the opportunity to stretch their legs. Again, as the mounds of ash and clinker testify, this is a corner of the railway where a lot of work goes on unseen by the general public.

The locomotive in the distance is an ex-London & North Eastern Railway L1 class 2–6–4 tank engine, designed by Edward Thompson and introduced at the end of the war in 1945. One hundred of this class were built, and they were the LNER equivalent of the very successful 2-6–4 tank engines on the LMS (see page 106). Close to us on the left is ex-Great Eastern Railway B12 class 4-6-0 61572 (see pages 64, 76 and 112). As mentioned before, this class was extensively rebuilt in the 1930s and 40s by Sir Nigel Gresley. On the right of the picture is another old friend, the ex-Great Eastern Railway J15 class 0-6-0 and as we have seen it was used over a very long period on the Eastern Region of the railways (see pages 4, 48, and 118). This example, number 65462 has a very good head of steam, probably too much in the eyes of the depot authorities. The two locomotives show the two different types of crest used by British Railways.

There is a story attached to these two locomotives. Bill Harvey was the shed master at Norwich during this period, and 61572 became his personal pride and joy. As you can see she is in superb condition, both cosmetically and mechanically, given that she is already about fifty years old. This was the period when steam traction was being phased out, as engines became due for expensive overhauls. Bill received notice on more than one occasion that the B12 should be withdrawn. For some reason, however, he was unable to comply with the instruction at that particular moment – perhaps the locomotive was in pieces or being used as a standby. The weeks slipped by and became months, and still the cherished B12 worked quietly out of Norwich shed together with the J15 also shown. Eventually, because of the delay, the steam preservationists were able to save the engines when the end of steam traction finally came, and both locomotives were moved to the newly-opened North Norfolk Railway, where they work happily today looking very smart in their preserved state.

Tribute must be paid to the vast army of dedicated volunteers who have given endless time and raised hundreds of thousands of pounds to restore and preserve our railway heritage all over the country, and are constantly expanding the whole operation today.

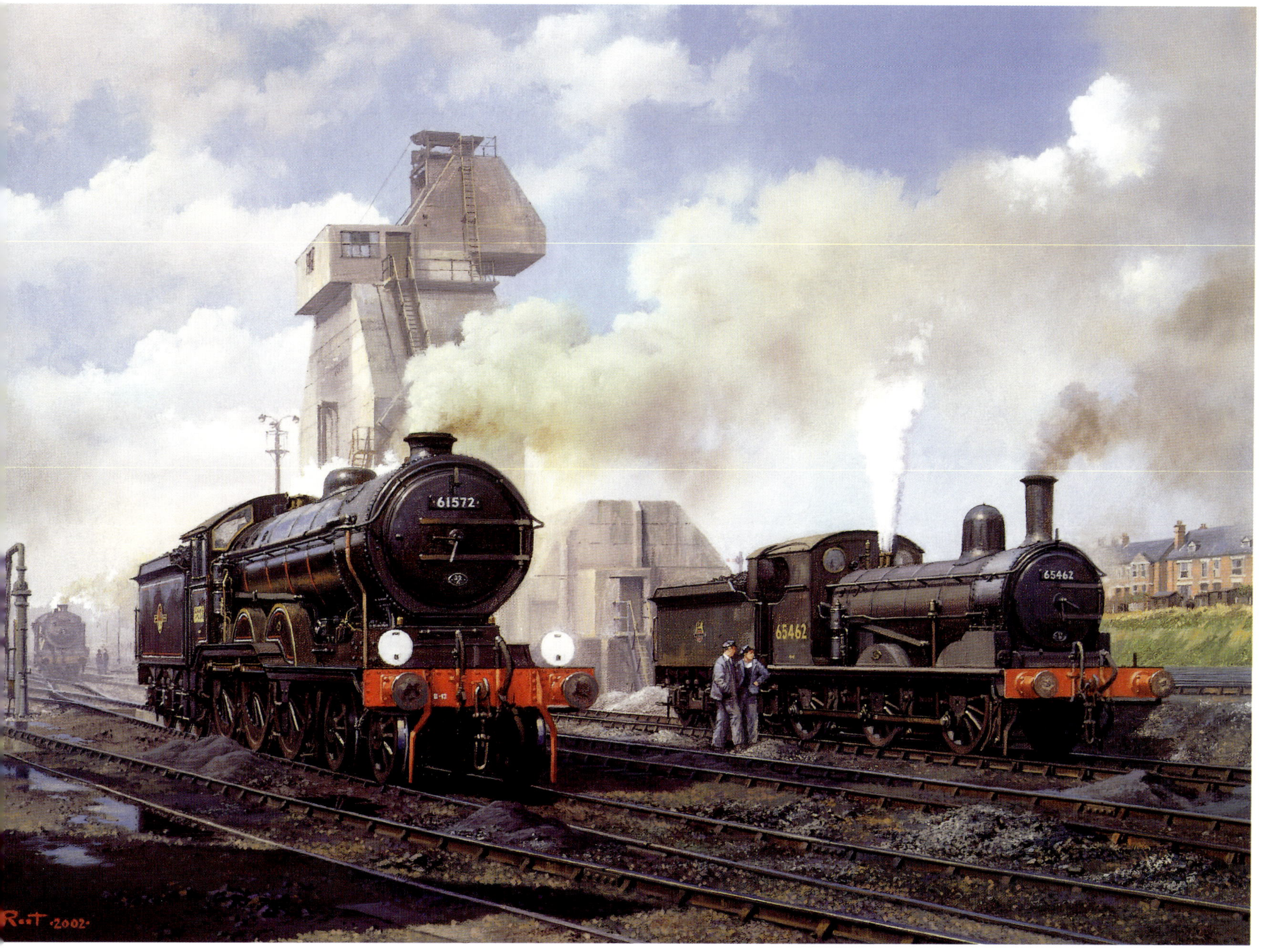
61572
65462
65462
ROOT 2002

Capital Bound

Painted 2000

This express does not stop at Winchester, to the obvious disgust of the station cleaner who watches as the slipstream from the train whirls his carefully-swept pieces of paper across the track. Winchester, the ancient capital of Wessex was established first as a Roman town, and later as an important cathedral city with a huge diocese. From the commercial point of view it tended to be overshadowed by the nearby coastal developments of Southampton, Fareham and Portsmouth, with their important ferry services and shipping and naval interests. Thus it came about that a lot of trains originating at Southampton and bound for London would not stop at Winchester. The old Southern Railway then ran through Basingstoke and Woking, and so into London Waterloo, which is almost the route that the M3 motorway follows today.

It is about 8pm on a warm autumn evening in the 1960s with only a solitary employee on the platform. The semaphore signal on the left shows a green light, easily visible to the train driver, and the electric lamps cast pools of light on the platform. Above the nearer platform the station announcer's voice has just come over the hanging loudspeaker proclaiming to a non-existent audience that this train will not stop at Winchester. Over the years station announcers have won a justified reputation for being almost totally incomprehensible!

The gleaming locomotive hauling the express has probably been recently cleaned as is evident by the multitude of reflections along the boiler. Providing the power is a Merchant Navy Pacific number 35005, *Canadian Pacific* designed by Oliver Bulleid, which first entered service in 1941. This locomotive was one of the first batch to be built, and was then re-built with the removal of the streamlined casing in the late 1950s. Although too heavy for many of the lines on the Southern Railway, the class was ideal for the Southampton to London route. This particular locomotive worked on British Railways until the end of steam traction in 1967, and then was saved from scrap and restored, and until recently was again working steam specials over main lines.

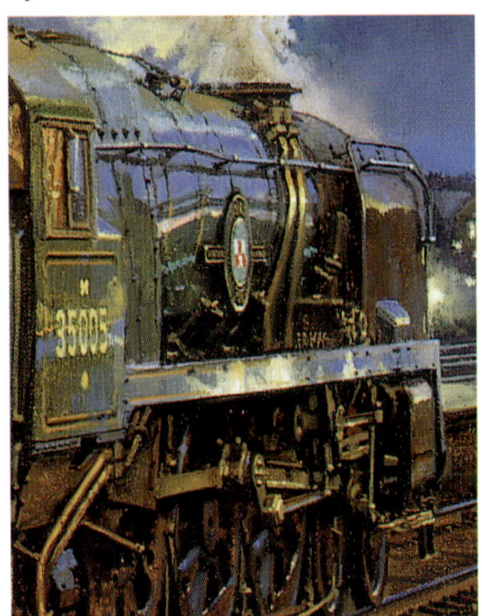

The Canadian Pacific Line was one of the most famous shipping lines operating from Europe to Canada via the St Lawrence River, and operating liners such as the *Empress of Britain*, the fastest on the route. The St Lawrence was ice-bound in winter so the company used its liners for cruising elsewhere during that period. The North Atlantic could promote a lot of sea sickness for susceptible passengers, so the Canadian Pacific Line advertised that their route involved 1½ fewer days open ocean!

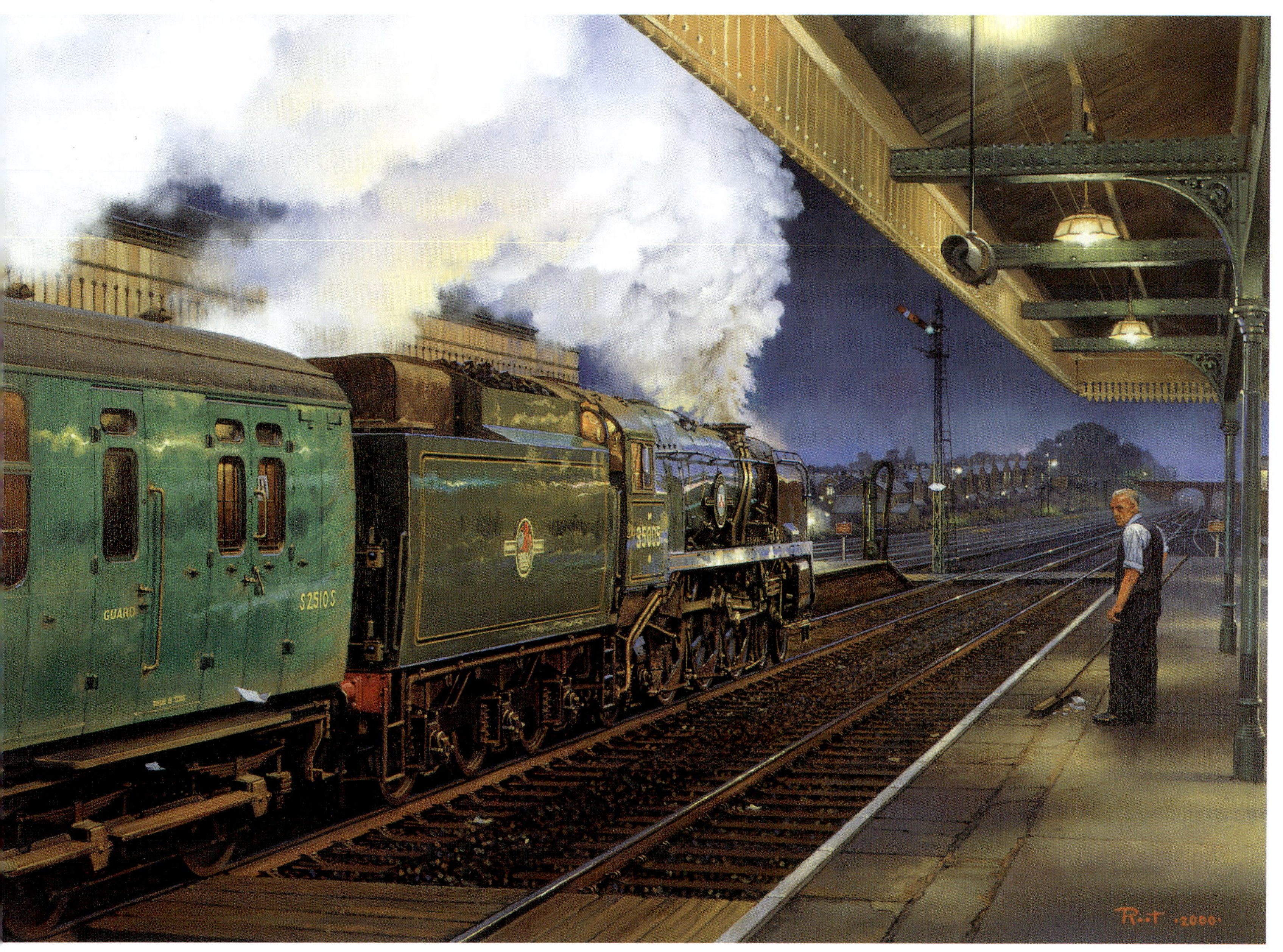
GUARD
S2510 S
Root ·2000·

Ivatt in the Snow

Painted 1997

We end as we began, with a branch line after a moderate snowfall, and it is the familiar Colne Valley Railway which we have come to know well as it was Malcolm's local railway. It is one of those clear, crisp winter days when the temperature plummets with the fading light. In areas where the grass has been fairly high at the end of summer the tussocks are weighed down with the snow, but they still show, and the painting beautifully captures this familiar aspect of a snowfall in the countryside. Away to the left the Halstead town gas holder appears to be completely full, which will be encouraging to the local population as they strive to keep warm. A gentle breeze from the south blows the smoke from the locomotive away, as the fireman builds up his fire for the journey to Haverhill. To the left of the locomotive can be seen a factory building and a sports pavilion, and behind the train on the right are the signal box and level crossing, seen closer on page 125.

The locomotive pulling a three-coach train comprising Thompson branch line stock is the familiar Ivatt class 2-6-0 introduced on the LMS in 1946, just before the nationalisation of the railways. Five of these locomotives were allocated for work on the Colne Valley branch line in British Railways days. Like the J15s before them, their low axle weight was ideal for the lightly laid track and the bridges, and their tractive effort was more than adequate for the mixed-traffic trains they normally had to haul. This said, on Sundays during the summer, excursions were run from Cambridge to either Clacton or Walton on the Naze via the Colne Valley line. The trains, made up to eight coaches would require the best from both engines and crew.

Our paintings have taken us to almost every corner of the British Isles, and covered great and spectacular main lines, and small meandering branch lines. We have become familiar with the mightiest of express locomotives, and the small fussy tank locomotives doing a vital job on the feeder lines of the railway system. Hot summer days have been mixed with crisp snow and frost, and a number of wet days as well when the station platforms gleam in reflected water. It has truly been a journey capturing the great days of steam on Britain's railways as portrayed in a series of wonderful paintings by Malcolm Root, and we hope you have enjoyed them.

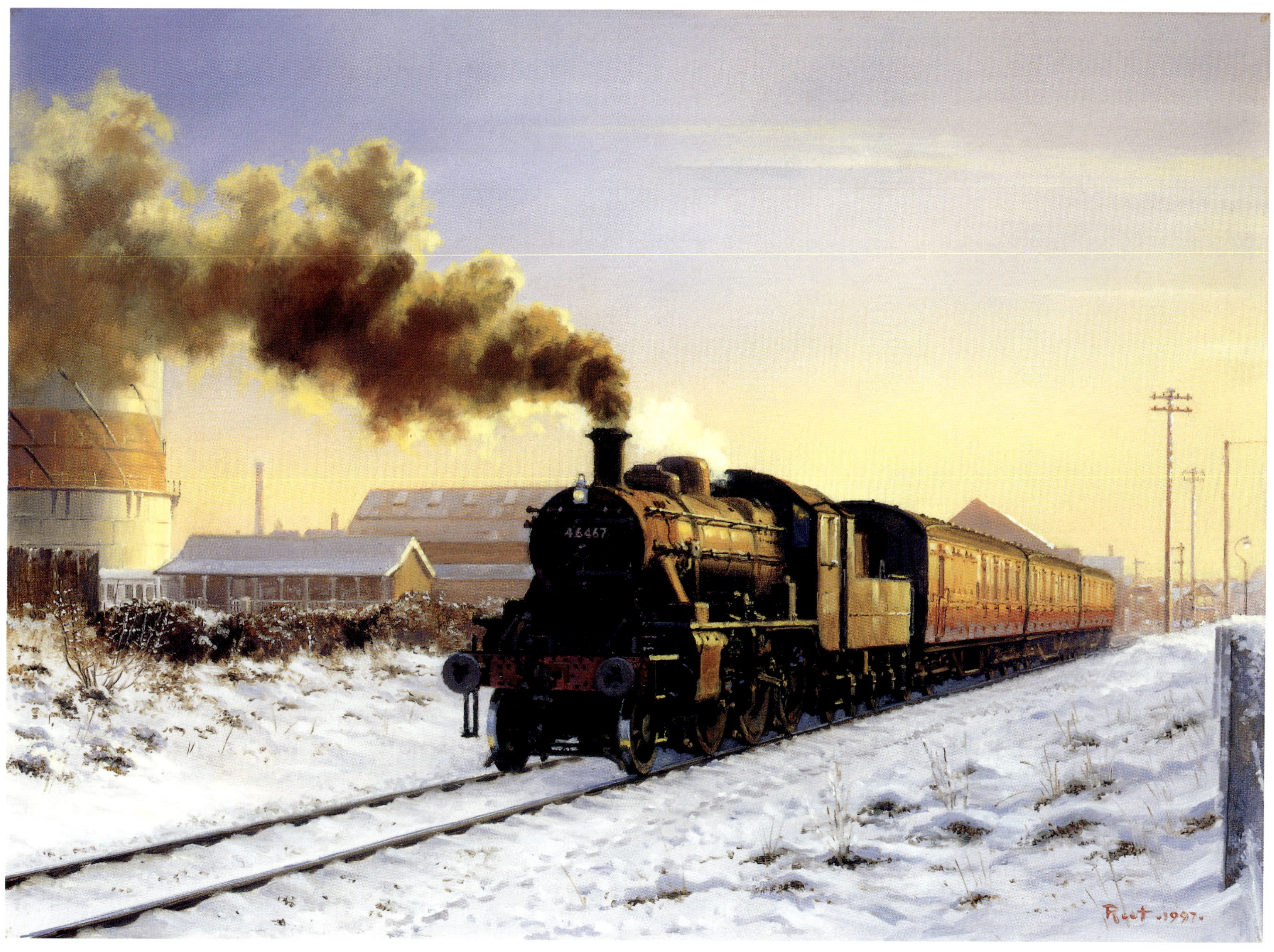
46467
Root .1997.

Bibliography

Ahrons, E.L. *Locomotive and Train Working in the Latter Part of 19th Century*. Vol. 4. Heffer & Sons Ltd. Cambridge. 1953.

Allan, Ian. *Locomotives Illustrated*. Sept. 1992.

Allen, Cecil J. *The Great Eastern Railway*. Ian Allan Ltd. London. 1955.

Allen, Cecil J. *Titled Trains of Great Britain*. Ian Allan Ltd. London. 1946.

Awdry, W & Cook. C. *Guide to the Steam Railways of Great Britain*. Pelham Books. London. 1979.

Bowtell, Harold D. *Rails through Lakeland*. Vol 1. Silver Link Publishing. Kettering. 1989.

Carter, Ernest F. *The Observer's Book of Railway Locomotives of Britain*. Frederick Warne and Co Ltd. London. 1955.

Casserley, H.C. *The Observer's Book of British Steam Locomotives*. Frederick Warne and Co Ltd. London. 1974.

Cone, Philip J. *100 Years of Parkeston Quay and its Ships*. Harwich Printing Co. Harwich. 1983.

Cooper, B.K. *Great Western Railway Handbook*. Ian Allan Ltd. London. 1986.

Deacon, Tim. *Swanage Railway in Colour*. Ian Allan Ltd. London. 1996.

Ellaway, K.J. *The Great British Railway Station: Euston*. Irwell Press. Oldham. 1994.

Flinders, T.G. *On the Settle & Carlisle Route*. Ian Allan Ltd. London. 1981.

G.W.R. Engines. Names, Numbers, Types Classes etc. Great Western Railway. Paddington. 1938.

Gammell, C.J. *The Steam Age*. Moorland Publishing Co. Buxton. 1978.

Hamilton Ellis, C. *The Trains We Loved*. George Allen & Unwin. 1947.

Harris, Nigel. *L.N.E.R. Reflections*. Silver Link Publishing. Carnforth. 1985.

Hay, Peter. *Steaming through the Isle of Wight*. Middleton Press. Midhurst. 1988.

Hughes, Geoffrey. *L.N.E.R. 4-6-0s at Work*. Ian Allan Ltd. London. 1988.

Johnson, Peter. *The British Travelling Post Office*. Ian Allan Ltd. London. 1985.

Jones, Robin. *Heritage Railway Magazine*. July 2002.

Kingston, Patrick. *Royal Trains*. David & Charles Ltd. Newton Abbot. 1985.

L.A.M.A. *British Locomotives*. Locomotive & Allied Manufacturers Association of Great Britain. London.

Le Fleming, H.M. Durrant, A.E. & Snell, J.B. *International Locomotives*. Institution of Mechanical Engineers. London. 1972.

Marsden, Colin J. *Locomotives*. Ian Allan Ltd. London. 1981.

Nock, O.S. *British Locomotives of the 20th Century*. Volumes 1 & 2. Guild/B.C.A. 1983/4.

Nock, O.S. *Engine 6000. The Saga of King George V* .David & Charles. Newton Abbot. 1972.

Nock, O.S. *The Great Western Railway in the 20th Century*. Ian Allan Ltd. London. 1964.

Newman, Marcus. *The Birth of the Cornish Riviera*. Ian Allan Ltd. London.

Page, Hugh. *Rambles around the Cambrian Coast*. Great Western Railway, Paddington. 1936.

Rear, W.G. & Williams, M.F. *The Cambrian Coast. Dovey Junction to Pwllheli*. Foxline Publishing. Stockport. 1994.

Ross, David. *British Steam Railways*. Paragon. Bath. 2002.

Townend, Paul. *The Modern World Book of Railways*. Sampson Low, Marston & Co. Ltd. 1947.

Tyler, Tom. *Malcolm Root's Transport Paintings*. Halsgrove. Tiverton. 2002.

Williams, Archibald. *Brunel and After*. Great Western Railway. Paddington. 1925.

Whitehouse, Patrick & St John Thomas, David. *The Great Western Railway, 150 Glorious Years*. David and Charles. Newton Abbot. 1984.

Index

INDEX OF
NAMED LOCOMOTIVES

INDEX OF LOCOMOTIVE
TYPES AND CLASSES

INDEX OF TRAINS

INDEX OF RAILWAY LINES
AND COMPANIES

GENERAL INDEX